MAGIC, WITCHCRAFT, AND PAGANISM IN AMERICA

GARLAND BIBLIOGRAPHIES ON
SECTS AND CULTS
(General editor: J. Gordon Melton)
Vol. 1

GARLAND REFERENCE LIBRARY
OF SOCIAL SCIENCE
Vol. 105

MAGIC, WITCHCRAFT, AND PAGANISM IN AMERICA
A Bibliography

J. Gordon Melton

compiled from the files of
The Institute for the Study of American Religion

GARLAND PUBLISHING, INC. • NEW YORK & LONDON
1982

Library of Congress Cataloging in Publication Data

Melton, J. Gordon.
  Magic, witchcraft, and paganism in America.

  (Garland bibliographies on sects and cults ; v. 1)
(Garland reference library of social science ; v. 105)
  Includes indexes.
  1. Magic—United States—Bibliography. 2. Witch-
craft—United States—Bibliography. 3. Paganism—
United States—Bibliography. 4. Cults—United
States—Bibliography. 5. Sects—United States—
Bibliography. I. Institute for the Study of American
Religion. II. Title. III. Series. IV. Series:
Garland reference library of social science ;
v. 105.
Z6878.M3M44 [BF1622.U6]   016.299   81–43343
ISBN 0–8240–9377–1   AACR2

Printed on acid-free, 250-year-life paper
Manufactured in the United States of America

to June

CONTENTS

Preface   ix

I. Introductory Material
   A. This Bibliography: Its Scope and Construction   3
   B. An Introduction to the Magical Community   6

II. Background Material
   A. Magic, Witchcraft, and Paganism—
      A Reader's Guide   25
   B. The Magical Worldview   28
   C. Magic in History   34
   D. Witchcraft and Magic in the Third World   38
   E. Magic in Ancient Times   40
   F. European Witchcraft   44

III. Ritual Magic
   A. Modern Ceremonial Magic   49
   B. The Grimoires   56
   C. The Kabbalah   59
   D. The Hermetic Tradition   62
   E. Magnum Opus Hermetic Sourceworks   70
   F. Sex in Magic and Religion   71
   G. Aleister Crowley   74
   H. Ritual Magic in Modern America   79

IV. Witchcraft
   A. Witchcraft in Colonial America   89
   B. Salem   92
   C. Powwow   97
   D. Pre-Modern Witchcraft   100
   E. Gerald B. Gardner   105

10-4-83

F. Modern British Wicca   109
G. Directories   111
H. Modern Wicca in America   113
I. Feminist Wicca   131
J. Songbooks and Poetry   137
K. Calendars   139

V. Neo-Paganism
A. Paganism   141
B. Egyptian Paganism   148
C. Norse Paganism   150
D. Druids   151
E. The Discordians and Illuminati   153

VI. Afro-American Magical Religions
A. Voodoo   155
B. Santeria   161
C. Hoodoo   163
D. Macumba   167
E. The Yorubans of South Carolina   168

VII. Kahuna   169

VIII. Bruja   173

IX. Periodicals
A. American Periodicals   177
B. Foreign Periodicals   189

Appendixes
Appendix I. "List of Works in the New York
    Public Library Relating to Witchcraft
    in the United States," by George F. Black   195

Appendix II. "The Curriculum of the A.A."   213

Author Index   219

Periodical Index   231

PREFACE

During the last few years, I have been in a unique position and had open to me a rather singular opportunity. Though a minister in the United Methodist Church, I have been welcomed into a still largely secret and underground movement in America, that of Pagans, Witches, and ceremonial magicians. Their existence on the edge of the much larger and open occult community in America had been known to me for many years, but their revival in the 1970s brought them to my attention as an important but forgotten element in the broader scene of New Religions. As books began to appear in the early 1970s, I became painfully aware of the distinction between what Pagans and Witches described concerning their life and beliefs and what I had been taught to think of "Witchcraft" and "magic," which carried the most sinister of connotations.

While on a lecture tour of California, I met, for the first time people who called themselves Witches and Pagans. From them I learned that Pagans were everywhere. There was even a community of them in Chicago, where I resided.

As I spent more time around real Witches, I went from one shock to another as all of my images of dark rites, demon curses, voodoo dolls, and evil magicians were wrenched away. I found the Pagans to be a gentle folk, in love with nature, celebrating the joy of living and worshipping the Earth Mother. Signs of Satanism were nowhere to be found, and they condemned black magic as thoroughly as the Church in which I was raised. Harmlessness was advocated as a way of life and the idea of animal sacrifice considered more of a sacrilege than desecrating an altar.

Over a decade of researching the Pagan community, I attended many Pagan gatherings, both small coven meetings and large festivals. I wrote several articles and monographs attempting to interpret the Pagan movement to the scholarly world and to my fellow Christians. Slowly, as my work appeared and a trust level established itself, I was admitted to the more closed rituals, those usually reserved for initiates, and allowed to read instructional material marked with the Witch's equivalent of "Top Secret." I also became increasingly concerned about the continuing publication of material by well meaning but ignorant Christian brothers and sisters who confuse Witchcraft with Satanism and black magic. They were showing their lack of direct contact with the phenomena they were discussing and, to my regret, have continued to circulate through the mass media and Christian publications their completely warped picture of the Pagan world. I hope that this publication can begin to offer a corrective to such misinformation.

Very early in my research, I constructed an outline for a proposed history of the magical religious community in America. Though the article was well received, even by those I described above, I know now just how naive and limited was the perspective I presented. During each phase of my continuing research I was given new material which necessitated my reconceptualizing a significant portion of my data.

Now, after a decade of contact, I feel ready to report the results of my work. This volume is the first part of that report. It is an exhaustive listing of all the material I have been able to locate on the magical religious community in America from Colonial times to the present. The more than 1500 items document the existence of Witches and Pagans and magicians throughout American history. A second volume which will, I hope, be finished in the not-too-distant future will tell the story of Pagans in America beginning with the surfacing of Witches in New England in the 1640s to the current revival of Witchcraft in the 1970s.

Acknowledgments

During the preparation of this volume and while doing my general research, I have incurred many debts and have been helped by far too many people to begin to mention them all. With a few, however, I have had long-term contact and to them I directed my day-to-day questions. Selena Fox, Jim Alan, and De-Anna Alba opened their home and library to me on many occasions and guided me to resources of which I would have otherwise been ignorant. These three constitute the core of a Pagan group called simply Circle, and their center near Madison, Wisconsin, contains the only Pagan-Wicca library open to the public other than the one at ISAR.

Margot Adler, who has been the major chronicler of contemporary Paganism, opened her files to me and has provided much critical reflection on my research through the years.

The members of the Midwest Pagan Council, even at times over the suspicions of some members, opened their meetings to me and cooperated in my research in a most gracious manner. Each has my thanks, but particular gratitude goes to Christa Heiden, Stan Modryzk, and Ginny Brubaker.

William Wheeler, who puts together the annual Gathering of the Tribes for Pagans in the Southeast United States, also opened the doors for me to conduct my research at the Gathering in 1980.

For the supplying of important material for this volume, thanks go to Isaac Bonewits, Grady McMurtry, Yvonne Moore, Carroll Runyon, Richard Sells, Carl Weschcke, Nelson and Anne White, and Tim Otter Zell.

I hope that the following pages present an accurate picture of modern Paganism, although I have learned by painful experience that if there are points which any Pagans feel are inaccurate, they will assuredly let me know about it.

J. Gordon Melton
Chicago, Illinois

MAGIC, WITCHCRAFT,
AND PAGANISM IN AMERICA

I

INTRODUCTORY MATERIAL

A. THE BIBLIOGRAPHY:
ITS SCOPE AND CONSTRUCTION

This bibliography surveys the literature produced by and about the American magical community. That community, while existing more-or-less continuously since Colonial days, has emerged powerfully in the 20th century due to the creation of two new gestalts of magical formation--the thelemic magick of Aleister Crowley (1875-1947) and the goddess-centered Witchcraft of Gerald Gardner (1884-1964). In the years since Crowley and Gardner the large community of magicians, Witches, and Pagans has come into existence. The great majority of them have come to so identify themselves during the 1970s.

While doing my research on the Neo-Pagans, I discovered a great body of material which the magicians and Pagans produced, or which was written about them, that had never been indexed. This material had been privately printed for limited circulation, published in more or less obscure journals or periodicals, or published in journals with no immediate and obvious connection to the occult world. I also discovered a segment of American history largely ignored by historians. While they had spilled tons of ink on Colonial Witchcraft, they neglected the phenomenon after 1750. Even Russell's excellent *A History of Witchcraft* (184) jumps from the early 18th century to the modern revival with mention of only some romantic writings about Witchcraft in the early 19th century and the revival of ritual magic in Europe at the end of the century. As a historian I was forced into the writings of folklorists, local chroniclers, and occult books and periodicals. From the effort to compile the material from which a history of the American magical community can be constructed, I saw the need for a separate volume treating just the mass of somewhat hidden material that has been found and informing potential users of its existence.

My goal, admittedly a heuristic one, has been to list all of the material available on the magical community in America from Colonial times to the present. This list includes all books, booklets, pamphlets, calendars, periodical articles about the magical community, and periodicals issued by the magical community. Where copies have been located and are on file for researchers, substantive newspaper articles are listed (though I have probably missed far more of these than have surfaced during the decade of searching). While standard indices have been scanned, I am sure that some magazine articles have also been missed and possibly some booklets produced by various Pagan groups. I am confident, however, that all of the items representative of anything more than an odd coven or small group of Pagans have been found and included.

Some material I excluded. During the years of moving through the Pagan community, I have been given and become privy to much "secret" material including secret rituals, instructional manuals, and confidential items circulating among magicians and Pagan leaders. While I keep what has been given to me on file for scholars and others to use in research, it has not seemed prudent either to publish a list of exactly what I have been given or to reveal what many Pagans and Witches sincerely hold as sacred texts. Finally, I have not included the large file of ephemera--flyers, meeting notices, festival programs, and ads for Pagan books.

Copies of most of the material mentioned in this work can be found in the collection of the Institute for the Study of American Religion, whose collection includes about 90% of all the items listed below. *It should be noted that the "secret" material and the more valuable and hard-to-replace items in the collection have been separated from the main ISAR collection and placed under lock-and-key at an alternate location. They are available for use by making an appointment with the Institute's director.*

Obviously the American magical community was not created *de novo*. It began as a European (primarily British) transplant, and it has continued to interact with the European scene from which it received the impulse of the occult revival in the 19th century, wave after wave of immigrants, and more recently the writings of Britishers Crowley and Gardner. It also received independent impulses from Africa and the Caribbean.

Any understanding of the American magical community would be hindered without some understanding of what has been called magic and Witchcraft in other times and places. The search for American magic continually led to African Witchdoctors, European Witchhunters, ancient goddess worshippers, and the scholarly dialogue on the nature of Witchcraft and magic. Material on such topics sets the context from which a wider perspective on the unique American community can be gained.

Thus supplementing the list on American magic and Witchcraft, material about magic and Witchcraft in Western history and in pre-technological societies around the world and general works on the nature of magic make up the first section of this bibliography. In Section II, "Background Material," will be found chapters on the magical worldview, magic in history, magic in pre-technological societies, magic in ancient times, and European Witchcraft.

The background material was assembled so as to include relevant bibliographic works and a few scholarly works on each topic. Prime importance was placed on the numerous items currently circulating in the Pagan and magical groups. During the 1960s and 1970s publishing houses specializing in the occult, such as Samuel Weiser, Health Research, and University Books, reprinted numerous books, many in inexpensive paperback editions, which because of their availability have had a great influence on the contemporary magical community. These books have supplied to contemporary Pagans and magicians (and to much of the public as well) their view of magic and Witchcraft.

Within Section II, one will also note the presence of a number of articles from popular magazines, occult periodicals, little-known journals, and even newspapers. These items, frequently omitted from selective bibliographies, constitute a set of materials encountered during my research which offer additional perspective on various topics not found elsewhere. I have included them in this listing in order to call the reader's attention to their existence. Also, during the preparation of this bibliography, I indexed every item on magic and Witchcraft in *Fate* Magazine, the largest circulating occult periodical in America during the last thirty years, and placed the items in the relevant sections.

While completeness in Sections III-IX has been attempted, I am sure items have been missed. Knowledge (and where possible, copies) of such items is earnestly desired both to list in future, revised editions of this work and to include in the library of the Institute for the Study of American Religion, whose collection now constitutes a virtual archive of the American magical/Neo-Pagan community. The reader is invited to write:

> Institute for the Study of American Religion
> Box 1311
> Evanston, Illinois 60201

B. AN INTRODUCTION TO THE MAGICAL COMMUNITY

Within the much larger occult community there exists a smaller community of individuals whose particular beliefs clearly distinguish them from other occultists. These persons not only believe in "real" magic but practice it. They believe in a plurality of deities, the gods and goddesses of pre-Christian polytheism. They revere the earth and the forces of nature and attempt to attune themselves to them. They form groups that practice elaborate initiation rituals and offer members the opportunity to progress through a series of three to ten or more degrees, depending upon the group.

The members of the various segments of the magical community in America acknowledge that despite very real differences, all--whether they call themselves ritual magicians, Witches, Pagans, Druids, or even Voodooists--are part of the same movement. They also possess a strong sense of being not-Christian. Some, openly hostile to Christianity, recount horror stories from childhood experiences in church. Others, the majority, view themselves as members of a new religion which, like Buddhism or Islam, is simply not the Christian religion. Most occultists tend to see themselves as teaching a deeper or truer or Gnostic version of Christianity.

This magical community, which came into being after World War II, inherits a tradition of magical practice and belief that has continued unabated in America since Colonial times. However, that tradition was reinvigorated in the 1950s by Gerald Gardner (1884-1964), who created a new form of magical religion based upon the worship of the Great Mother Goddess and her consort, the Horned God. While Gardner took much from traditional material, he presented a new religion to the world in his first book. Behind Gardner stands Aleister Crowley, who in the early 20th century reconstructed magic as "magick," to distinguish his creation from both stage conjurations and the alchemical and hermetic traditions that preceded him.

GERALD B. GARDNER

While working as a government official in Southeast Asia, Gardner became fascinated with the local magic and supernaturalism. He became an expert on native weapons and picked up their occultism. Upon his return to England in 1936 he was initiated into a coven of Witches headed by "Old Dorothy" Clutterbuck. In the freer climate resulting from the repeal of the British laws against Witchcraft in 1951, Gardner published his first book, *Witchcraft Today*, in which his brand of Wicca first came before the world. Gardner said he published the volume so that at least a record of a dying group would survive. The book itself, however, became a tool for the group's rebirth.

How much of the material of Gardnerian Wicca Gardner inherited from Dorothy and how much he wrote himself remain questions for future generations to answer. But it is likely that he himself composed the rituals that he passed on to others. He was responsible for the emphasis on nudity (a practice he learned in Southeast Asia) and scourging as a means of creating an altered state of consciousness. He also emphasized the preeminent Mother Goddess and the role of the High Priestess. Within Gardnerian Wicca, worship may proceed without the priest but not without the priestess. Also Gardnerian covens are linked through a lineage of High Priestesses who form a chain similar to an apostolic succession.

Gardner possibly inherited much material from the coven-- the use of magical instruments, the eight annual festivals, the practices of British folk (low) magic, and the idea of a coven itself. There is good evidence that some covens existed in England in the early years of this century. Sybil Leek claims to have joined a coven, one of four in the New Forest area, that dates to the Middle Ages. While the claim to antiquity might be doubted, there is little question that covens existed before World War II. Doreen Valiente, among others, documents the existence of a set of nine covens headed by George Pickingill near East Anglia in the late 1800s. Both Aleister Crowley and his friend Allan Bennett were reportedly members.

The folklorist Margaret Murray (1863-1963) raised the issue of early British covens in her two books, *The Witchcult in Western Europe* (1921) and *The God of the Witches* (1933). She stirred a storm of controversy (as well as a myth which modern Witches quickly absorbed) with her assertion that Witches still existed and that they practiced a polytheistic, nature-oriented religion that had survived, despite all persecution, since pre-Christian times. Murray's theories have been discarded by all but a few, but the rumor that she was

herself a practicing Witch, if true, offers further evidence
that covens operated in pre-Gardnerian England and that they
thought of themselves as continuing Pagan traditions.

Pre-Gardnerian groups of witches almost certainly existed
in America at least on a small scale. Several sources affirm
the presence of covens in Rhode Island, New York, Michigan,
and Louisville, Kentucky, during the 1930s and 1940s. Some of
these covens were exclusive to one ethnic group. A group of
Scottish covens, four in number, which still operate in Southeastern Michigan, claim that one of their number has been
functioning since its original members immigrated to America
in the early 1800s.

These covens had widely varying practices, but none gave
special emphasis to the Mother Goddess nor did they keep the
biweekly gatherings at the full moon and new moon which Gardner
practiced. They practiced "low" magic (blessings, healings,
occasional curses, and the use of talismans and amulets) but
not "high" magic (mystical alchemy).

Folk magic and Witchcraft from rural Europe came to
America with the first Colonists in the 17th century. They
have been practiced ever since by individual Witches living
on the edge of urban culture, in the mountains, or in farm
country.

As early as 1648 Alse Young was tried and convicted of
Witchcraft in Windsor, Connecticut, while Margaret Jones of
Charlestown, Massachusetts, and Mary Johnson of Withersfield,
Connecticut, were arrested and sentenced the following year.
All were executed, the first of a succession of victims to
die in the years leading up to 1692 and the famous episode
at Salem Village (now Danvers), Massachusetts.

The incident at Salem Village, now so much a part of
American lore, had a worldwide impact. The 19 deaths, the
fervor of the Witchhunt, the disruption of the community--all
finally shocked the perpetrators. The waves of revulsion did
much to stop further trials. Others did occur, however. In
1721, for example, Grace Sherwood was tried in Virginia.

The Salem events took on mythlike qualities. Their occurrence in holy New England, like the occurrence of the Holocaust in civilized Germany, demanded explanation. The explanation usually offered is hysteria. No doubt emotions did
get out of hand. But recent reexaminations of the trials
indicate "hysteria," whatever that is, accounts for only part
of the event.

The discovery of images--Voodoo dolls, if you prefer--in
the homes of two of the accused lends credence to the notion
that Witchcraft was indeed being practiced. Malevolent Witchcraft does work in communities that believe in its power.
Salem was not yet secularized enough to believe in the non-
effectiveness of Witchcraft.

Recent sociological studies have also pointed to a pattern of accusation and victimization in the trials. A simple line through Salem Village separated persecutors and persecuted, suggesting that the trials marked a dramatic--and for some fatal--playing-out of community tensions.

After Salem, intellectuals grew skeptical of Witchcraft, discounting its existence except as silly superstition. In fact Witches continued to exist but fled to places where their presence was little-noticed. But as ethnographers, anthropologists, folklorists, and local historians began to collect their data in the 19th century, they discovered Witches all across the country, quietly practicing their craft in their small communities.

In Pennsylvania, largely free of the Colonial trials, German magical practices were brought over by Johann Kelpius and a group of Rosicrucian hermeticists who established a colony on Wissahickon Creek near Germantown. The men of the group were apocalypticists, but when the second coming failed to occur, the colony dissolved and the remnants of the group stayed on to teach and practice their arts in the area. They passed on the oral tradition of low magic brought from Germany and were most assuredly joined through the years by new immigrants who also brought magical practices with them.

In 1819 Johann Hohman gathered the folk magic into printed form and published it as *Der lange verborgene Freund*, more popularly known today as *The Long-Lost Friend*, which has become the Bible of the hexmeisters of Pennsylvania Dutch country. The *Friend*'s magic typically sets the magician in a very assertive position, commanding God and the angels to do his/her bidding. Like the *bruja*, the Witches of the Mexican communities, the hexmeisters still live within a community where they are feared for the malevolent powers they are supposed to possess.

The *conjureman*, who works hoodoo, is another product of the British folk magic tradition. That tradition was adapted by slaves who picked up the magic of their masters and practiced it in the black communities. The conjureman still flourishes in the South and in urban centers across the country. His power continues to fascinate the medical profession, members of which are frequently called upon to treat victims of hoodoo.

Because of the name "hoodoo," the operation of *hoodoo* in black communities, and the general ignorance of *Voodoo*, many writers confuse hoodoo with Voodoo, an African magical religion (to be discussed below) that has almost nothing to do with hoodoo. Thus, in using the literature, the reader must exercise caution because the two terms (and often *bruja*) are used indiscriminately and imprecisely.

ALEISTER CROWLEY

The second prophet of the magical revival of the last half
of the 20th century, Aleister Crowley (1875-1947), reacted
to his fundamentalist upbringing in the Plymouth Brethren by
proclaiming himself the Beast 666 of the Book of Revelation
and the "Wickedest Man in the World." While still a teenager,
he began to experiment with sex with both men and women. He
also became fascinated with magic and in 1898 joined the
Hermetic Order of the Golden Dawn, a group that pioneered
much of the magical revival. After a quarrel with the leader
he was expelled.

Crowley went on to more positive experiences. Two in
particular did much to shape his life. First, in 1904 in
Cairo, Egypt, Crowley engaged in a three-day working during
which he contacted an entity named Aiwass. Aiwass communicated a manuscript known as *Liber Al vel Legis, The Book of the
Law*. He announced to Crowley the coming of a new era, that
of Horus, the child of Nuit, and proclaimed Crowley the ini-
tiator and herald of that new eon.

From that book Crowley began to develop a reconstructed,
highly psychologized magical system, thelemic magick. The
era of Horus is dominated by "thelema" or "will." A summary
of thelemic magick appears in the three famous sentences:
"Do What Thou Will is the Whole of the Law," "Love is the
Law, Love under Will," and "Every Man and Woman is a Star."
Crowley directs each individual to move in his/her own true
orbit, as marked by the nature of his/her position, the law
of his/her own growth, and the impulse of his/her past. One's
duty is to experience the suitable act in each moment. Love,
the art of uniting with a part of Nuit, opens one to the
possibilities of each moment. Each act of the magician must
be willed in accord with his/her true nature.

The second major event occurred after Crowley left the
OGD and joined the Ordo Templi Orientis, a German magical
group. In 1912, in his *The Book of Lies*, Crowley, who claimed
not to know the secrets of the higher levels of the OTO, published material that implied knowledge of OTO secrets. Theodore
Ruess accused him of revealing the secrets. The encounter
helped Crowley to fully understand what he had written, and
Ruess, impressed with him, appointed Crowley head of the
British OTO. Crowley eventually succeeded Ruess as head of
the entire order.

The secret Crowley inadvertently discovered was sex magic.
The upper levels of the OTO, to which Crowley had not been
privy, taught a form of magic that used sexual energies to
work magical operations and in which the sex act was central
to the rituals being performed. Almost immediately Crowley

plunged into experimentation with the new magical format which soon dominated his life and defined the groups that came afterwards.

Crowley, of course, had not been the first to attempt sexual magic. (He was, however, the first to do it so openly and to promote it so vigorously.) During the 19th century travellers to the East were bringing back word of the sexual magic of the Tantric Yogis and of the Sufis. One traveller, Paschal Beverly Randolph, was taught the secrets of sexual magic which he subsequently used to found the first sexual magic group, the Society of Eulis, in Nashville, Tennessee, in 1874. The Society functioned as the inner court of the Rosicrucian Fraternity he also created. When Randolph died, the Society of Eulis dissolved. A group of French students evidently passed Randolph's material along to the founders of the OTO. Thus, teachings originally promulgated in America returned there through the OTO.

The American branch of the OTO was founded by Frater Achad, Charles Stansfeld Jones, a close student of Crowley, in Vancouver in 1914. Achad eventually broke with Crowley over some fine points of magical teachings and formed his own group, the Fellowship of Ma-Ion. Wilfred Smith took over the American group and moved it to Southern California. It operated out of a Pasadena headquarters through the 1930s and 1940s.

Crowley replaced Smith with Jack Parsons in the early 1940s, and for the last years of Crowley's life the Agape Lodge, as it was called, was the only organized group under the OTO. The death of Parsons in an explosion in his home signaled the demise of the now-leaderless group.

Crowley was succeeded by Karl Germer (1885-1962) as Outer Head of the Order. Unfortunately for the OTO, during his time as OHO, Germer initiated almost no one and left no designated successor. The Order in America fell into disarray, and leaders in Brazil, England, and Switzerland each claimed succession. Marcelo Motta now heads one branch. In England Kenneth Grant asserts his rightful role as leader, and in Switzerland Herr Metzger (Frater Paragranus) heads a branch with membership confined to the Continent.

In the 1970s Grady McMurtry, a former member of the Agape Lodge, declared himself OHO on the strength of some Crowley-written documents naming himself Caliph and giving emergency powers. McMurtry has rebuilt an OTO in the past decade and now heads a number of lodges in the United States from his Berkeley, California, headquarters.

One other group growing out of the OTO, the Choronzon Club, began in Chicago in the 1930s. C.F. Russell, operating with Crowley's blessing, taught the practice of kerazza.

First promulgated in America by John Humphrey Noyes as a means of birth control at his Oneida Community, kerazza is a technique of prolonged sexual intercourse without the male reaching climax. Louis Culling, head of the Southern California branch of the Club, published the ritual and teaching material of the group in 1969. During the last years of his life Culling was also associated with the Ordo Templi Astarte, a nonthelemic ritual magic group in Pasadena.

THE HERMETIC AND KABBALISTIC TRADITION

Crowley did not originate magic, although he reworked the tradition in a significant manner. While most magicians today work thelemic magick, by no means all have abandoned the hermetic and Kabbalistic systems of medieval times.

During the Middle Ages, when magic reached its maturity in Western Europe, two systems predominated: the hermetic (alchemical) and the Kabbalistic. The hermetic system, which drew upon the teachings of Hermes Trismegistus, offered the magician a means to power and transformation of the self. Hermes taught, "As above, so below." Each part of the whole was modeled upon the world. Hence by mastering the part, one mastered the whole, and once having mastered the whole, one had mastered any part of it. Thus the magician's work centered on learning the mundane correspondences to cosmic reality and using them to contact the cosmic world.

As the main hermetic tradition, alchemy constructed a model of the universe from alchemical elements and the process of magic from chemical reaction. The Great Work, that of transforming the magician, was pictured as the ultimate chemical achievement, the transforming of lead into gold.

The Kabbalistic tradition was rooted in the Jewish community, but a Christianized version was created during the Renaissance. The original Jewish form survived and flourished until the Holocaust destroyed most of the Hassidic communities of Europe. It was, however, the Kabbalah in the Christianized version that was transmitted through the occult groups.

Kabbalists believe that the world can be symbolically represented through number and letter. The basic organizing principle of the universe is the number 10. Through the 10 numbers the principles of life are organized and pictured in a diagram, the Tree of Life. The 10 numbers appear as circles in an ascending/descending pattern connected by 22 branches or paths. Above the trees is the realm of God and at the bottom the realm of man, which God created by the succession of 10 emanations.

Each circle, called a Sephirot, represents an aspect of life as well as a realm of attainment for the Kabbalistic

student. Above the first Sephirot is the Ein Soph, the in-
effable ground of being, i.e., God. Each Sephirot has a name
and quality assigned to it, as follows:

1. Kether--being or existence.
2. Chochmah--wisdom.
3. Binah--intelligence or understanding.
4. Chesed--mercy or love.
5. Geburah--strength and/or beauty.
6. Tiphareth--beauty.
7. Netzach--firmness.
8. Hod--glory.
9. Yesod--foundation.
10. Malkuth--kingdom.

An eleventh Sephirot, not often pictured on the tree,
lies concealed behind it. It is Daath--Knowledge (of the
sexual kind, as spoken of in the Book of Genesis). In magical
groups that use sexual techniques, Daath often takes on great
prominence.

In actual practice the Kabbalistic and hermetic systems
(owing in part to the problems of using the alchemical model)
mix inseparably, and groups often draw material from both
sources.

THE HERMETIC TRADITION IN AMERICA

Like Witchcraft, the hermetic tradition that flourished on
the Continent was transferred to America by the Colonists.
Unlike the Craft it attained a certain level of respectability,
and while New Englanders were hunting down Witches, bringing
them to trial, and in some cases hanging them, hermetic alchemists were operating openly and with the blessing of the
powers running the Colonies. In at least one case the local
alchemist *was* the power.

The most famous alchemist/hermeticist in Colonial America,
John Winthrop, Jr. (1606-1676), governor of Connecticut,
brought a collection of alchemical texts with him to America
in 1631. Among his collection were volumes from the personal
library of John Dee (1527-1608), England's most famous hermetic
philosopher. Winthrop kept up a correspondence with several
British alchemists who had visited him in New England--Robert
Child and George Starkey, for example. The latter studied
with Winthrop before moving to England.

Cotton Mather praised the Winthrops, both John and his
son Wait Still Winthrop (1642-1717), who had continued his
father's interest in medicine. During the late 17th and
early 18th centuries the alchemists spearheaded a heated

medical controversy over the introduction of nonorganic medi-
cines, i.e., chemical preparations, for the treatment of illness. Mather himself had taken much abuse from New England
doctors for his attempts to introduce smallpox vaccination
into the colonies. Thus a basis for affinity had been established.

Alchemists continued to work in the Colonial wilderness
throughout the 1700s. The most famous was Ezra Stiles,
president of Yale College. Eventually, with the introduction
of chemistry, the practice met the same fate it had on the
Continent: a slow death.

But in the 19th century, after decades of silence, a
voice in defense of alchemy and hermeticism spoke. Ethan
Allan Hitchcock's *Remarks upon Alchemy and the Alchemists*
(1857) signaled a new interest in the hermetic alternative
(philosophically if not scientifically). In the book's 307
pages Hitchcock argued that "the subject of Alchemy was Man;
while the object was the perfection of Man, which was supposed
to centre in a certain unity with the Divine nature." Hitchcock would be criticized for distilling the hermetic philosophy
into mere mortal teaching, thereby missing the depth of its
transformative, i.e., magical, component. But the popular
book found its audience in the United States and opened the
way for the post-Civil War hermetic groups.

After the War the United States, following Europe's
example of a few years earlier, underwent an occult revival.
Earlier the magnetists and the Spiritualists had established
a foothold, but the 1870s saw the emergence of genuine occult
non-Spiritualist alternatives. P.B. Randolph founded the
Rosicrucian Fraternity in 1868. In 1875 one of the most influential occult bodies, the Theosophical Society, was established by Henry Steele Olcott and H.P. Blavatsky in New York
City. Hermeticists were among the wide variety of occultists
who embraced Theosophy. Many who were to found hermetic
groups had been Theosophists first, most notably Anna Kingsford
and William Maitland.

In America Emily Hardinge Britten, one of the original
members of the Olcott/Blavatsky circle, published the teachings
of an occult order, the Brotherhood of Light, said to date from
ancient Egypt. In the 1880s Thomas Burgoyne contacted the
European head of the order, one M. Theon. With the help of
Norman Astley, his wife, Genevieve Stebbins, and Henry and
Belle M. Wagner, he founded the American branch of the Brotherhood. Burgoyne and the Wagners wrote the lesson material.

During the first decade of this century a young man named
Elbert Benjamine became the council's astrologer and eventually
its leader. He prepared a complete series of occult lessons,
and the voluminous writings began to roll off the presses.

Under Benjamine's direction the Brotherhood of Light evolved into the Church of Light. Benjamine's books, written under the pen name C.C. Zain, are still read in American occult circles.

Olney H. Richmond (1844-1920), founder of the Order of the Magi, was introduced to the occult on the battlefield where a mysterious stranger informed Richmond that he had been designated the new leader of the ancient Order. After the Civil War Richmond moved to Chicago and taught a class that grew into the Order of the Magi. In 1890 he opened a Temple which functioned at least until the 1940s. Richmond's daughter Arline took over leadership of the group after his death.

The Rosicrucians, the Theosophists, and Magi were joined soon after the turn of the century by other occult bodies that either were hermetic or included hermeticism as a strong component of their teachings. The Theosophical Publishing House printed and reprinted hermetic books, and independent hermetic teachers such as David Patterson Hatch, whose two books were published in 1898, appeared on the scene.

Two more Rosicrucian bodies joined the original Rosicrucian Fraternity and the Societas Rosicruciana in America which had immigrated to this country from England in the 1880s. The A.M.O.R.C., chartered by the Ordo Templi Orientis, started in 1909, just three years after Theosophist Max Heindel (d. 1919) had formed the Rosicrucian Fellowship.

The most famous hermetic group and the father of many children in the 20th century, the Hermetic Order of the Golden Dawn, was formed in 1888 in England by a group of Masons. During the several decades of its existence it produced a complete set of magical rituals, and its leaders wrote and translated a number of texts. The Order did not generate spontaneously, of course. It had been anticipated in the writings of such men as British magician Francis Barrett, author of the 1801 classic *The Magus*, and Eliphas Levi. The latter had spearheaded the occult revival in France in the mid-19th century.

During the early 20th century the OGD established itself in the United States. Michael Whitty, editor of the *Azoth*, an occult journal, became Praemonstrator General. He brought Paul Foster Case (1884-1954) into the Order, and Case later succeeded Whitty at both jobs. Case, however, left the OGD (which died in a few years) and founded the Builders of the Adytum, the largest of the hermetic schools in the United States today.

Shortly after World War II, several major occult teachers appeared--Manly Palmer Hall, Marc Edmund Jones, and Albert Sidney Raleigh. Hall, one of the most widely-read occultists in America, started his career as head of the Church of the

People in Los Angeles and continues to speak and write today
as head of the Philosophical Research Society. Marc Edmund
Jones, an early associate of Hall's, integrated hermeticism
into what he called the Sabian philosophy. The Sabian Assembly, though known mostly for its emphasis on astrology, has
continued to teach occult doctrines throughout its existence.

Albert Sidney Raleigh, a Chicago-based independent occult
teacher who wrote voluminously, taught hermeticism and magic
to his students during the 1920s and 1930s. His writings,
published by Chicago's Hermetic Publishing Company, were much
sought-after during the occult explosion of the 1970s.

The main exponent of the alchemical tradition in America
today is Frater Albertus, who heads the Paracelsus Research
Society in Salt Lake City, Utah. Founded in 1962, the Society
offers students instruction in esoteric astrology, Kabbalah,
and alchemy. Frater Albertus has written a number of alchemical books and edits the quarterly *Parachemy*.

THE FLOWERING OF PAGANISM

In the 1960s Americans heard of Gerald Gardner, whose form of
Wicca arrived by at least four routes. First, Rosemary and
Raymond Buckland traveled to England in the mid-1960s and in
a few weeks progressed through the degrees. Upon their return
to America as High Priestess and High Priest, they set up
Gardnerian covens across the country. Soon afterwards Donna
Cole, a Chicago Witch, visited England and was initiated into
a Gardnerian coven. From her work and that of her early col-
league Herman Enderle, most Chicago Paganism derives.

On the West Coast much Witchcraft can be traced to Victor
Anderson, who learned as a child that he was a Witch. He
became active only after reading Gardner's *Witchcraft Today*
but soon became a teacher of many of the Wiccans of California.

Meanwhile, in England, Alexander Sanders created a variation of the Gardnerian tradition, in part by adding some
ritual magic material. Alexandrian Wicca came to the United
States through a group in Boston headed by James Baker and
one in New York headed by Mary Nesnick. Nesnick later broke
with Sanders to found her own tradition, which she termed
Algard.

Endless variations on Wicca now exist. Some are variations
on Gardner. Some have been made up entirely by people who got
the general idea from the Gardnerians on how to do it. The
most popular term among Witches who seek to describe themselves
is "eclectic." Margot Adler, who has written the most authori-
tative chronicle of them, says the real Wiccan tradition is
"creativity."

Representative of this new creative Wicca is Circle Wicca of Madison, Wisconsin. Founded by two students of the occult community in Madison, it combines general occult material--writings by C.G. Jung, Jane Roberts (the Seth Material), and the Theosophical Society--with Wiccan material received from other groups, much of it written by leaders Selena Fox, Jim Alan, and De-Anna Alba. Circle has created a national network of Witches and Pagans through its publications--several periodicals, a song book, a Pagan directory, and a great deal of artwork.

While Witchcraft was growing, so was a vision of Neo-Paganism that posited a Mother Goddess faith from anthropological, historical, and science-fictional elements. The vision was based in part on some of the same material that Gardner had found. Three groups illustrate this impulse.

From his reading of Jung and Robert Graves, Fred Adams, a graduate student at Los Angeles State College, had come to love the ancient deities. Then one day as he was walking across the campus, he had a vision of the female Goddess. Thus inspired, Adams formed Hesperides, which later grew into Fereferia, a religion centered on Kore, the maiden aspect of the Triple Goddess (mother, maiden, crone).

In Missouri a group built around Tim Zell found inspiration in a science fiction novel, Robert A. Heinlein's *Stranger in a Strange Land*. In the book Michael Smith, a human being born on Mars, founds a new religion, the Church of All Worlds. During the 1970s the Church of All Worlds, founded by Zell but modeled on Smith's, was one of the largest Neo-Pagan groups in the country.

In the early 1960s a group at Carleton College in Northfield, Minnesota, sought a means to protest the compulsory chapel attendance rules. From anthropology books such as James Frazer's *The Golden Bough*, they constructed the Reformed Druids of North America, whose worship services they attended instead of chapel. After a year of controversy the rules were lifted, but the Druids had discovered a new faith which they preferred. Today Druid groves are found in every section of America and at last report (1979) were still active at Carleton.

The 1970s saw the flowering of the Neo-Pagan religion. Wiccan covens emerged in every corner of the continent, and a multitude of Pagan traditions appeared: Druid, Norse, Egyptian, Strege, Welsh, Celtic, and others. Numerous newsletters, most limited in circulation and lasting only a few issues, came and went. As old ones died, however, new ones arose.

The community experienced steady growth during the 1970s and, beginning with the 1974 Witchmeet in Minneapolis, held both regional and national festivals annually. The Midwest

Pagan Council, based in Chicago, sponsored the largest of
these, the Pan-Pagan Festival, which attracted over 500
persons in 1980. Recent surveys of the Neo-Pagan community
suggest approximately 30-40,000 members.

The feminists who appeared in the early 1970s created
considerable controversy at first with their defense of
separatist covens and lesbianism, and with their definition
of Wicca as an exclusively female religion. The controversy
has slowly abated. Not only is the feminist presence accepted
in most Neo-Paganism, but feminists occupy key positions in
the national leadership and regularly appear on the programs
of the regional and national gatherings.

Neo-Paganism will continue to grow, and its visibility
is certain to increase. Still a first-generation movement,
it has yet to produce the stable structure that will enable
it to survive in a highly mobile society and to educate its
children in Pagan faith. But such structure will evolve and
begin to function in the next decade. Look for the emergence
of permanent Pagan retreat centers, the production of children's books, and stable national periodicals.

OTHER MAGICAL TRADITIONS

The rise of Neo-Paganism in the last two decades drew attention once again to the other magical traditions that have
operated on American soil for many years. Voodoo, possibly
the most famous, came to the United States in the early 19th
century as planters fled the slave revolts in Haiti and
brought their human property with them.

Voodoo derives from West African tribal religion, and
magic forms an essential part of its core. Like its cousins
Santeria and Macumba, Voodoo allows the individual to become
possessed of the deity while in a trancelike state. While
possessed, the Voodoo practitioner assumes the role of the
deity. Through magical acts the deities are asked for assistance in the wide range of matters that fill human life.

Voodoo, again like Santeria and Macumba, is polytheistic
in the extreme but has several main deities, the chief one
being Damballah, usually pictured as a snake.

Voodoo derives from the Ibo tribe and has been filtered
through French Catholicism. Santeria, with which Voodoo is
often confused, is derived from Yoruban religion and filtered
through Spanish Catholicism. Macumba, like Santeria, is
Yoruban and comes from Portuguese Brazil. The chief deity
of Santeria is Chango.

The Voodoo family of African faiths has followed immigrants
from Haiti, Puerto Rico, Cuba, and Brazil to the United States.

A huge growth took place in the 1970s as immigration from
Latin America increased, and almost every major city in America
has its botanicas, shops that sell Santeria and Voodoo supplies
and artifacts.

Also surviving in the Mexican-American community is the
bruja, who like the hexmeister practices a system of low magic
and is feared for possible malevolent intentions. The bruja
stands in contrast to the *curandero* or healer. The two are
seen in opposition within the Mexican communities in the
United States.

Finally, in the Hawaiian Islands, the traditional magical
religion *huna*, largely destroyed in the early 1800s, experienced
a comeback in the 1970s. Encouraged by new waves of ethnic
pride, several healing hunas made their presence known to the
public, and major journals published research in huna practices.
Most recently huna groups have established teaching centers.

THE NEW MAGIC

Historians have correctly laid the demise of magic in Western
society to the impact of science and scientific methodology.
The magical worldview in pre-technological societies is
dominated by superstitions, fears, and approaches to nature
that science has rendered obsolete. Yet while science killed
"primitive" magic, it did not kill the "occult," and within
a short period of time, shorn of its pre-scientific models,
it rose again. In its new form it no longer relied upon
supernatural worldviews. Science had not solved the central
problems of occultism, metaphysics, and the transformation
of human life. Thus in the 19th century, even as science was
embarking on its era of greatest accomplishment, the occult
reappeared.

The new occultism adopted science as its revised model.
Occult phenomena, historically described as "supernatural,"
were redefined as "natural" phenomena, and occultists believed
that such phenomena would soon be generally accepted as factual when science in due course widened its area of investiga-
tion. Most occultists now believe that while physical science
does well with that part of the world it has chosen to ex-
amine, it has examined only a limited part of the world.

Eliphas Levi (1810-1875), the French magician and author,
became the spokesman of a scientific model of magical power.
He absorbed the popular teachings of the Mesmerists, the
19th-century followers of French physician F.A. Mesmer
(1734-1815), who had postulated a mysterious etheric--but no
less scientifically described--power that caused paranormal
healings and allowed practitioners to induce hypnotic trances

in people. Levi claimed that this Mesmeritic fluid was the
real power by which magic can be performed. While Mesmer's
claims never gained wide scientific acceptance, they never
died and have been resurrected as a result of recent experi-
ments in psychokinesis.

Furthermore Levi, possibly without realizing what he had
done, redefined magical power in a second important way.
Besides giving it a scientific model, he radically diminished
its potential as the all-powerful force to be feared and
revered. It became just one force among others in the natural
world. It was a subtle force, a personal force, whose main
use was high magic--the mystical transformation of the individual magician. Yes, it could be used for low magic--the
working of change in the mundane world. But used for low
magic, the power was more an additive, a straw to break the
camel's back, that little extra which, working with other
forces, could create the desired change. Its power increased
greatly if aligned with the ardent belief and desire of the
magician.

If Levi saved magical power, the rise of psychical research
saved the magician. Psychical researchers documented the
existence of "paranormal" powers, seemingly in a few people
much of the time and in most people occasionally. Telepathy,
clairvoyance, precognition, communication with spirits, and
psychokinesis were attributes of the individual. Thus magic
became psychic ability and the magician an adept at extrasen-
sory perception.

And while Levi saved magical power and the psychical researchers the magician, the depth psychologists, particularly
psychoanalyst Carl Gustav Jung, saved the gods. Jung advanced
the idea of archetypes, images that were generated in the un-
conscious of the race, that reappeared in many cultural set-
tings and which related to specific psychic realities of
humanity. In passing, he noted that many of the ancient gods
and goddesses of Paganism appear in his collection of archetypes.

Thus out of Jung's work grew a new rationale for polytheism. The archetypes, the deities of old, existed. They
existed subjectively but more so as they were the product of
the combined psyche of the race. They could be venerated,
even worshipped, because they manifest and represent forces
that transcend the individual. They could also be manipulated
because they represent segments of the individual. To understand the deities is to understand the self. To worship them
is to grow. To become one with them is the aim of life.

This new magic--individualized and psychologized--with a
scientific model could be given to post-scientific people and
combined with the essentials of magical teachings to create a
new religion.

MAGIC AS RELIGION

That new religion exists now in many forms. The movement is organized into numerous small groups--covens, groves, lodges, and nests--few of which have anything beyond a possible friendly affinity to any other group. There is far more diversity than conformity, although within rampant diversity some consensus on matters of worship, belief, and lifestyle runs as a thread holding the movement together.

Most Neo-Pagans believe in the basic hermetic magical principle, "As above, so below." They see the world as a macrocosm that is known in the many microcosms that reflect it. They also believe that actions carried out in the microcosm are reflected in the macrocosm. Further, the hermetic principle implies the interconnection of all things.

The will and imagination activate magical power. The disciplined will calls up the powers of the magician, and the imagination focuses the direction of the power being used. The techniques of magic serve the magician as tools in raising the power, and Witches and magicians, early in their careers, master the various ways of creating the emotional and psychic (i.e., magical) energy--ritual, chanting, dancing, and meditation. Some, the minority, even use psychedelic drugs or various extraordinary techniques such as the scourging ritual devised by Gardner.

The magical operation usually begins with the creation of sacred space. Most magical people worship and perform magical operations in a circle. The circle drawn on the floor or visualized in the imagination becomes the microcosm of the macrocosm. The spherical working space inscribes a circle as it intersects the floor. The sacred space is both a meeting ground between the mundane world and the world of the gods, and a place of protection from the forces dealt with in magical operations. All magical ceremonies begin by "closing the circle," i.e., the sealing of the magical space, and end by banishing the forces raised and returning to the mundane world, i.e., opening the circle.

Within the circle two basic types of magical operations occur. Invocation is the process by which the magician or Witch calls from the cosmos a particular force. Witches call this "drawing down the moon," and it is their most popular ritual. The manifestation of this invocation is the intoxication and possession of the magician or Witch by the deity so that the individual or individuals doing the invocation become one with the deity. In Voodoo the possessed act as if they are momentarily the possessing deity. In contrast, evocation calls forces from within, forces often seen as an unbalanced or segmented aspect of the magician's own inner make-up. The

forces are personified as spirits and directed to the task at
hand.

The object of invocation is a mystical oneness with the
gods, and invocation is a basic religious act common to almost
all religious traditions. Evocation is a confrontation of
the magician with the magical forces within him/herself.
These forces are to be tamed and used either for the development of the magician or for a specific mundane magic task.

GROUP LIFE

Pagans are organized into small intimate groups. Witches form
covens. Neo-Pagans form groves, nests, and circles. Ritual
magicians typically form lodges and temples. Witch and Neo-
Pagan groups are usually led by a Priestess and/or Priest,
while the Master of a magical temple goes under a variety of
names.

The coven (and temple) frequently meets in the home of
the leader. In some cases (usually if the leader is affluent
enough) a separate room may be set aside exclusively for
ritual use, but such is the exception. The leaders are not
paid for their efforts as priests or priestesses, and the
only money that changes hands is for the few candles and
magical supplies and lesson materials that a coven might use.
Being a priest(ess) can be a major financial drain on one's
otherwise secular income.

The coven meets bi-weekly on the new and full moon
(esbats). It also meets eight times per year for major festivals. Frequently festival time will be the occasion for
several covens and groups to meet together for a ritual and
feast. The festival (sabbat) occasions are:

Samhain	October 31
Yule	December 21
Oimelc (Candlemas)	February 2
Spring Equinox	March 21
Beltane	April 30
Summer Solstice	June 21
Lammas	August 1
Fall Equinox	September 21

These festivals follow the agricultural cycle of spring rebirth, summer growth, harvest, and winter death. The Pagan
year begins at Hallowe'en or Samhain, which is celebrated as
a time of examination of the past and resolution for the
future.

The Pagan lifestyle is festive and happy, and even the
most somber gatherings have a certain lightness, gaiety, and

humor about them. The Pagans' moral stance centers on two
principles: respect for the earth and harmlessness. Often
called an earth religion, Paganism worships the Earth Mother
and sees the protection of the earth as a major responsibility.
Many Pagans can be found in ecology programs, though the
nature of their organization into small intimate groups works
against their forming ecology action groups themselves. Their
social interaction is governed by the Wiccan Rede, "That you
harm none, do what you will." Witches and Pagans are admon-
ished to concentrate on getting their lives in order and not
to interfere with others in accomplishing the same. This
style does allow for love bonding and for coming to the aid
of others, but cautions Pagans to refrain from meddling in
affairs into which they have not been invited.

A strain of sexual liberation runs through the movement.
The main deities are the Mother Goddess and her consort. To
the sexual metaphor at the heart of their faith, Crowley added
the emphasis on sex magic. This does not mean, however, that
Pagans are especially promiscuous or otherwise out of the
ordinary in their sexual practices. Individuals generally do
sex magic rituals only with their mates or more often conduct
them symbolically.

A final dominant aspect of the magical life is secrecy.
Witches and magicians carry with them the memory of the
"burning times," and though few fear a tortured death, they
do fear loss of job or home and trouble with family and
acquaintances from the revelation that they are Pagan. While
covens and magical groups exist in most urban centers, they
are difficult to locate, and potential members must work to
find a group. Secrecy has its reward, however. It creates
a certain elite sense in movement participants who believe
they are privy to the secret wisdom kept from the masses of
the secular world.

The secret life is bolstered by a system of initiations
and degrees. The typical Pagan, upon joining a group, is
first dedicated to the Goddess or the Gods. After a period
of study, members are initiated into full membership. Other
degrees, the number of which varies from group to group,
follow. In Witchcraft there are typically three degrees
which can only be administered a year and a day apart, after
a level of both learning and occult attainment has been
reached. The highest degree is for the coven leaders.

PAGANS AND CHRISTIANS

The encounter between Pagans and Christians fills a significant
part of the Pagan life, both because of the simple fact that

the Western world is still nominally Christian and because of the memory of the Witchhunting of past generations. Some Christians, mostly conservative Evangelicals, help keep alive this negative encounter by a continued attack upon Witchcraft and occultism in books and tracts.

The Christian attack has affected the Pagan community basically in only one way: it keeps the fear-level high. Many Pagans are genuinely afraid that the Christians will do more than just write against them. They also complain bitterly of the slander that much Christian literature continues to direct against them.

As noted above, the Pagans and Witches are part of a basically nature religion, worshipping the Mother Goddess and her consort, the Horned God. Much of the Christian literature repeats the myths of the Witchhunters who in medieval times identified Witchcraft with Satanism. Most Christians who write on Witchcraft know little of the Pagan/Wicca movement; moreover, they often are unwilling to learn about it, electing instead to perpetuate their errors. Witches are quick to note that not only do they not believe in the Devil, but that the Devil is a Christian personification of evil; Witches, like Hindus and Buddhists, accept neither the Christian God nor the Christian anti-God, Satan.

A lurid incident occurred during the 1970s involving one John Todd (aka Lance Collins). When Todd suddenly resigned as a leader of the Church of Wicca group in Dayton, Ohio, he announced that all along he had been an undercover agent whose purpose was to discover the Witches' secrets and to expose them to the world. Though only the head of a small coven in Dayton (most of whose members were from his immediate family), he declared that he had risen to an international position of leadership in a giant secret conspiracy by the Witches to take over the world, much of which they secretly controlled already. Fortunately, after only a short time, the inconsistencies and undeniable falsehoods in his story were uncovered, and his testimony was discredited.

Polemics between Christians and Pagans seem likely to continue. Too many Pagans have come into magic and Witchcraft from a negative experience as young people in the church. Also, Evangelical anti-cultists show no signs of discontinuing their attacks on Witchcraft and the occult. Meanwhile the Pagans take comfort in the growing pluralism of America and the Western world.

II

BACKGROUND MATERIAL

A. MAGIC, WITCHCRAFT, AND PAGANISM--
A READER'S GUIDE

No single volume has attempted to cover the territory mapped out by this volume--the presence of magic, Witchcraft, and Paganism in America both historically and in the recent revival. There are, however, a number of volumes that can aid the new reader to attain some background in the area and to begin to understand the world of modern Pagans. By far the best single volume, Margot Adler's *Drawing Down the Moon* (818), written in the mid-1970s, chronicles the burgeoning Neo-Pagan movement in great detail. Adler mixes the insight of her two roles as Wiccan priestess and investigative reporter.

Second only to Adler, P.F. Isaac Bonewits' *Real Magic* (5) offers a perspective on the contemporary practice of magic by someone with formal training in anthropology and occult history, as well as the practice of being a Pagan priest. Francis King's several books (243-245) trace the modern magical revival from the perspective of ritual magic with the Ordo Templi Orientis and Aleister Crowley as central actors.

Little in the way of academic reflection on Neo-Paganism as part of the "new" religions scene has yet occurred. Both Ellwood (12) and Melton (33) have included chapters in their books, and the latter has produced several items as precursors to this volume (34-35). Truzzi (47-49) has provided valuable comment on the role of the new Witch, as opposed to the traditional one.

Other than Ellwood, Truzzi, and Melton, one must look to actual practitioners for the best description of the Neo-Pagan world, a not altogether unhappy situation. In trying to comprehend the world of Neo-Paganism and contemporary magic, to rely upon the works produced by outside observers, even scholarly ones, can easily lead one astray. Few writers have

taken the time of either Ellwood or Truzzi to actually experience and talk to magicians and Witches about their faith
and life. With Witches especially, since so much of their
lives are occult, i.e., hidden, and because there is so much
diversity in the movement, writers who rely on a few inter-
views or on other people's writings can do naught but produce
superficial and error-filled observations. Hans Holzer's
books (904-908, 1189) provide a ready case in point. Though
a large segment of the Wiccan/Pagan community accepted Holzer,
his writings did not penetrate beyond the superficial level
and are replete with errors. Though laudatory of the movement, they were quietly and quickly discarded and never found
their way to the Pagan reading lists.

What do Pagans and magicians read, and what books do they
identify as books most representative of their shared thoughts?
A sample list of the main books, after Adler and Bonewits,
which might find their way to the shelf of a new Pagan or
Witch would include:

Raymond Buckland. *Witchcraft from the Inside* (768)
William E. Butler. *The Magician, His Training and Work* (202)
Stewart Farrar. *What Witches Do* (771)
Dion Fortune. *Practical Occultism in Everyday Life* (213)
————. *Training and Work of the Initiate* (218)
Selena Fox. *Circle Guide to Wicca and Pagan Resources* (810)
Gerald Gardner. *Witchcraft Today* (775)
Leo L. Martello. *Witchcraft: The Old Religion* (961)
David L. Miller. *The New Polytheism* (1198)
Israel Regardie. *The Middle Pillar* (566)
Susan Roberts. *Witches U.S.A.* (991)
Lady Sheba. *The Grimoire of Lady Sheba* (1003)
Starhawk. *The Spiral Dance* (1121)
A Book of Pagan Rituals (1160)

Eventually, Aleister Crowley's works would also be included,
but more for the advanced student.

American Witchcraft and magical practices are, of course,
set within the broader context of Witchcraft and magic as
they have occurred historically in the West and in pre-technological societies around the world. The modern Wiccan and
ritual magic phenomenon, however, is more notable for its
contrasts with what has been called Witchcraft and magic in
other contexts than its likenesses. As one reads the standard
histories and anthropological reports of magical groups and
practitioners, careful attention to exactly what phenomenon
the author is describing is of the greatest importance.

Given that warning, a library of excellent writing on the
broad spectrum of magic and Witchcraft awaits the reader. For

those not yet ready to tackle Thorndike's massive work (86),
several one-volume surveys of magic and Witchcraft have appeared, the best being Jeffery B. Russell's *A History of
Witchcraft* (184). Cohn (152) and Cavendish (60) cover additional material from different perspectives.

From the surveys of Western magic, one turns to the
specialized studies of magical practice, most notably Witchcraft and sorcery in Europe from the Middle Ages to the
Enlightenment. During the last decade a number of outstanding
works have appeared. Begin with Thomas (83), Russell (184),
and Yates (97), but do not neglect Baroja (151), Kieckhefer
(165), Monter (177), or Trevor-Roper (193).

Within the area of history of religions and anthropology,
one can do well to begin with Marwick's *Witchcraft and Sorcery*
(101), which contains a collection of articles on the nature
of Witchcraft in pre-technological society, as well as extensive bibliographic references for further reading. Mircea
Eliade has also recently published his mature reflection on
the nature of magic (11).

Little consensus on the nature of magic exists within
scholarly circles as yet, and few attempts to integrate historical and anthropological materials with modern magical
thought in the West have appeared. The student is left with
the problem of sampling a variety of reflections and integra-
ting them him/herself. For example, Mauss (32) supplies an
anthropological approach while Tiryakian (46) offers a sociological one. See the items below in Section II-B, not forgetting the major treatises by the modern magicians--Conway
(10), Crowley (459), and Levi (250).

The phenomenon of modern forms of traditional (pre-technological) magical systems currently functioning in the United
States presents another problem. Thought about the essential
character of Voodoo and its cousins, Santeria and Macumba, is
undergoing radical revision (see Desmangles, 1292-1293), and
no satisfactory book is available. One might begin with
Tallant (1338), an older work on Voodoo in New Orleans, or
Gilfond's more recent treatment (1298). Gonzalez-Wippler
(1355) has done the best survey of Santeria.

The treatment of folk magic traditions such as hoodoo and
bruja remains in the writings of folklorists and medical practitioners (who must deal with "bewitched" patients), and
little work of an historical nature has been attempted. On
hoodoo see McTeer (1384), Mitchell (1389), and Puckett (1394).
For bruja, see Simmons (1456).

Finally, huna has received renewed attention in the 1970s,
and the volumes by Gutmanis (1417), Kamakau (1421-1422), and
Rodman (1433) provide ready access to the tradition.

B. THE MAGICAL WORLDVIEW

Magic, according to Aleister Crowley, is the art of employing
the cosmic paranormal forces which underpin the universe for
the purpose of creating change by an act of the will. That
definition came out of two centuries of development within the
magical occult community, development forced by the impact of
science. Pre-scientific magicians, at least the ones in the
West, conceived of their task as the evocation and invocation
of spirit entities. Science challenged that worldview, and
Eliphas Levi reworked the tradition using the magnetic categories of Franz Anton Mesmer. Levi defined magic as the control and manipulation of the universal magnetic fluid or
astral light.

The final reworking under Aleister Crowley psychologized
the magical act and interpreted magic with primary reference
to the magician. "Every intentional act is a magical act,"
asserted Crowley at one point, thus fully demythologizing the
concept.

Following Crowley's lead, modern magicians have redefined
the occult tradition. They have searched for the essence of
real magic, the core that remained when the centuries of
occult lore were stripped away. They discarded quaint traditions, superstitions, and pre-technological science. The
small but all-important bit that remained was a subtle occult
power frequently identified with the power investigated by
parapsychologists as psychokinesis.

Thus while the general public and most scholars still see
occultists as believers in a supernatural, all-powerful
spirit-directed force, magicians see themselves as possessors
of a force that operates within the context of other well-
defined natural forces. In the hands of the adept, that
subtle force can be the balance of power that directs a
situation one way or another. Combined with other forces--
psychological sets, suggestion, wish fulfillment, body chemistry, etc.--it can be a powerful energy.

The major use of magical power is the transformation of
the magician. The power changes the dross of the soul into
the pure gold of spirit. Thus the true magician concentrates
first on changing the self. Magicians will learn to attune

themselves to occult forces, to train the will with discipline, to meditate, and to perfect ritual precision.

The works in this section bring together the wide variety of opinion, both popular and scholarly, on the nature of magic, the magical community, and the rationale for individuals' becoming magicians. As with other highly selective listings included in this bibliography, the section was constructed from relevant items representative of the scholarly debates and works circulating in the contemporary magical community, including some obscure periodical citations, newspaper articles, and even a few books to which I felt attention should be drawn. This list should be viewed as presenting the range of opinion on the nature of magic rather than an attempt to resolve the ongoing discussion.

Bibliographically, Black, Galbreath, Hall, and Melton (33) explore areas tangential to this bibliography.

For scholarly reflection on magic see Eliade, Greeley, Marty, Rony, and Wax. Sociologist Tiryakian offers a sympathetic perspective on the confluence of creativity in society and the occult. Other sociological perspectives come from Jarvis and Agassi, Scott, Truzzi, and Webster. Psychological speculations are offered by Huxley, Leininger, Masters, and Wilson.

Occultists can speak articulately for themselves, and Bonewits and Conway both do capable jobs. Druid High Priest Bonewits, in a lighthearted, carefree style, demythologizes much of current magical practice and Pagan belief, and his book has become standard reading for most new Pagans. Conway's book, an introductory text used by many groups, offers a basic introduction to magic, a rationale for how it works, the disciplines required, and simple rituals.

In surveying the magicians' self-understanding, one should not forget the works of Aleister Crowley (459), W.E. Butler (201), and William Gray (225), found elsewhere in this bibliography.

1. Anderson, Robert D. "Witchcraft and Sex." *Sexual Behavior* (1972) 8-14.

2. Banis, Victor. *Charms, Spells and Curses for the Millions.* Los Angeles: Sherbourne Press, 1970. 154 pp.

3. Black, George Fraser. "List of Works Related to Druids and Druidism." *Bulletin of the New York Public Library* 24 (1920) 11-24.

4. ———. "List of Works Related to Witchcraft in Europe." *Bulletin of the New York Public Library* 15 (1911) 727-55.

5.   Bonewits, P.E. Isaac. *Real Magic*. New York: Coward,
     McCann & Geoghegan, 1971. 236 pp.

6.   Brennan, J.H. *An Occult History of the World*. London:
     Futura, 1976. 320 pp.

7.   Cavendish, Richard. *The Black Arts*. New York: G.P.
     Putnam's Sons, 1967. 373 pp.

8.   Cohen, Daniel. *Magicians, Wizards & Sorcerers*. Phila-
     delphia: J.B. Lippincott Company, 1973. 159 pp.

9.   ————. *The New Believers*. New York: M. Evans and Com-
     pany, 1975, pp. 127-74.

10. Conway, David. *Magic: An Occult Primer*. New York: E.P.
     Dutton & Co., 1972. 286 pp.

11. Eliade, Mircea. *Occultism, Witchcraft, and Cultural
     Fashions*. Chicago: University of Chicago Press, 1976.
     148 pp.

12. Ellwood, Robert S., Jr. *Religious and Spiritual Groups
     in Modern America*. Englewood Cliffs, NJ: Prentice-
     Hall, 1973. 334 pp.

13. Galbreath, Robert, ed. *The Occult: Studies and Evalua-
     tions*. Bowling Green, OH: Bowling Green University
     Popular Press, 1972. 126 pp.

14. Godwin, John. *Occult America*. Garden City, NY: Doubleday
     & Co., 1972. 314 pp.

15. Gonzalez-Wippler, Migene. *The Complete Book of Spells,
     Ceremonies and Magic*. New York: Crown Publishers,
     1978. 376 pp.

16. Greeley, Andrew. *The Sociology of the Paranormal*.
     Beverly Hills, CA: Sage Publications (A Sage Research
     Paper).

17. Gregor, Arthur S. *Witchcraft and Magic*. New York:
     Charles Scribner's Sons, 1972. 148 pp.

18. Hall, Manly P. *Great Books on Religion and Esoteric
     Philosophy*. Los Angeles: Philosophical Research
     Society, Inc., 1966. 85 pp.

19. Hartman, Patricia A. "Social Dimensions of Occult Par-
     ticipation: The Gnostica Study." *British Journal of
     Sociology* 27,2 (June 1976) 169-83.

20. Hill, Douglas, and Pat Williams. *The Supernatural.* New
     York: New American Library, 1965. 240 pp.

21. Huxley, Elspeth. "Science, Psychiatry--or Witchery?"
     New York Times Magazine (May 31, 1959).

22. Jarvie, I.C., and Joseph Agassi. "The Problem of the
     Rationality of Magic." *British Journal of Sociology*
     18 (March 1967) 55-76.

23. Kenyon, Richard L. "Bias Against 'Pagans' Is Termed a
     Refusal to Face Self." *Milwaukee Journal* (September 16,
     1978) 4.

24. Klander, J.I. "Archives on Witchcraft." *Fate* 20,7
     (July 1967) 68-70.

25. Larner, Christina. "Is All Witchcraft Really Witchcraft?"
     New Society (October 10, 1974) 81-83.

26. Leininger, Madeline. "Witchcraft Practices and Psycho-
     logical Therapy with Urban U.S. Families." *Human
     Organization* 32,1 (Spring 1973) 74-82.

27. Lippman, Deborah, and Paul Colin. *How to Make Amulets,
     Charms and Talismans.* New York: M. Evans and Company,
     1974. 208 pp.

28. McFerran, Douglas. "The New Magic." *Commonweal* 94
     (September 17, 1971) 477-80.

29. Madsen, William, and Claudia Madsen. *A Guide to Mexican
     Witchcraft.* Mexico: Minutiae Mexicana, 1972. 96 pp.

30. Marty, Martin. "The Occult Establishment." *Social Re-
     search* 37 (Summer 1970) 212-30.

31. Masters, Robert E.L. *Eros and Evil.* New York: Julian
     Press, 1962. 322 pp.

32. Mauss, Marcel. *A General Theory of Magic.* London:
     Routledge and Kegan Paul, 1972. 148 pp.

33. Melton, J. Gordon. *The Encyclopedia of American Reli-gions*. Wilmington, NC: McGrath Publishing Company, 1978, II, 249-308.

34. ————. *The Literature of Magick, Witchcraft and Neo-Paganism*. Evanston, IL: Institute for the Study of American Religion, 1979. 62 pp.

35. ————. "Neo-Paganism: Report on the Survey of an Alterna-tive Religion." A paper presented to the Society for the Scientific Study of Religion. Cincinnati, OH, October 30-November 2, 1980.

36. ————. "Toward a History of Magical Religion in the United States." *Listening* 9,3 (Autumn 1974) 112-33.

37. Nugent, Donald. "The Renaissance and/of Witchcraft." *Church History* 40,1 (March 1971) 69-78.

38. "The Occult: A Substitute Faith." *Time* 99,25 (June 19, 1972) 62-68.

39. "The Psychology of Witches." *Time* (September 3, 1956) 62-63.

40. Rony, Jerome-Antoine. *A History of Magic*. New York: Walker and Company, 1962. 160 pp.

41. Rowley, Peter. *New Gods in America*. New York: David McKay Company, 1971, pp. 78-83.

42. Scott, Gini Graham. *Cult and Countercult*. Westport, CT: Greenwood Press, 1980. 213 pp.

43. Seabrook, William. *Witchcraft: Its Power in the World Today*. New York: Harcourt, Brace & Co., 1940. 387 pp.

44. Sepharial. *The Book of Charms and Talismans*. New York: Arc Books, 1969. 118 pp.

45. Singer, Dale. "Voodoo Shop Owner Keeps the Faith." *Chicago Daily News* (September 19, 1977).

46. Tiryakian, Edward A. "Towards the Sociology of Esoteric Culture." *American Journal of Sociology* 78,3 (November 1972) 491-511.

47. Truzzi, Marcello. "The Occult Revival as Popular Culture: Some Random Observations on the Old and Nouveau Witch." *Sociological Quarterly* 13 (Winter 1972) 16-34.

48. ————. "The Old and the Nouveau Witch." *Fate* 26,2-3, I (February 1973) 58-65; II (March 1973) 97-104.

49. ————. "Toward a Sociology of the Occult: Notes on Modern Witchcraft." In I.I. Zaretsky and M.P. Leone, eds., *Religious Movements in Contemporary America*. Princeton, NJ: Princeton University Press, 1972, pp. 628-45.

50. *The Unknown: A National Tattler Special Report*. Chicago: Publishers Promotion Agency, 1976. 20 pp.

51. Vetter, George B. *Magic and Religion*. New York: Philosophical Library, 1958. 555 pp.

52. Wax, Rosalie, and Murray Wax. "The Magical World View." *Journal for the Scientific Study of Religion* 1,2 (April 1962) 179-88.

53. Webster, Hutton. *Magic, A Sociological Study*. Stanford, CA: Stanford University Press, 1948. 524 pp.

54. Wedeck, Harry E. *Treasury of Witchcraft*. New York: Philosophical Library, 1961. 271 pp.

55. Wilson, Arnold W. "Magic in Contemporary Life and in Psychoanalysis." *Psychoanalytic Review* 59,1 (Spring 1972) 5-18.

56. *Witchcraft, Magic and the Supernatural*. London: Octopus Books, 1974. 176 pp.

57. Woods, Richard. *The Occult Revolution*. New York: Herder and Herder, 1971. 240 pp.

58. Wright, Walter. "File 1004--Police Study Witchcraft." *Seattle Post-Intelligencer* (February 1, 1976).

59. Zolar. *Book of Forbidden Knowledge*. New York: Zolar, n.d. 128 pp.

C. MAGIC IN HISTORY

Numerous books treat the history of magic, witchcraft, sorcery, and the occult. Survey books generally begin in ancient times and end with Salem or the Enlightenment in Europe. This selection of such titles includes a few of the better items produced by recent scholarship and those titles most frequently encountered within the magical community.

Specialized studies in Medieval and Renaissance magic helped create a new interest in the 1970s in the largely neglected study of the impact of occultism on the development of modern thought. The works by Shumaker, Thomas, Walker, and Yates are "must" reading.

The pre-modern magical tradition reached its culmination in the alchemical tradition, largely misunderstood as merely a pre-scientific chemistry. A selection of books on the history and nature of alchemy are cited, though no attempt has been made in this work to begin to cite the numerous alchemical volumes written over the years. Among the specialized studies, Debus offers an interesting perspective on the effect of alchemy on the advancement of medicine.

Rosicrucianism, a philosophy and occult school, stands in close proximity to both magic and alchemy, and at times has been a cover for alchemical and magical activity. The history of this movement can be found in Jennings, McIntosh, Waite, and Yates.

60. Cavendish, Richard. *A History of Magic*. New York: Taplinger Publishing Company, 1977. 180 pp.

61. Crow, W.B. *A History of Magic, Witchcraft and Occultism*. North Hollywood, CA: Wilshire Book Company, 1968. 316 pp.

62. Debus, Allen G. *The English Paracelsians*. New York: Franklin Watts, 1966. 222 pp.

63. Eliade, Mircea. *The Forge and the Crucible*. New York: Harper & Brothers, 1962. 208 pp.

64. Federmann, Reinhard. *The Royal Art of Alchemy*. Phila-
    delphia: Chilton Book Company, 1964. 264 pp.

65. Gardner, Helena. *Witchcraft*. Chatsworth, CA: Brandon
    Books, 1974. 192 pp.

66. Godwin, Joscelyn. *Robert Fludd*. Boulder, CO: Shambhala,
    1979. 96 pp.

67. Hartmann, Franz. *The Life and Doctrines of Paracelsus*.
    New York: John W. Lovell Company, 1891. 367 pp.

68. Hutin, Serge. *A History of Alchemy*. New York: Tower
    Book, 1962. 120 pp.

69. Jaffé, Aniela. "The Influence of Alchemy on the Works of
    C.G. Jung." In Ian Macphail, comp., *Alchemy and the
    Occult*. New Haven: Yale University Library, 1968, I,
    xv-xxxiii.

70. Jennings, Hargrave. *The Rosicrucians*. London: George
    Routledge & Sons, 1907. 486 pp.

71. McIntosh, Christopher. *The Rosy Cross Unveiled*. Well-
    ingsborough, Northamptonshire: Aquarian Press, 1980.
    160 pp.

72. Macphail, Ian, comp. *Alchemy and the Occult*. New Haven:
    Yale University Library, 1968. 4 vols.

73. Magus Incognito. *The Secret Doctrine of the Rosicrucians*.
    Chicago: Occult Press, 1949. 256 pp.

74. Mead, George R.S. *Thrice Greatest Hermes*. London:
    Theosophical Publishing Society, 1906.

75. Nicolaus. *The Little Mystic-Magic Picture Book*. Chicago:
    Aries Press, 1937. 231 pp.

76. Redgrove, H. Stanley. *Alchemy: Ancient and Modern*.
    London: Rider, 1922. Rpt. New Hyde Park, NY: Univer-
    sity Books, 1969. 144 pp.

77. Rohmer, Sax. *The Romance of Sorcery*. New York: Causeway
    Books, 1973. 320 pp.

78. Ronan, Margaret. *Hunt the Witch Down!* New York:
    Scholastic Book Services, 1976. 122 pp.

79. Sadoul, Jacques. *Alchemists and Gold*. New York: G.P. Putnam's Sons, 1972. 253 pp.

80. Seligmann, Kurt. *The History of Magic*. New York: Pantheon Books, 1948. Rpt. as *Magic, Supernaturalism and Religion*. New York: Pantheon Books, 1971. 342 pp.

81. Shumaker, Wayne. *The Occult Sciences in the Renaissance*. Berkeley: University of California Press, 1972. 284 pp.

82. Silberer, Herbert. *Hidden Symbolism of Alchemy and the Occult Arts*. New York: Dover Publications, 1971. 451 pp.

83. Thomas, Keith. *Religion & the Decline of Magic*. New York: Charles Scribner's Sons, 1971. 716 pp.

84. Thompson, C.J.S. *The Mysteries and Secrets of Magic*. New York: Causeway Books, 1973. 320 pp.

85. Thompson, R. Campbell. *Semitic Magic*. London: Luzac & Co., 1908. 286 pp.

86. Thorndike, Lynn. *A History of Magic and Experimental Science*. New York: Columbia University Press, 1923-58. 8 vols.

87. Trachtenberg, Joshua. *Jewish Magic and Superstition*. New York: Sherman's Jewish Book House, 1939. 356 pp.

88. Waite, Arthur Edward. *The Brotherhood of the Rosy Cross*. London: Rider & Company, 1924.

89. ———. *The Real History of the Rosicrucians*. London: George Redway, 1887. 446 pp. Rpt. Mokelumne Hill, CA: Health Research, 1960. 311 pp.

90. ———. *The Secret Tradition in Alchemy*. New York: Samuel Weiser, 1969. 415 pp.

91. Walker, D.P. *Spiritual and Demonic Magic*. Notre Dame, IN: University of Notre Dame Press, 1975. 244 pp.

92. Webb, James. *The Occult Establishment*. LaSalle, IL: Open Court Publishing Company, 1976. 535 pp.

93. ———. *The Occult Underground*. LaSalle, IL: Open Court Publishing Company, 1974. 387 pp.

94. Wittemans, Frans. *A New & Authentic History of the Rosicrucians.* Chicago: Aries Press, 1938. 224 pp.

95. Yates, Frances A. *Majesty and Magic in Shakespeare's Last Plays.* Boulder, CO: Shambhala, 1978. 140 pp.

96. ————. *The Occult Philosophy in the Elizabethan Age.* Boston: Routledge and Kegan Paul, 1979. 217 pp.

97. ————. *The Rosicrucian Enlightenment.* Boston: Routledge and Kegan Paul, 1972. 267 pp.

D. WITCHCRAFT AND MAGIC IN THE THIRD WORLD

In a pre-literate and pre-technological society in which the
majority of the members believe in the close proximity of the
spirits, magic varies considerably from the phenomenon in a
post-technological one. Most anthropological literature on
magic and Witchcraft grows out of the study of pre-modern
societies. In turn the experience of pre-modern occultism
strongly informs anthropological reflection upon the nature
of magic.

This highly selective list includes not only standard
works (Evans-Pitchard, Malinowski, Marwick, and Parrinder)
but works reflecting on Australian (Rose), South American
(Sharon), and Native American (Walker) Witchcraft as well.
These works describe a phenomenon quite different from modern
Paganism and Witchcraft.

98.   Douglas, Mary, ed. *Witchcraft Confessions and Accusa-
        tions*. New York: Tavistock Publications, 1970.
        387 pp.

99.   Evans-Pitchard, E.E. *Witchcraft, Oracles and Magic
        Among the Azande*. Oxford: Clarendon Press, 1937.
        588 pp.

100. Malinowski, Bronislaw. *Magic, Science and Religion*.
        Garden City, NY: Doubleday, 1954.   274 pp.

101. Marwick, Max, ed. *Witchcraft and Sorcery*. Baltimore,
        MD: Penguin Books, 1970.   416 pp.

102. Middleton, John, and E.H. Winter, eds. *Witchcraft and
        Sorcery in East Africa*. New York: Frederick A.
        Praeger, 1963.   302 pp.

103. Nash, June. "Devils, Witches, and Sudden Death."
        Natural History 81,3 (March 1972) 52-58, 82-83.

104. Newell, Venetia, ed. *The Witch Figure*. Boston: Routledge and Kegan Paul, 1973. 239 pp.

105. Parrinder, E.G. "African Ideas of Witchcraft." *Folklore* 63 (1956) 142-50.

106. ————. *Witchcraft: European and African*. London:
Faber and Faber, 1963. 215 pp.

107. Rose, Ronald. *Living Magic*. New York: Rand McNally
and Company, 1956. 240 pp.

108. Sharon, Douglas. *Wizard of the Four Winds*. New York:
Free Press, 1978. 222 pp.

109. Walker, Deward E., Jr., ed. *Systems of North American
Witchcraft and Sorcery*. Moscow, ID: University of
Idaho (Anthropology Monograph of the University of
Idaho, #1), 1970. 295 pp.

110. "Witchcraft: It Works Says Sociologist at ASU." *Tempe*
(Ariz.) *Daily News* (March 28, 1978).

111. Wright, Harry B. *Witness to Witchcraft*. New York:
Funk and Wagnalls Company, 1957. 246 pp.

E. MAGIC IN ANCIENT TIMES

During the past century a steady increase of scholarly works
has drawn attention to occult religion and magic in ancient
times. Pagan religion in Western Europe was an occult and
magical faith.

Today's magical practitioners consider themselves the
modern representatives of the old Paganism. They have, however, learned of the "Old Religion" from the material here
cited, not from any ancient traditions passed orally through
the centuries. An examination of the modern Pagan writings
will confirm this observation. Modern Paganism also needed
the production of this literature as a prior condition of its
emergence.

This section was compiled almost completely from references
in Pagan publications and Pagan groups' reading lists, and
from examining the personal libraries of a number of Pagans.
Thus it represents not the flow of recent scholarship (except
possibly by accident) but the flow of information into the
Pagan community. These books have been most influential in
shaping the opinions of Pagans about their adopted faith.
More than one group has constructed its belief system and
ritual from a single book or a small selection of books.

Within the literature of modern Paganism Frazer, Graves,
James, and Leland have been most frequently cited as sources,
though writers have freely used Spence, often without giving
him due credit. Many modern Pagan writers, while taking
material from these relatively mundane sources, suppress the
references to modern authors and prefer to project an image
of having received material from some ancient oral wisdom
tradition. In this manner they can create a belief that
Pagans are practicing an old tradition instead of a modern
reconstruction of one.

112. Brier, Bob. *Ancient Egyptian Religion*. New York:
      William Morrow and Company, 1980. 322 pp.

113. Dale-Green, Patricia. *The Cult of the Cat*. New York:
      Weathervane Books, 1963. 189 pp.

40

114. Dexter, T.F.G. *Fire Worship in Britain.* London: Watts
     and Co., 1931. 47 pp.

115. Dumézil, Georges. *Gods of the Ancient North Men.*
     Berkeley: University of California Press, 1977.
     157 pp.

116. Evans-Wentz, W.Y. *The Fairy Faith in Celtic Countries.*
     N.p.: University Books, 1966. 524 pp.

117. Frankfort, Henri. *Ancient Egyptian Religion.* New
     York: Harper and Row, 1961. 181 pp.

118. Frazer, James G. *The Golden Bough.* New York: Macmillan
     Company, 1960. 864 pp.

119. Graves, Robert, trans. *The Golden Ass.* New York:
     Farrar, Straus and Giroux, 1951. 293 pp.

120. ————. *The White Goddess.* New York: Farrar, Straus
     and Giroux, First American amended and enlarged edi-
     tion, 1966. 511 pp.

121. Guthrie, Kenneth Sylvan. *The Mithraic Mysteries.*
     Yonkers, NY: Platonist Press, 1925. 214 pp. Rpt.
     Mokelumne Hill, CA: Health Research, 1967. 214 pp.

122. Harrison, Jane Ellen. *Themis.* Cleveland: World Pub-
     lishing Company, 1962. 559 pp.

123. James, Edwin Oliver. *The Ancient Gods.* New York:
     G.P. Putnam's Sons, 1960. 359 pp.

124. ————. *The Cult of the Mother-Goddess.* New York:
     Barnes and Noble, 1959. 300 pp.

125. Kraemer, Ross S. "Ecstasy and Possession: The Attrac-
     tion of Women to the Cult of Dionysius." *Harvard
     Theological Review* 72,1-2 (January-April 1979) 55-80.

126. Leland, Charles Godfrey. *Aradia, Gospel of the Witches.*
     London: David McNutt, 1899. Rpt. New York: Hero
     Press, 1971.

127. ————. *Etruscan Magic and Occult Remedies.* New Hyde
     Park, NY: University Books, 1963. 384 pp.

128. ————. *Gypsy Sorcery and Fortune Telling.* London:

T.F. Unwin, 1891.   271 pp.   Rpt. New Hyde Park, NY:
University Books, 1962.   271 pp.

129.   ————.   *The Mystic Will*.   New York: Hero Press, 1972.
       120 pp.

130.   Neumann, Erich.   *The Great Mother*.   New York: Pantheon
       Books, 1954.   493 pp.

131.   Nilsson, Martin P.   *Greek Folk Religion*.   New York:
       Harper and Brothers, 1961.   166 pp.

132.   Patai, Raphael.   *The Hebrew Goddess*.   New York: Ktav
       Publishing House, 1968.   347 pp.

133.   Pearson, Karl.   "Woman as Witch--Evidences of Mother-
       Right in the Customs of Medieval Witchcraft."   In
       Chances of Death.   London: Edward Arnold, 1897, pp.
       1-50.

134.   Pennell, Elizabeth R.   *Charles Godfrey Leland, Biography*.
       Boston: Houghton Mifflin, 1906.   2 vols.

135.   Picard, Barbara Leonie.   *Celtic Tales*.   New York: Cri-
       terion Books, 1964.   159 pp.

136.   Spence, Lewis.   *The History and Origins of Druidism*.
       London: Rider and Company, 1949.   Rpt. New York:
       Samuel Weiser, 1971.   199 pp.

137.   ————.   *Magic Arts in Celtic Britain*.   London: Rider
       and Co., n.d.   198 pp.

138.   ————.   *The Mysteries of Britain*.   Philadelphia: David
       McKay Company.   Rpt. Mokelumne Hill, CA: Health
       Research, 1972.   256 pp.

139.   Squire, Charles.   *Celtic Myth and Legend*.   Hollywood,
       CA: Newcastle Publishing Co., 1975.   450 pp.

140.   Steiner, Rudolf.   *Egyptian Myths and Legends*.   New
       York: Anthroposophic Press, 1971.   151 pp.

141.   Thompson, C.J.S.   *The Mystic Mandrake*.   London: Rider
       and Co., 1934.   253 pp.   Rpt. Detroit: Gale Research
       Company, 1975.   253 pp.

142. Wallis Budge, E.A. *Egyptian Magic*. Rpt. London: Routledge and Kegan Paul, 1979. 234 pp.

143. Warner, Marina. *Alone of All Her Sex: The Myth & Cult of the Virgin Mary*. New York: Alfred A. Knopf, 1976. 419 pp.

144. Wedeck, Harry E., and Wade Baskin. *Dictionary of Pagan Religions*. New York: Philosophical Library, 1971. Rpt. Secaucus, NJ: Citadel Press, 1973. 363 pp.

145. Wright, Dudley. *Druidism: The Ancient Faith of Britain*. London: Ed. J. Borrow and Co., 1924. 192 pp.

F. EUROPEAN WITCHCRAFT

Since World War II scholarship has with renewed zeal attempted
to reformulate an understanding of the role of Witchcraft in
Western history. Baroja, Cohn, Hole, Kieckhefer, Monter,
Robbins, Rose, Russell, and Trevor-Roper have been major
voices in the debates. Their work reflects doubly on the
modern revival.

First, what these writers have described as Witchcraft in
the Middle Ages bears little resemblance to modern Paganism
and Wicca. They outline the history of the pre-Christian
Satanic occultism, largely the product of Christian Witchhunters and antiestablishment ideas of social dissidents.
Whatever the phenomenon being described as Witchcraft in the
Middle Ages, it lacks the essential elements of the modern
variety: the Mother Goddess, the joyful approach to life, and
the fertility cult.

On the other hand, the literature on European Witchcraft,
particularly that published prior to 1960, has had a marked
effect upon the modern revival. Modern Wiccans consciously
copied their practice from the literature concerning European
Witches. Many modern Witches would deny that they picked up
their craft from old books. Rather they view old accounts
of practices they now follow as confirmation of the Murray
Hypothesis. Following this lead, more than one priest and/or
priestess has cited the death of an ancestor at the hands of
a Witchhunter as one credential in their claim to be a
hereditary Witch, along with their claims to have been initiated in their skills by a grandparent.

Possibly most important of all, this literature defines a
history of a persecuted minority. Some modern Witches experience a high level of alienation from society and fear that
society (including the religious establishment) is basically
against them. There is enough evidence to confirm this belief, so they keep on guard lest the "time of burning" return.
When strong social pressure from acquaintances or media attacks
occur, modern Witches perceive a connection between themselves
and the European Witchhunt victims.

For a more complete bibliographical treatment of European
Witchcraft than we are able to give here, see Nugent (178) and

Midelfort (176). As with other sections, this list has been compiled almost exclusively from those items circulating in contemporary Pagan circles. In this case, not only are popular works such as those by Haining and O'Connell finding an audience, but the best scholarly works are also being read.

146. Ahl, Henry Curtis. *Witchcraft and Witches*. N.p.: The Author, 1947. 15 pp.

147. Alderman, Clifford Lindsey. *A Cauldron of Witches*. New York: Pocket Books, 1973. 182 pp.

148. Anderson, Alan, and Raymond Gordon. "Witchcraft and the Status of Women--the Case of England." *British Journal of Sociology* 29,3 (1973) 171-84.

149. Anderson, Robert D. "The History of Witchcraft: A Review with Some Psychiatric Comments." *American Journal of Psychiatry* 126,12 (June 1970) 1727-35.

150. Aylesworth, Thomas G. *Servants of the Devil*. Reading, MA: Addison-Wesley Publishing Company, 1970. 127 pp.

151. Baroja, Julio Caro. *The World of Witches*. Chicago: University of Chicago Press, 1965. 313 pp.

152. Cohn, Norman. *Europe's Inner Demon*. New York: Basic Books, 1975. Rpt. New York: New American Library, 1977. 304 pp.

153. Connor, John W. "The Social and Psychological Reality of European Witchcraft." *Psychiatry* 38 (1975) 366-80.

154. de Plancy, Collin (trans. by Wade Baskin). *Dictionary of Witch-Craft*. New York: Philosophical Library, Inc., 1965. 125 pp.

155. Donovan, Frank. *Never on a Broomstick*. New York: Bell Publishing Company, 1971. 256 pp.

156. Dyer, B.R. *Kent Witchcraft*. St. Ives, Cornwall, Eng.: James Pike Ltd., 1977. 32 pp.

157. Gupta, Marie, and Fran Brandon. *A Treasury of Witchcraft and Devilry*. Middle Village, NY: Jonathan David Publishers, 1975. 180 pp.

158. Haining, Peter. *An Illustrated History of Witchcraft*.
      London: New English Library, 1975. 127 pp.

159. Harper, Clive. "The Witches' Flying Ointment." *Folk-
      lore* 88,1 (1977) 105-6.

160. Harris, Anthony. *Night's Black Agents*. Manchester,
      Eng.: Manchester University Press, 1980. 210 pp.

161. Harrison, Michael. *The Roots of Witchcraft*. Secaucus,
      NJ: The Citadel Press, 1974. 278 pp.

162. Hole, Christina. *Witchcraft in England*. New York:
      Charles Scribner's Sons, 1947. 168 pp.

163. Holmes, Ronald. *Witchcraft in History*. Secaucus, NJ:
      The Citadel Press, 1977. 272 pp.

164. Hueffer, Oliver Madox. *The Book of Witches*. Totowa,
      NJ: Rowman & Littlefield, 1973. 336 pp.

165. Kieckhefer, Richard. *European Witch Trials*. Berkeley,
      CA: University of California Press, 1976. 181 pp.

166. Kohn, Bernice. *Out of the Cauldron*. New York: Holt,
      Rinehart and Winston, n.d. 119 pp.

167. Kors, Alan C., and Edward Peters. *Witchcraft in Europe:
      1180-1700; A Documentary History*. Philadelphia:
      University of Pennsylvania Press, 1972. 382 pp.

168. Lea, H.C. *Materials Toward a History of Witchcraft*.
      Philadelphia: University of Pennsylvania, 1939.
      3 vols.

169. Lethbridge, T.C. *Witches, Investigating an Ancient
      Religion*. New York: Citadel Press, 1968. 162 pp.

170. McCormick, Jane. "Witchcraft in Literature." *Psychic*
      5,1 (September-October 1973) 50-54.

171. MacFarlane, A.D.J. *Witchcraft in Tudor and Stuart
      England*. New York: Harper and Row Publishers, 1970.
      334 pp.

172. Maple, Eric. *The Complete Book of Witchcraft and
      Demonology*. New York: A.S. Barnes and Company, 1966.

173. Marshburn, Joseph H. *Murder and Witchcraft in England, 1550-1640.* Norman: University of Oklahoma Press, 1971. 287 pp.

174. Martin, Kevin. *The Complete Booke of White Magic.* New York: A.S. Barnes and Company, 1976. 144 pp.

175. Michelot, Jules. *Satanism and Witchcraft.* New York: The Citadel Press, 1939. 332 pp.

176. Midelfort, H.C. Erik. "Recent Witch Hunting Research, or Where Do We Go From Here?" *Papers of the Bibliographical Society of America* 62,3rd quarter (1968) 373-420.

177. Monter, E. William. *European Witchcraft.* New York: John Wiley & Sons, 1969. 177 pp.

178. Nugent, Donald. "Witchcraft Studies, 1959-1971: A Bibliographical Survey." In Robert Galbreath, ed., *The Occult: Studies and Evaluations.* Bowling Green, OH: Bowling Green University Popular Press, 1972, pp. 710-825.

179. O'Connell, Margaret F. *The Magic Cauldron.* New York: S.G. Phillips, 1975. 192 pp.

180. Paine, Lauran. *Witches in Fact and Fantasy.* New York: Taplinger Publishing Company, 1972. 188 pp.

181. Robbins, Rossell Hope. *The Encyclopedia of Witchcraft and Demonology.* New York: Crown Publishers, Inc., 1965. 571 pp.

182. ————. *Witchcraft.* Millwood, NY: KTO Press, 1978. 121 pp.

183. Rose, Elliott. *A Razor for a Goat.* Toronto: University of Toronto Press, 1964. 257 pp.

184. Russell, Jeffery Burton. *A History of Witchcraft.* London: Thames and Hudson, 1980. 192 pp.

185. ————. *Witchcraft in the Middle Ages.* Ithaca, NY: Cornell University Press, 1972. 394 pp.

186. Sargeant, Philip W. *Witches and Warlocks.* East Aadsley, Yorks., Eng.: EP Publishing, 1974. 290 pp.

186a. Schieneman, Thomas J. "The Role of Mental Illness in the European Witch Hunts of the Sixteenth and Seventeenth Centuries: An Assessment." *Journal of the History of Behavioral Sciences* 13 (1977) 337-53.

187. Seth, Ronald. *Children Against Witches*. New York: Taplinger Publishing Company, 1969. 190 pp.

188. ————. *In the Name of the Devil*. New York: Tower Books, 1969. 218 pp.

189. ————. *Witches and Their Craft*. New York: Award Books, 1969. 253 pp.

190. Seymour, St. John D. *Irish Witchcraft*. New York: Causeway Books, 1973. 256 pp.

191. Summers, Montague. *The Geography of Witchcraft*. New York: Alfred A. Knopf, 1927. 623 pp.

192. ————. *The History of Witchcraft and Demonology*. New York: Alfred A. Knopf, 1926. 353 pp.

193. Trevor-Roper, H.R. *The European Witch-Craze of the 16th and 17th Centuries*. New York: Harper, 1969. 246 pp.

194. Williams, Charles. *Witchcraft*. New York: Meridian Books, 1959. 316 pp.

III

RITUAL MAGIC

A. MODERN CEREMONIAL MAGIC

Occultists consider the ceremonial or ritual magician as the elite of his/her field. He/she inherits the alchemical tradition, and is considered the more learned and disciplined and most ritually precise and adept practitioner of the occult arts. The ritual magician frequently practices his/her art alone rather than in a group, though some associate in lodges and orders.

The literature in this section describes and defines ritual magic and its key role in the rebirth of the magical community. King (245) gives the most complete overview while Colquhoun, Grant (224), Howe, King (243), McIntosh, and Williams offer more specialized studies.

The initial step in reviving the tradition came from Francis Barrett who wrote *The Magus* (1801) and began an occult school in England. However, Eliphas Levi's monumental volumes in the mid-19th century, and his reworking of the tradition using Mesmer, signaled the first wave of more popular attention to magical practice. Levi's work was part of a general wave of revised occultism in Europe in the 19th century.

In England, the most important magical group emerged in 1888--The Hermetic Order of the Golden Dawn (O.G.D.). Founded by some Masons, the O.G.D. flourished for a generation and included among its members many of the people who put magic back on the agenda of Western society--MacGregor Mathers, Dion Fortune (pseudonym of Violet Mary Firth), William Butler Yeats, A.E. Waite, and, preeminently, Aleister Crowley.

Included in this section are the major works of the prominent European magicians of the last century. Most of these works freely circulate among American ritual magicians, as well as Pagans and Witches, and form a large percentage of the teaching material. The works of Butler, Fortune, Gray, and Knight stand second only to Crowley in their influence.

49

195. Bardon, Franz. *Initiation into Hermetics*. Wupperthal,
      West Germany: Dieter Ruggeberg, 1971. 294 pp.

196. ————. *The Key to the True Quabbalah*. Wupperthal,
      West Germany: Dieter Ruggeberg, 1971. 270 pp.

197. ————. *The Practice of Magical Evocation*. Wupperthal,
      West Germany: Dieter Ruggeberg, 1970. 279 pp.

198. Barrett, Francis. *The Magus*. London: Lackington,
      Allen and Co., 1801. 198 pp. Rpt. New Hyde Park,
      NY: University Books, 1967. 198 pp.

199. Blavatsky, Helen Petrovna. *Dynamics of the Psychic
      World*. Wheaton, IL: Theosophical Publishing House,
      1972. 132 pp.

200. Butler, E.M. *Ritual Magic*. Hollywood, CA: Newcastle
      Publishing Company, 1971. 329 pp.

201. Butler, William E. *Magic: Its Ritual, Power and Purpose*.
      London: Aquarian Press, 1952. 76 pp.

202. ————. *The Magician: His Training and Work*. London:
      The Aquarian Press, 1959. 176 pp.

203. Chevalier, Georges. *The Sacred Magician*. St. Albans,
      Herts.: Paladin, 1976. 99 pp.

204. Colquhoun, Ithell. *The Sword of Wisdom*. New York:
      G.P. Putnam's Sons, 1975. 307 pp.

205. Drury, Neville. *Don Juan, Mescalito and Modern Magic*.
      London: Routledge and Kegan Paul, 1978. 229 pp.

206. ————. *Inner Visions*. Boston: Routledge and Kegan
      Paul, 1979. 141 pp.

207. ————, and Stephen Skinner. *The Search for Abraxas*.
      London: Neville Spearman, 1972. 138 pp.

208. Edwards, David. *Dare to Make Magic*. London: Regel
      Press, 1971. 94 pp.

209. Fortune, Dion. *Applied Magic*. New York: Samuel Weiser,
      1962. 110 pp.

210. ————. *The Cosmic Doctrine*. Cheltenham, Glos., Eng.:
      Helios, 1966. 157 pp.

211. ————. *The Esoteric Orders and Their Work.* St. Paul,
      MN: Llewellyn Publications, 1971. 150 pp.

212. ————. *The Mystical Qabalah.* London: Ernest Benn,
      1935. 327 pp.

213. ————. *Practical Occultism in Daily Life.* London:
      Williams & Norgate, 1935. 93 pp.

214. ————. *Psychic Self-Defense.* London: Rider & Co.,
      1930. 218 pp.

215. ————. *Sane Occultism.* London: Rider & Co., 1939.
      192 pp.

216. ————. *The Secrets of Dr. Taverner.* London: Noel
      Douglas, 1926. 253 pp.

217. ————. *Through the Gates of Death.* New York: Samuel
      Weiser, 1968. 94 pp.

218. ————. *The Training and Work of an Initiate.* London:
      Rider & Co., n.d. 139 pp.

219. Galbreath, Robert A. "Arthur Edward Waite, Christian
      Mystic and Occult Scholar: A Chronological Bibliog-
      raphy." *Bulletin of Bibliography* 30,2 (April-June
      1973) 55-61.

220. Gilbert, Robert A. "A.E. Waite and the Later Workings
      of The Golden Dawn." *Spectrum* 1,2 (December 1974) 3-7.

221. ————. "Arthur Machen and A.E. Waite—A Forgotten
      Collaboration." *Antiquarian Book Monthly Review* 2,4
      (April 1975) 7-8.

222. Grant, Kenneth. *Aleister Crowley & The Hidden God.* New
      York: Samuel Weiser, 1974. 245 pp.

223. ————. *Images & Oracles of Austin Osman Spare.* London:
      Frederick Muller, 1975. 96 pp.

224. ————. *The Magical Revival.* New York: Samuel Weiser,
      1973. 244 pp.

225. Gray, William G. *Inner Traditions of Magic.* New York:
      Samuel Weiser, 1970. 287 pp.

226. ———. *The Ladder of Lights*. Cheltenham, Glos., Eng.:
      Helios Book Service, 1968. 230 pp.

227. ———. *Magical Ritual Methods*. Cheltenham, Glos.,
      Eng.: Helios Book Service, 1969. 301 pp.

228. ———. *The Office of the Holy Tree of Life*. Dallas,
      TX: Sangreal Foundation, 1970. 65 pp.

229. ———. *An Outline of Our Inner Western Way*. New York:
      Samuel Weiser, 1980. 156 pp.

230. ———. *The Qabalistic Mass of Light*. Dallas, TX:
      Sangreal Foundation, 1970.

231. ———. *The Rite of Light*. Cheltenham, Glos., Eng.:
      privately printed, 1976. 40 pp.

232. ———. *Seasonal Occult Rituals*. N.p.: Savitria Press,
      n.d. 11 pp.

233. ———. *A Self Made by Magic*. New York: Samuel Weiser,
      1976. 198 pp.

234. ———. *The Simplified Guide to the Holy Tree of Life*.
      Pasadena, CA: Labrys Press, 1973. 60 pp.

235. ———. *The Talking Tree*. New York: Samuel Weiser,
      1977. 256 pp.

236. ———. *The Tree of Evil*. Cheltenham, Glos., Eng.:
      Helios Book Service, 1974. 119 pp.

237. H.I., Sorer. *Oracles*. Wolverhampton, Staffs., Eng.:
      The Order of the Cubic Stone, 1969. 46 pp.

238. Harper, George Mills. *Yeats' Golden Dawn*. London:
      Macmillan, 1979. 322 pp.

239. Hartmann, Franz. *In the Pronaos of the Temple of
      Wisdom*. Boston: Theosophical Society, 1890. Rpt.
      Chicago: Aries Press, 1941. 96 pp.

240. ———. *Magic Black and White*. New Hyde Park, NY:
      University Books, 1970. 298 pp.

241. Howe, Ellic. *The Magicians of the Golden Dawn*. London:
      Routledge and Kegan Paul, 1972. 306 pp.

242. Kearton, Michael. *The Magical Temple*. Wellingborough, Northamptonshire, Eng.: The Aquarian Press, 1980. 95 pp.

243. King, Francis, ed. *Astral Projection Magic and Alchemy*. New York: Samuel Weiser, 1971. 254 pp.

244. ———. *Magic: The Western Tradition*. New York: Avon Books, 1975. 128 pp.

245. ———. *Ritual Magic in England*. London: Neville Spearman, 1970. 224 pp.

246. ———, and Stephen Skinner. *Techniques of High Magic*. New York: Destiny Books, 1976. 254 pp.

247. Knight, Gareth. *Experience of the Inner Worlds*. Cheltenham, Glos., Eng.: Helios Book Service, 1975. 254 pp.

248. ———. *Occult Exercises and Practices*. Toddington, Eng.: Helios Book Service, 1969. 68 pp.

249. ———. *The Practice of Ritual Magic*. Toddington, Eng.: Helios Book Service, 1969. 74 pp. Rpt. New York: Samuel Weiser, 1976. 64 pp.

250. Levi, Eliphas. *The History of Magic*. London: W. Rider & Son, 1913. 535 pp. Rpt. New York: Samuel Weiser, 1971. 384 pp. (Trans. by A.E. Waite of *Histoire de la Magie*.)

251. ———. *The Key of the Mysteries*. London: Rider & Co., 1959. Rpt. New York: Samuel Weiser, 1970. 215 pp. (Trans. by Aleister Crowley of *Le Clef des Grandes Mystères*.)

252. ———. *The Magical Ritual of the Sanctum Regnum*. New York: Samuel Weiser, 1970. 108 pp.

253. ———. *The Paradox of the Highest Science*. Adyar: Theosophical Publishing House, 1922. 172 pp. Rpt. Mokelumne Hill, CA: Health Research, 1969. 22 pp.

254. ———. *Transcendental Magic*. London: G. Redway, 1896. 406 pp. Rpt. New York: Samuel Weiser, 1970. 438 pp. (Trans. by A.E. Waite of *Dogma et Rituel de la Haute Magie*.)

255. McIntosh, Christopher. *Eliphas Levi and the French Occult Revival*. New York: Samuel Weiser, 1974. 238 pp.

256. Mathers, S.C. MacGregor. *Kabbalah Unveiled*. London: Routledge and Kegan Paul, 1926. 360 pp.

257. Morrish, Furze. *The Ritual of Higher Magic*. London: Oak Tree Books, n.d. 128 pp.

258. Oakes, Philip. "Philip Oakes Meets a Magician from Somerset House." *London Sunday Times* (January 30, 1972).

259. Papus (pseudonym of Gerard Encausse). *The Qabalah*. New York: Samuel Weiser, 1977. 384 pp.

260. Raine, Kathleen Jessie. "Yeats, the Tarot and the Golden Dawn." *Sewanee Review* 77,7 (Winter 1969) 112-48.

261. ————. *Yeats, the Tarot and the Golden Dawn*. Dublin: Dolmen Press, 1972. 60 pp.

262. S.M.R.D., Frater, et al. *The Secret Workings of the Golden Dawn; Book "T": The Tarot*. Cheltenham, Glos., Eng.: Helios Book Service, 1967. 149 pp.

263. Sadhu, Mouni. *Meditation*. No. Hollywood, CA: Wilshire Book Company, 1974. 364 pp.

264. ————. *Theurgy*. London: George Allen & Unwin, 1965. 263 pp.

265. Skinner, Stephen. *Terrestrial Astrology: Divination by Geomancy*. London: Routledge and Kegan Paul, 1980. 293 pp.

266. Spare, Austin Osman. *The Book of Pleasure*. London: The Author, 1913. 59 pp.

267. Torrens, Robert George. *Secret Rituals of the Golden Dawn*. Wellingborough, Northamptonshire, Eng.: Aquarian Press, 1973. 304 pp.

268. Turner, Robert, and David Edwards. *The Outer Court*. Wolverhampton, Eng.: Order of the Cubic Stone, 1968. Second ed., 1969. Rev. ed., 1976. 33 pp.

269. Waite, Arthur Edward. *The Life of Louis Claude de Saint-Martin*. London: P. Wellby, 1901. 464 pp. Rpt. as *The Unknown Philosopher*. Blauvelt, NY: Rudolph Steiner Publications, 1970. 464 pp.

270. ————. *Shadows of Life and Thought*. London: Selwyn and Blount, 1938. 288 pp.

271. Wang, Robert. *An Introduction to the Golden Dawn Tarot*. New York: Samuel Weiser, 1978. 158 pp.

272. ————. *The Secret Temple*. New York: Samuel Weiser, 1980. 91 pp.

273. Williams, David, trans. *The Book of Lambspring*. London: Rigel Press, 1972. 35 pp.

274. Williams, Thomas A. *Eliphas Levi: Master of Occultism*. University: University of Alabama Press, 1975. 174 pp.

275. Yeats, William Butler. *Autobiography*. New York: Macmillan Company, 1938. 479 pp.

276. ————. *Memoirs*. New York: Macmillan Publishing Company, 1973. 318 pp.

B. THE GRIMOIRES

A necessary item in any magician's library, the grimoire contains the rituals and magical formulae by which the magician does magic. A number of old grimoires, mostly written in German, Latin, or Hebrew, circulated among medieval magicians. They were objects of awe and mystery until popular editions began to appear in the 1880s. In the early part of this century, publishers released the first American edition, and the de Laurence Company in Chicago has kept them in print.

Listed below are the English-language editions of the most-circulated grimoires. The startling fact about them is not their mystery or the diabolical nature of their content so much as the size of an audience large enough to keep them in print for so many years.

Nahigan surveys the various grimoires, offers some information about the origin and content of each, and suggests some rationale for their having been written.

The *Necronomicon*, a newly-published grimoire, has attained some popularity because of its apparent connection with a fictional volume of the same name mentioned frequently in the works of H.P. Lovecraft.

Selections from these grimoires found their way into the rituals of the Witches in the 1950s and 1960s, most notably in the case of Alex Sanders, who needed specific ritual material and instruction that most older books on Paganism and Witchcraft did not have. No evidence exists to suggest that ritual material, apart from a few fragmentary prayers, invocations, and low magic formulae, survived from ancient or medieval times to become a part of contemporary Neo-Paganism. Hence modern Witches and Pagans had either to lift materials from the grimoires or to write their own.

277. Best, Michael R., and Frank H. Brightman, eds. *The Book of Secrets of Albertus Magnus*. London: Oxford University Press, 1973. 128 pp.

278. *The Black Pullet*. New York: Samuel Weiser, 1972. 80 pp.

279. Briggs, Katherine Mary. "Some Seventeenth Century Books of Magic." *Folklore* 64 (1955) 445-62.

280. de Laurence, L.W. *The Book of Secret Hindu Ceremonial and Talismanic Magic*. Chicago: The de Laurence Company, n.d. 279 pp.

281. ————. *The Great Book of Magical Art, Hindu Magic and Indian Occultism*. Chicago: The de Laurence Company, 1915. 635 pp.

282. ————, ed. *The Lesser Key of Solomon; Goetia; The Book of Evil Spirits*. Chicago: The de Laurence Company, 1916. 80 pp.

283. ————, ed. *Raphael's Ancient Manuscript of Talismanic Magic*. Chicago: The de Laurence Company, 1916. 104 pp.

284. Malchus, Marius. *The Secret Grimoire of Turiel*. New York: Samuel Weiser, 1960. 42 pp.

285. Mathers, S.L. MacGregor, trans. & ed. *The Book of the Sacred Magic of Abra-Melin*. Chicago: The de Laurence Company, 1932. 268 pp. Rpt. New York: Causeway Books, 1974. 268 pp.

286. ————, trans. *The Greater Key of Solomon*. Chicago: The de Laurence Company, 1914. 129 pp.

287. Nahigan, Ken. "Grimoires and Black Books." *Fate* 25, 3-4; I (March 1972) 98-109; II (April 1972) 66-75.

288. Shah, Sayed Idries. *The Secret Lore of Magic*. New York: Citadel Press, 1957. 316 pp.

289. Simon, ed. *The Necronomicon*. New York: Schlangekraft Inc./Barnes Graphics, 1977. 218 pp.

290. Waite, Arthur Edward. *The Book of Ceremonial Magic*. New Hyde Park, NY: University Books, 1961. 337 pp. Rpt. New York: Bell Publishing Company, 1969. 337 pp.

291. ————. *The Secret Tradition in Goëtia*. London: W. Rider & Son, 1911. 336 pp.

292.   White, Nelson, and Anne White, comps. *Index and Refer-
       ence Volume to: The Lemegeton of Solomon.* Pasadena,
       CA: The Technology Group, 1979.   68 pp.

293.   —————, trans.   *Lemegeton; Clavicula Salomonis: or the
       Complete Lesser Key of Solomon the King.* Pasadena,
       CA: The Technology Group, 1979.   63 pp.

C. THE KABBALAH

The Kabbalah (spelled variously Cabala and Quabbalah), a mystical magical system developed within Judaism, became Christianized in the Renaissance. Among Jews, the Hasidim built their teachings around Kabbalistic speculations, while the Christianized version became popular among occultists.

The Kabbalah describes God, the Infinite, Hidden Divine radiating the Divine Light by which the universe comes into being. This process is pictured as a diagram (the Tree of Life) made up of 10 circles (termed *sephirot*) connected by 22 lines or paths. In understanding the tree the magician/mystic comprehends the nature of the world and the process by which individuals can be transformed as they metaphysically climb the tree.

From the vast literature on the Kabbalah, the selection below is representative of volumes circulating in the occult community in the 1970s.

Gonzalez-Wippler provides a good introduction as does Ginsburg, one of the earliest books on the Kabbalah in English. The two volumes by Gershom Scholem represent the finest in modern Jewish scholarship on the subject.

The reader will find additional volumes on the Kabbalah in the sections on modern magic, Aleister Crowley, and ritual magic in America, as modern magicians have made Kaballistic concerns central to their practice. (See 197, 214, 228, 234, 256, 259, 461, 492, 542, 571, and 577.)

294. Ashlag, Yohuda. *Kabbalah: Ten Luminous Emanations, Vol. 1.* New York: Research Centre of Kabbalah, 1972. 128 pp.

295. Berg, Philip S. *An Entrance to the Zohar.* New York: Research Centre of Kabbalah, 1974. 153 pp.

296. Bokser, Ben Zion. *From the World of the Cabala.* New York: Philosophical Library, 1954. 210 pp.

297. Bond, Bligh, and Thomas Simcox Lea. *Gematria*. London:
     Research into Lost Knowledge Organization Trust, 1977.
     113 pp.

298. de Camp, L. Sprague. "The Mysterious Kabbalah." *Fate*
     9,10 (October 1956) 55-60.

299. Epstein, Perle. *Kabbalah: The Way of the Jewish Mystic*.
     Garden City, NY: Doubleday & Company, 1978. 171 pp.

300. Franck, Adolphe. *The Kabbalah*. New York: Bell Pub-
     lishing Company, 1940. 224 pp.

301. Gewurz, Elias. *The Hidden Treasures of the Ancient
     Qabalah*. Krotona: Theosophical Publishing House,
     1915. 133 pp.

302. Ginsburg, Christian D. *The Kabbalah*. London: Longmans,
     Green & Company, 1863. Rpt. London: Routledge and
     Kegan Paul, 1955. 241 pp.

303. Gonzalez-Wippler, Migene. *A Kabbalah for the Modern
     World*. New York: Julian Press, 1974. 171 pp.

304. Gruberger, Philip S., comp. & ed. *Kabbalah: Ten
     Luminous Emanations, Vol. 2*. New York: Research
     Centre of Kabbalah, 1973. 186 pp.

305. Halevi, Z'ev ben Shimon. *Adam and the Kabbalistic
     Tree*. London: Rider and Company, 1974. 333 pp.

306. ————. *Kabbalah and Exodus*. Boulder, CO: Shambhala
     Publications, 1980. 234 pp.

307. ————. *The Way of Kabbalah*. New York: Samuel Weiser,
     1976. 224 pp.

308. Krakovsky, Levi Isaac. *Kabbalah: The Light of Redemp-
     tion*. New York: Research Centre of Kabbalah, 1970.
     264 pp.

309. Kushner, Lawrence. *Honey from the Rock*. San Francisco:
     Harper & Row, 1977. 151 pp.

310. Meltzer, David, ed. *The Secret Garden*. New York:
     Seabury Press, 1976. 233 pp.

311. Pick, Bernhard. *The Cabala*. Chicago: Open Court Pub-
      lishing Co., 1913. 115 pp.

312. Pullen-Burry, Henry B. *Qabalism*. Chicago: Yogi Publi-
      cation Society, 1925. 167 pp.

313. Scholem, Gershom. *Kabbalah*. New York: Quadrangle,
      1974. 492 pp.

314. ————. *On the Kabbalah and Its Symbolism*. New York:
      Schocken Books, 1969. 216 pp.

315. Sepharial. *The Kabala of Numbers*. New York: Samuel
      Weiser, 1970. 387 pp.

316. Waite, Arthur Edward. *The Holy Kabbalah*. New Hyde
      Park, NY: University Books, 1960. 636 pp.

D. THE HERMETIC TRADITION

The central magical occult tradition in the West follows the teachings of the *Corpus Hermeticum*, a body of magical, astrological, and alchemical writings which appeared early in the Christian era. Marcilio Ficino published a translation of the *Corpus* in 1471, and it became the basis of the Renaissance revival of magical alchemy. The 1906 English version by G.R.S. Mead significantly bolstered the modern revival.

As Wilkerson's articles show, European hermetics (at this time in the form of alchemy) came to Colonial New England and survived well into the 18th century. Then, as on the Continent, it appears to have died out. Renewed interest, coincidental with that on the Continent, is manifest in the writings of Hitchcock. He thoroughly demythologized the magical content while becoming a major hermetic advocate.

In the several decades before World War I, a flowering of interest in hermetics appeared in the Theosophical and Rosicrucian groups. Two Theosophists, Anna Kingsford and William Maitland, formed the London-based Hermetic Society in 1884. Mead followed their lead and formed the Quest Society in 1909.

The most influential hermetic group, the Hermetic Order of the Golden Dawn, combined the hermetic philosophy with the practice of magic, a step many hermetic groups stop just short of.

By the 1870s hermetic groups began to appear in America around teachers like T.H. Burgoyne, Manly Palmer Hall, A.S. Raleigh, Olney H. Richmond, and C.C. Zain. Paul Foster Case, an American leader in the Order of the Golden Dawn, left the Order and founded the Builders of the Adytum, currently one of the largest occult groups in America.

In the 1970s Frater Albertus, as head of the Paracelsus Research Society of Salt Lake City, Utah, emerged as the major voice of hermetic alchemy and the author of a number of books. Carroll Runyon leads the Church of the Hermetic Sciences (also known as the Ordo Templi Astarte), a hermetic ritual magic group in Pasadena, California. Christensen and Ellwood describe the O.T.A.

In passing, it should be noted that alchemy owes no small part of its current popularity to Carl Gustav Jung, whose sympathetic treatments have offered support to occultists of various strains. Both Jaffé (69) and Pagel (369) appraise Jung's perspective on alchemy.

317. Aima. *The Ancient Wisdom and Rituals*. Hollywood, CA: Foibles Publications, 1979. 121 pp.

318. Albertus, Frater. *The Alchemist of the Rocky Mountains*. Salt Lake City, UT: Paracelsus Research Society, 1976. 167 pp.

319. ————. *The Alchemist's Handbook*. Rev. ed. New York: Samuel Weiser, 1974. 124 pp.

320. ————. *From "One" to "Ten."* Salt Lake City, UT: Paracelsus Research Society, 1966. 48 pp.

321. ————. *The Seven Rays of the Q.B.L.* Salt Lake City, UT: Paracelsus Research Society, 1968. 206 pp.

322. *The Arithmosophy of Martines de Pasqually*. N.p.: Martinist Study and Research Group, n.d. 8 pp.

323. Blavatsky, Helena Petrovna. *Secret Instructions to Probationers of an Esoteric Occult School*. Mokelumne Hill, CA: Health Research, 1969. 122 pp.

324. Brown, Robert T. *Hermes, the Logos-Creator*. New York: Hermetic Society for World Service, 1955. 12 pp.

325. Burgoyne, Thomas H. *Celestial Dynamics*. Denver, CO: Astro-Philosophical Publishing Co., 1896. 107 pp.

326. ————. *The Language of the Stars*. Denver: Astro-Philosophical Publishing House, 1892. 100 pp.

327. ————. *The Light of Egypt*. Chicago: Religion-Philosophical Publishing House, 1889. 2 vols.

328. Burridge, Gaston. "Alchemist 1956?" *Fate* 9,9 (September 1956) 16-22.

329. Case, Paul Foster, ed., with commentary. *The Book of Tokens*. Los Angeles: B.O.T.A., Ltd., 1934. Second ed. 1947. 191 pp.

330. ———. *A Brief Analysis of the Tarot*. Buffalo, NY:
      Ellicott Press, 1927. 102 pp.

331. ———. *The Great Seal of the United States*. Santa
      Barbara, CA: J.F. Rowny Press, 1935. 34 pp.

332. ———. *An Introduction to the Study of the Tarot*.
      New York: Azoth Publishing Company, 1970. 59 pp.

333. ———. *The Oracle of the Tarot*. East Pasadena, CA:
      The Author, 1933.

334. ———. *The Tarot*. Richmond, VA: Macoy Publishing
      Company, 1947. 215 pp.

335. ———. *The True and Invisible Rosicrucian Order*.
      N.p.: The Author, 1928. 101 pp. Rev. ed. San Marino,
      CA: The Author, 1933. 147 pp.

336. Christensen, Cheryl JoAnne. "Magical Epistemic Communi-
      ties: The Construction of Specialized Social Realities
      in Bunyoro, Uganda and Los Angeles, California."
      Cambridge, MA: Massachusetts Institute of Technology,
      Ph.D. dissertation, 1975.

337. Clymer, R. Swinburne. *A Compendium of Occult Laws*.
      Quakertown, PA: Philosophical Publishing House, 1938.
      270 pp.

338. *Constitution of the Aurum Solis (Order of the Sacred
      Word)*. N.p., n.d. 20 pp.

339. Crabb, Judy, and Riley Crabb. *You Live in Four Worlds*.
      Vista, CA: Borderland Sciences Research Foundation,
      n.d. 68 pp.

340. Davis, Ann. *This Is the Truth about the Self*. Los
      Angeles: Builders of the Adytum, 1960. 23 pp.

341. de Claremont, Lewis. *The Ancient Book of Magic*.
      Dallas, TX: Dorene Publishing Company, 1936. 137 pp.

342. ———. *The Legends of Incense, Herb and Oil Magic*.
      New York: Oracle Publishing Co., 1936. 102 pp.

343. ———. *The Ten Lost Books of the Prophets*. New York:
      Dorene Publishing Co., 1936.

344. Dequer, John H. *Arrows of Light from the Egyptian Tarot*. New York: The Author, 1930. 263 pp.

345. Ellwood, Robert S. *Mysticism and Religion*. Englewood Cliffs, NJ: Prentice-Hall, 1980, pp. 136-38.

346. Gamache, Henri. *The Magic of Herbs*. New York: Power Thoughts Publishing Co., 1942. 79 pp.

347. ————. *The Master Key to Occult Secrets*. Highland Falls, NY: Sheldon Publications, 1945. 92 pp.

348. ————. *Mystery of the Long Lost 8th, 9th, and 10th Books of Moses*. Highland Falls, NY: Sheldon Publications, 1967. 103 pp.

349. Hall, Manly P. *An Encyclopedic Outline of Masonic, Hermetic, Qabbalistic and Rosicrucian Philosophy*. San Francisco: For the Author by H.S. Crocker Company, 1928. 245 pp. Rpt. Los Angeles: Philosophical Research Society, 1945. 245 pp.

350. ————. *An Essay on the Fundamental Principles of Operative Occultism*. Los Angeles: Hall Publishing Company, 1930. 53 pp.

351. ————. *The Hermetic Marriage*. Los Angeles: Hall Publishing Company, 1929. 60 pp.

352. ————. *Magic: A Treatise on Natural Occultism*. Los Angeles: Hall Publishing Company, 1930. 59 pp.

353. ————. *The Sacred Magic of the Qabbalah*. Los Angeles: Philosophical Research Society, 1929. 64 pp.

354. Hatch, David Patterson. *Some More Philosophy of the Hermetics*. Los Angeles: B.R. Baumgardt & Co., 1898. 232 pp.

355. ————. *Some Philosophy of the Hermetics*. Los Angeles: B.R. Baumgardt & Co., 1898. 109 pp. Rpt. Detroit: Hermes Press, Inc., 1978. 109 pp.

356. *Highlights of Tarot*. Los Angeles: Builders of the Adytum, 1931. 8th ed., 1970. 64 pp.

357. Hitchcock, Ethan Allen. *Remarks on the Sonnets of*

Shakespeare ... Showing They Belong to the Hermetic Class of Workings.... New York: J. Miller, 1865. 258 pp.

358. ————. *Remarks upon Alchemy and the Alchemists.* Boston: Crosby, Nichols, 1857. 307 pp. Rpt. New York: Arno Press, 1976. 307 pp.

359. ————. *Swedenborg, an Hermetic Philosopher.* New York: D. Appleton & Co., 1858. 352 pp.

360. Hoeller, Stephen A. *The Royal Road.* Wheaton, IL: Theosophical Publishing House, 1975. 119 pp.

361. Hurley, Phillip. *Herbal Alchemy.* N.p.: A Lotus Publication, 1977. 100 pp.

362. Jones, Marc Edmund. *Occult Philosophy.* Stanwood, WA: Sabian Publishing Society, 1971. 436 pp.

363. Kasdin, Simon. *Jacob's Ladder.* Convent, NJ: Emerson Society, 1969. 36 pp.

364. Khedemel, Frater. "The What and Why of Magick." *Cosmos* 6,7 (March-April 1972) 28-29.

365. MacPhail, Ian. "The Mellon Collection of Alchemy and the Occult." *Ambix* 14,3 (October 1967) 198-202.

366. Meade, George Robert Stowe. *The Hymns of Hermes.* London: Theosophical Publishing House, 1907. 84 pp. Rpt. Detroit: Hermes Press, Inc., 1978. 84 pp.

367. Mohan, Rasheed, ed. *The Original Key to the 6th and 7th Books of Moses.* N.p., n.d. 97 pp.

368. *The Open Door.* Los Angeles: Builders of the Adytum, n.d. 9 pp.

369. Pagel, Walter. "Jung's Views on Alchemy." *Isis* 39, 1-2 (1948) 44-48.

370. Phylotus. *Esoteric Masonry.* Chicago: Hermetic Publishing Company, n.d. 77 pp.

371. ————. *Private Lessons.* Chicago: Hermetic Publishing Company, n.d. 78 pp.

372. Raleigh, Albert Sidney. *The Hermetic Art*. Chicago: Hermetic Publishing Company, 1919. 142 pp.

373. ————. *Hermetic Fundamentals Revealed*. Chicago: Hermetic Publishing Company, 1928. 127 pp.

374. ————. *Hermetic Science of Motion and Number*. Chicago: George W. Wiggs, 1924. Rpt. Mokelumne Hill, CA: Health Research, n.d. 68 pp.

375. ————. *An Interpretation to Rudyard Kipling's Brushwood Boy and Map*. Chicago: Hermetic Publishing Company, 1932. 40 pp.

376. ————. *An Interpretation to Rudyard Kipling's They*. Chicago: Hermetic Publishing Company, 1932. 38 pp.

377. ————. *Magic*. Chicago: Hermetic Publishing Company, 1928. 54 pp.

378. ————. *Philosophic Hermetica*. Chicago: Sterling Publishing Company, 1916. 127 pp.

379. ————. *Philosophy of Alchemy*. Chicago: Hermetic Publishing Company, 1924. 153 pp.

380. ————. *Phrenogarten System of Education*. Chicago: Hermetic Publishing Company, 1932. 90 pp.

381. ————. *Scientifica Hermetica*. Chicago: Sterling Publishing Company, 1916. 113 pp.

382. ————. *A Series of Private Lessons on the Science of Alchemy*. Chicago: Hermetic Publishing Company, 1928. 172 pp.

383. ————. *The Shepherd of Men*. Chicago: Sterling Publishing Company, 1916. 145 pp.

384. ————. *Speculative Art of Alchemy*. Chicago: Hermetic Publishing Company, 1926. 191 pp.

385. ————. *The Two Paths or the Parting of the Ways*. Chicago: Hermetic Publishing Company, 1929. 33 pp.

386. Richmond, Arlene L., comp. *Yenlo and the Mystic Brotherhood*. Chicago: The Author, 1945. 138 pp.

387. Richmond, Olney H. *Evolutionism*. Chicago: Temple Pub-
     lishing Company, 1896. 253 pp.

388. ————. *Temple Lectures of the Order of the Magi*.
     Chicago: Al Fyfe, 1892. 270 pp. Rpt. as *Religion
     of the Stars or the Temple Lectures*. Chicago: B.C.
     Peterson, 1905. 318 pp.

389. Roback, C.W. *The Mysteries of Astrology, and the Wonders
     of Magic*. Boston: The Author, 1854. 238 pp. Rpt.
     Mokelumne Hill, CA: Health Research, 1970. 238 pp.

390. Selig, Godfrey. *Secrets of the Psalms*. Dallas, TX:
     Dorene Publishing Company, 1958. 128 pp.

391. *The Sixth and Seventh Books of Moses*. N.p., n.d. 190 pp.

392. Straughn, R.A. *The Realization of Neter Nu*. Brooklyn,
     NY: Maat Publishing Company, 1975. 98 pp.

393. Thibodeau, Robert. *The Hermetic Dream*. Detroit:
     Hermes Press, 1979. 90 pp.

394. ————. *Laws of Hermetic Wisdom*. Detroit: Hermes Press,
     1978. 56 pp.

395. Three Initiates. *The Kybalion: A Study of the Hermetic
     Philosophy of Ancient Egypt and Greece*. Chicago: Yogi
     Publication Society, 1912. 223 pp.

396. Wagner, Belle. *Within the Temple of Isis*. Denver, CO:
     Astro-Philosophical Publishing Co., 1890. 156 pp.

396a. Wagner, Henry. *The Duality of Truth*. Denver, CO:
     Astro-Philosophical Publishing Co., 1899. 206 pp.

397. Wagner, Dr. and Mrs. Henry. *A Treasure Chest of Wisdom*.
     Denver, CO: H.O. Wagner, 1967. 251 pp.

398. Wilkinson, Ronald Sterne. "The Alchemical Library of
     John Winthrop, Jr. (1606-1676) and His Descendents
     in Colonial America." *Ambix* 11,1 (February 1963)
     33-51.

399. ————. "New England's Last Alchemists." *Ambix* 10,3
     (October 1962) 128-38.

400. Zain, C.C. *Organic Alchemy*. Los Angeles: Church of
        Light, 1944. 236 pp.

401. ————. *Spiritual Alchemy*. Los Angeles: Church of
        Light, 1931. 160 pp.

E. MAGNUM OPUS HERMETIC SOURCEWORKS

One sign of revived interest in alchemy and magic, the Magnum Opus Hermetic Sourceworks project initiated by Adam McLean of Edinburgh, Scotland, "seeks to make available important works of great esoteric value." McLean, himself an alchemist and editor of the *Hermetic Journal*, draws primarily on 16th- and 17th-century alchemical and Rosicrucian texts. Some are new publications from old manuscripts, others first English translations of German and Latin volumes, and a few are new editions of hard-to-find alchemical volumes.

During the 1970s McLean emerged as an important alchemical personality among magical communities on both sides of the Atlantic. Five titles have appeared to date.

402. *The Crowning of Nature*, ed. by Adam McLean. Edinburgh: Magnum Opus Hermetic Sourceworks, 1980. 137 pp.

403. Fludd, Robert. *The Mosaical Philosophy*. Edinburgh: Magnum Opus Hermetic Sourceworks, 1979. 125 pp.

404. *The Hermetic Garden of Daniel Stolcius*, trans. by Patricia Tahil. Edinburgh: Magnum Opus Hermetic Sourceworks, 1980. 169 pp.

405. *The Magical Calendar*, trans. and ed. by Adam McLean. Edinburgh: Magnum Opus Hermetic Sourceworks, 1979. 109 pp.

406. *The Rosicrucian Emblems of Daniel Cramer*, ed. by Adam McLean, trans. by Fiona Tait. Edinburgh: Magnum Opus Hermetic Sourceworks, 1980. 56 pp.

McLean has projected several titles for future editions. They include: *The Ampitheatre Engravings of Heinrich Khunrath; The Mylus Series; The Art of St. Cyprian; Jane Leade's Revelation of Revelations; Salomon Trismosin's Flower of Treasures; Reusner's Pandora Series;* and *The Ripley Scroll.*

F. SEX IN MAGIC AND RELIGION

During the 19th century the West slowly rediscovered the
element of sex in religion and magic. Emphasis on sex and
religion in the early books such as Knight's called attention
to phallic worship in ancient cults. These volumes were followed by works describing the continuing sexual component in
Eastern tantric religions.

At the end of the 19th century the spreading knowledge of
tantric magic led to the marriage of tantra and the Western
occult tradition and the development of a magical tradition
in which the sexual act was used to accomplish magical ends.
Possibly the first to combine Western occultism with Eastern
sexual teaching was Paschal Beverly Randolph, who founded the
Temple of Eulis in 1875 (see Section III-H). His teaching
became the basis for the most famous sexual magic group, the
Ordo Templi Orientis.

The volumes in this section sample some of the most popular
books on sex worship and the sexual metaphor in religion.
King (417-418) describes the development of Western sex magic
and the role of such men as Randolph and Edward Sellon. He
also published the texts of the O.T.O. rituals.

Karezza, a technique involving prolonged intercourse
without a climax, originally developed as a birth control
technique by John Humphrey Noyes for his Oneida colonists,
has a long history in the occult community. It was adopted
by several magical orders in the early 20th century and
taught to members as one of the "secret" practices. At the
time, of course, the quantity of material on various sexual
practices now easily attainable by anyone was still somewhat
secret.

407. Bach, Charlotte M. *What Is Human Ethology About?* N.p.:
        The Author, n.d. 275 pp.

408. Buckley, Edmund. *Phallicism in Japan.* Chicago: Univer-
        sity of Chicago Press, 1895. 34 pp.

409. Cutner, H. *A Short History of Sex Worship.* London:
        Watts & Co., 1940. 222 pp.

410. Douglas, Nik, and Penny Slinger. *Sexual Secrets*. New
     York: Destiny Books, 1979. 383 pp.

411. Dulaure, Jacques Antoine. *The Gods of Generation*.
     New York: Ponurge Press, 1933. 280 pp.

412. Gamble, Eliza Burt. *The God Idea of the Ancients*.
     New York: G.P. Putnam's Sons, 1897. 339 pp.

413. Goldberg, Ben Zion. *The Sacred Fire*. New York: H.
     Liveright, 1930. 386 pp.

414. Hannay, J.B. *Sex Symbolism in Religion*. London:
     Religious Evolution Research Society, 1922. 2 vols.

415. Howard, Clifford. *Sex Worship*. Chicago: Medical Book
     Co., 1899. 215 pp.

416. Jennings, Hargrave. *Phallicism*. London: George Redway,
     1884. 298 pp. Rpt. Mokelumne Hill, CA: Health Re-
     search, 1972. 298 pp.

417. King, Francis, ed. *The Secret Rituals of the O.T.O.*
     New York: Samuel Weiser, 1973. 239 pp.

418. ————. *Sexuality, Magic, and Perversion*. Secaucus,
     NJ: The Citadel Press, 1972. 207 pp.

419. Knight, Richard Payne. *A Discourse on the Worship of
     Priapus*. Rpt. Secaucus, NJ: University Books, 1974.
     294 pp.

420. Krishnar, Maravedi el. *Gran-Sexron*. Escondido, CA:
     Krishnar Institute, 1953. 154 pp.

421. Laurent, Emile. *Magica Sexualis*. New York: Falstaff
     Press, 1934. 294 pp.

422. Lloyd, J. William. *The Karezza Method*. Roscoe, CA: The
     Author, 1931. 64 pp. Rpt. Mokelumne Hill, CA: Health
     Research, 1964. 64 pp.

423. Long, Richard B. *Suburban Phallic Cults*. San Diego,
     CA: Phenix Publishers, 1969. 158 pp.

424. Miller, George Noyes. *After the Sex Struck or Zugassent's
     Discovery*. Boston: Arena Publishing Company, 1895.
     124 pp.

425. ————. *The Strike of a Sex*. New York: G.W. Dilling-
      ham, 1890. 235 pp.

426. Mumford, John (Swami Anandakipila). *Sexual Occultism*.
      St. Paul, MN: Llewellyn Publications, 1975. 178 pp.

427. Muses, Charles Arthur. *Esoteric Teachings of the Tibetan
      Tantra*. Lausanne, Switzerland: Falcon's Wing Press,
      1961. 305 pp.

428. Noyes, John Humphrey. *Male Continence*. Oneida, NY: Of-
      fice of the Circular, 1866. 4 pp. Rpt. Oneida, NY:
      Office of the American Socialist, 1877. 32 pp.

429. Rocco, Sha (pseudonym of Alisha S. Hudson). *The Mascu-
      line Cross*. New York: Asa K. Butts & Co., 1874. 65 pp.
      Rpt. as *The Masculine Cross and Ancient Sex Worship*.
      New York: Commonwealth Co., 1904.

430. Scott, George Ryley. *Phallic Worship*. London: Luxor
      Press, 1966. Rpt. London: Panther Books, 1970. 255 pp.

431. Sellon, Edward. *Annotations on the Sacred Writings of
      the Hindus*. London: The Author, 1902. 59 pp.

432. Stockham, Alice B. *Kerezza/Ethics of Marriage*. Chicago:
      A.B. Stockham, 1896. 136 pp. Rpt. Mokelumne Hill,
      CA: Health Research, n.d. 39 pp.

433. Stone, Lee Alexander. *The Story of Phallicism*. Chicago:
      P. Covici, 1927. 2 vols.

434. Wall, Otto Augustus. *Sex and Sex Worship*. St. Louis:
      C.V. Mosby Company, 1919. 607 pp.

435. Wellesley, Gordon. *Sex and the Occult*. New York: Bell
      Publishing Company, 1973. 224 pp.

436. Westropp, Hodder M. *Primitive Symbolism as Illustrated
      in Phallic Worship*. London: George Redway, 1875.
      64 pp.

437. ————, and C. Stanisland Wake. *Ancient Symbol Worship.
      Influence of the Phallic Idea in the Religions of An-
      tiquity*. New York: J.W. Bouton, 1875. 98 pp.

438. Wright, Thomas. *The Worship of the Generative Powers
      During the Middle Ages of Western Europe*. London:
      Dilettanti Society, n.d. 196 pp.

G. ALEISTER CROWLEY

Aleister Crowley (1875-1947), the single most influential
magician and most prolific magical writer of the 20th century,
lived with controversy and at times seemed to draw the appro-
bation of society upon his head. He sought to gather disciples,
but few stayed close over a period of time, and only after his
death did a following big enough to support popular publication of his writing appear.

At present almost all of Crowley's magical works have
been published and are readily available in relatively inexpensive editions. Both hostile and sympathetic writers chose
him as the subject of their biographical studies. His papers
now rest in the Warburg Institute in London under lock and
key.

From the 1904 dictation of *The Book of the Law*, Crowley
announced the beginning of the New Eon and proclaimed himself
its prophet. Crowley termed his magick (he added the "k")
"Thelemic" magick. *Thelema*, the Greek word for "will," key-
notes the new age whose watch word asserts, "Do what thou Will
is the Whole of the Law." Thelemic magic emphasizes the
discipline of the will and the individual's search for his
true will. Upon perception of his true will, the magician
is to follow it in all things.

Crowley also added the emphasis on sex to the Western
magical tradition. During the late 19th century, taking the
new knowledge of Tantra and the ancients' integration of sex,
magic, and religion, several groups began to practice sex
magic. Crowley picked up the practice, promoted it during
most of his life, and through his writings supplied to a
waiting public the material necessary if they were to join in.

The Crowley material appears below in two sections. The
first section lists Crowley's major magical writings with
citations biased toward the readily available American editions. The second lists books and articles about Crowley.

Besides his own writings, Crowley established a curriculum
for his students. The books of that curriculum constitute a
basic list of sources for Crowley's mature thought and modern
magical speculation in general. See Appendix II, pp. 213-18.

74

1. CROWLEY'S MAJOR WRITINGS

Between 1909 and 1912, Crowley assembled the largest collection of his writings in a semi-annual periodical, *The Equinox*
(London: 1909-1913, 10 volumes). Each of the 10 issues had
300-500 pages. An eleventh volume, popularly termed the
"blue" *Equinox*, appeared during Crowley's stay in America
(Detroit: Universal Publishing Co., 1919. 439 pp.). Page
proofs of a twelfth issue survive, but Crowley never published
it. *The Equinox*, including the blue volume, have all been reprinted (New York: Samuel Weiser, 1972). In the late 1970s
the O.T.O. branch headed by Marcelo Motta began issuing a new
Equinox series, two issues of which have appeared. They contain much Crowley material along with new writings by Motta
and members of the O.T.O. *Gems from the Equinox* contains a
selection of major works from the first 10 issues as selected
by Israel Regardie.

Liber Al vel Legis, Crowley's most important item, is the
manifesto of the New Eon. In *Magick Without Tears*, Crowley
makes his most systematic presentation of magical theory,
while the *Magical Diaries* and *Magical Record* give the best
picture of the day-to-day routine of a magician. In the
Confessions and *The Equinox of the Gods*, Crowley writes auto-
biographically.

439. Crowley, Aleister. *Aha.* Dallas, TX: Sangreal Founda-
     tion, 1969. 76 pp.

440. ———. *De Arte Magica.* Schmiedeberg, Germany: Die
     Oriflamme, 1914. Rpt. San Francisco: Level Press,
     n.d. 40 pp.

441. ———. *Book 4.* Dallas, TX: Sangreal Foundation,
     1969. 76 pp.

442. ———. *The Book of Lies.* London: Wieland & Co., 1913.
     131 pp. Rpt. New York: Samuel Weiser, 1970. 196 pp.

443. ———. *The Book of the Law* (*Liber al vel Legis*).
     Pasadena, CA: Church of Thelema, 1926. 49 pp.
     Rpt. New York: Samuel Weiser, 1976. 115 pp.

444. ———. *Book of Thoth.* London: The O.T.O., 1944.
     287 pp. Rpt. New York: Samuel Weiser, 1969. 287 pp.
     Rpt. San Francisco: Level Press, 1972. 287 pp.

445. ———. *Collected Works* I-III. Foyers, Scotland: S.P.R.T.,
     1905-7. 3 vols. Rpt. Chicago: Yogi Publication
     Society, 1973. 3 vols.

446. ————. *The Complete Astrological Writings*. London:
     Duckworth, 1974. 224 pp. Rpt. London: Tandem, 1976.
     235 pp.

447. ————. *The Confessions of Aleister Crowley*. Edited
     by John Symonds and Kenneth Grant. New York: Hill
     and Wang, 1969. 960 pp. Rpt. New York: Bantam Books,
     1971. 1058 pp.

448. ————. *Crowley on Christ*. Edited by Francis King.
     London: C.W. Daniel Company, 1974. 232 pp.

449. ————. *The Equinox of the Gods*. London: The O.T.O.,
     1936. 138 pp.

450. ————. *Gems from the Equinox*. Selected by Israel
     Regardie. St. Paul, MN: Llewellyn Publishing Co.,
     1974. 1134 pp.

451. ————, ed. *Goetia*. Foyers, Scotland: Society for
     the Propagation of Religious Truth, 1904. 65 pp.
     Rpt. Chicago: Occult Publishing House, n.d. 82 pp.

452. ————. *The Heart of the Master*. London: The O.T.O.,
     1938. 40 pp. Rpt. Montreal: 93 Publishing, 1973.

453. ————. *The Holy Books*. Dallas, TX: Sangreal Founda-
     tion, 1969. 116 pp.

454. ————. *The Law Is for All*. Edited by Israel Regardie.
     St. Paul, MN: Llewellyn Publications, 1975. 350 pp.

455. ————. *Liber Aleph*. West Point, CA: Karl Germer,
     1961. 219 pp. Rpt. San Francisco: Level Press, 1972.
     219 pp.

456. ————. *Magical and Philosophical Commentaries on the
     Book of the Law*. Edited by John Symonds and Kenneth
     Grant. Montreal: 93 Publishing, 1974. 343 pp.

457. ————. *Magical Diaries of Aleister Crowley*. Edited
     by Stephen Skinner. New York: Samuel Weiser, 1979.
     251 pp.

458. ————. *The Magical Record of the Beast 666*. Edited
     by John Symonds and Kenneth Grant. Montreal: Next
     Step Publications, 1972. 326 pp.

459. ———. *Magick in Theory and Practice*. New York:
     Castle Books, n.d. 436 pp.

460. ———. *Magick Without Tears*. New Jersey: Thelema
     Publishing Co., 1954. 400 pp. Rpt. St. Paul, MN:
     Llewellyn Publications, 1973. 522 pp.

461. ———. *The Qabalah of Aleister Crowley*. London: Cape,
     1969. 960 pp. Rpt. New York: Samuel Weiser, 1973.
     301 pp.

462. ———. *777*. London: Walter Scott Publishing Co.,
     1909. 54 pp. Rpt. Berkeley, CA: Ordo Templi Orientis,
     1980. 54 pp.

463. ———. *777 Revised*. London: The O.T.O., 1956. 150
     pp. Rpt. New York: Samuel Weiser, 1970. 150 pp.
     Rpt. San Francisco: Level Press, 1971. 150 pp.

464. ———. *Shih Yi*. California: Church of Thelema, 1971.
     70 pp.

465. ———. *Tao Teh King*. New York: Samuel Weiser, 1976.
     116 pp.

2. WORKS ABOUT ALEISTER CROWLEY

Crowley, being the colorful character that he was, inspired
friends to pen their memories of him and authors to attempt
to understand him. Roberts has come closest, though her work
has been neglected by many Thelemites who do not like her all-
too-human picture of Crowley. King has done a thorough job on
the magical side of Crowley, and Crammell, Fuller, Stephensen
& Regardie, and Symonds each add valuable insight.
    Parfitt and Drylie's cross-index lists all of Crowley's
works (with the exception of some poetry) under the several
titles most had, and begins to trace the numerous editions,
many privately printed in limited numbers. It is hoped that
others will carry on the work begun here.

466. Burnett-Rae, Alan. *Aleister Crowley*. London: Victim
     Press, 1971. 19 pp.

467. Carrington, Hereward. "Man of Mystery--Aleister Crow-
     ley." *Fate* 2,3 (September 1949) 66-71.

468. Clymer, R. Swinburne. *The Rosicrucian Fraternity in America*. Quakertown, PA: The Rosicrucian Foundation, 1935. 464 pp.

469. Crammell, C.R. *Aleister Crowley*. London: The Richards Press, 1951. Rpt. London: New English Library, 1969. 109 pp.

470. Dalton, David. "The Dope and Sex Magick of Aleister Crowley, Good Old 666." *High Times* 35 (July 1978) 71-76.

471. Fuller, J.F.C. *The Star in the West*. London: Walter Scott Publishing Co., 1907. 327 pp. Rpt. Mokelumne Hill, CA: Health Research, 1969. 327 pp.

472. Fuller, Jean Overton. *The Magical Dilemma of Victor B. Neuburg*. London: W.H. Allen, 1965. 295 pp.

473. Gilbert, Robert A. "Baphomat and Son: A Little-Known Chapter in the Life of 666." *Spectrum* 1,5 (May 1975) 3-8; and 1,6 (July 1975) 9-20.

474. King, Francis. *The Magical World of Aleister Crowley*. New York: Coward, McCann & Geoghegan, 1978. 210 pp.

475. Mannix, Daniel P. *The Beast*. New York: Ballantine Books, 1959. 140 pp.

476. ————. "The Great Beast." *True* 36,233 (October 1956) 29-31, 110-20.

477. Parfitt, Will, and A. Drylie. *A Crowley Cross-Index*. N.p.: ZRO, 1976. 36 pp.

478. Roberts, Susan. *The Magicians of the Golden Dawn*. Chicago: Contemporary Books, Inc., 1978. 337 pp.

479. Stephensen, P.R., and Israel Regardie. *The Legend of Aleister Crowley*. St. Paul, MN: Llewellyn Publications, 1970. 157 pp.

480. Symonds, John. *The Great Beast*. London: MacDonald & Co., 1971. 413 pp. Rpt. Frogmore, St. Albans, Herts., Eng.: Mayflower, 1973. 464 pp.

481. ————. *The Magic of Aleister Crowley*. London: Frederick Muller, 1958. 209 pp.

H. RITUAL MAGIC IN MODERN AMERICA

The teaching of ritual magic in the modern sense begins with
Paschal Beverly Randolph (1825-1871). Randolph, a learned
man, developed some ideas which did not exactly fit the re-
pressive mood of the Victorian era. He published many of
these ideas in his 1871 book *Eulis*, and also formed the
Fellowship of Eulis which embodied his full perspective on
what he termed "affectional alchemy," i.e., sex magic. He
stated his ideas clearly in his various books, a fact that
embarrassed his successor (Clymer) as head of the Rosicrucian
Fraternity that Randolph also founded.

From Randolph, the teachings and practice of sex magic
shifted to the Continent to the Ordo Templi Orientis and
hence to Aleister Crowley. Once Crowley began to spread the
magical gospel, though he never became the leader of the
large group toward which he worked, he infected the many
students who came into contact with him at one time or
another and spread the teachings throughout the West.

Frater Achad (magical name of Charles S. Jones), Crowley's magical son, broke with Crowley during the latter's
stay in America and developed his own system. Achad's side
of the schism is told in *Liber 31*, and his revised system is
spelled out in *Anatomy of the Body of God* and *Q.B.L. or the
Bride's Reception*. Damon, Alter, and Nemo are Achad's disciples.

Crowley gave C.F. Russell his blessing to come to America
and found a lodge. He started the Choronzon Club in Chicago
in the 1930s. Russell's story is told in his three-volume
Znuss Is Zness, and the teachings of the Club are fully ex-
posed in the works of Culling, one of its leaders.

Parsons was the leader for over a decade of Crowley's
only O.T.O. group during the 1940s. Some of his writings
were recently published in a booklet; others have appeared
as articles in the *Seventh Ray*, while the few remaining manuscripts have circulated privately.

After Crowley's death, Karl Germer headed the Order for
a decade but left no designated successor. At least four
people claim that distinction--Grady McMurty, Kenneth Grant,

Marcelo Motta, and Kurt Metzger. From Berkeley, McMurty has
slowly put prime O.T.O. documents back into print, partially
with the assistance of William Heidrick. Grant has written
voluminously and edited several works (including the writings
of Austin Spare). Motta has published a number of pamphlets
in recent years but more importantly has revived the *Equinox.*
Metzger's work is entirely in Europe.

Kenneth Grant, whose British-based O.T.O. has grown considerably in America during the 1970s, has written three books
describing not only the development of the O.T.O. (and giving
an apology for his leadership role in *The Magical Revival*)
but a number of other related magical systems (*Cults of the
Shadow* and *The Nightside of Eden*). These volumes offer the
only description in print of several of these groups.

No one can get seriously involved in ritual magic without
encountering the works of Israel Regardie. Regardie served
as Crowley's secretary for several years in the 1920s, then
returned to the United States and remained silent for many
years. Then in the 1930s he published a number of key books
that most people who practice magic read and recommend--*The
Tree of Life, The Middle Pillar, A Garden of Pomegranates,*
and *The Philosopher's Stone.*

Regardie, of course, gained his initial fame for the publication of the secret rituals of *The Golden Dawn.* Until
then, except for a few rituals printed by Crowley in the
Equinox, such rituals circulated only privately to members
of various occult orders.

Many items in this section have been written by what
might be considered the third generation of Crowley students--
Beth-Shin-Tau, Brennan, Feldman & Parshley, Grossinger, Heflin, Miller, Sandbach, Sommers, Toups, and White.

The remaining items refer to ritual magic groups and
teachers not in a direct lineage from Crowley. Aleta Baker
headed a feminist-oriented ritual magic group in Boston in
the 1930s. Other independent groups include the Order of
the Lily and the Eagle, Order of the Holy Grail, Bennu Phoenix
Temple of the Golden Dawn, the Fraternity of Light, Religious
Order of Templars in America, and the Grand Knights of Dorset.

482.   Achad, Frater. *Anatomy of the Body of God.* Chicago:
       Collegium ad Spiritum Sanctum, 1925. 111 pp.

483.   ———. *Ancient Mystical White Brotherhood.* Lakemont,
       GA: CSA Press, 1971. 174 pp.

484.   ———. *Chalice of Ecstasy.* Chicago: Yogi Publication
       Society, 1923. 83 pp.

485. ───. *Crystal Vision through Crystal Gazing*. Chicago: Yogi Publication Society, 1923. 116 pp.

486. ───. *The Egyptian Revival*. Chicago: The Collegium ad Spiritum Sanctum, 1923. 120 pp.

487. ───. *Liber 31*. San Francisco: Level Press, 1974. 82 pp.

488. ───. *Liber Q.N.A.* Manuscript.

489. ───. *Melchizedek Truth Principles*. Phoenix, AZ: Lockhart Research Foundation, 1963. 209 pp.

490. ───. *De Mysteriis R.R. et A.C.* North American Publishing Co., 1924.

491. ───. *Official Correspondence Concerning MA-ION*. Manuscript.

492. ───. *Q.B.L. or the Bride's Reception*. Chicago: The Author, 1922. 106 pp.

493. ───. *XXXI Hymns to the Star Goddess*. Chicago: Will Ransom, 1923. 38 pp.

494. Baker, Aleta Blanche. *The Divine Corpus-Christi*. Washington, D.C.: The Author, 1938. 39 pp.

495. ───. *The Causal Essence Personified*. Boston: The Rockwell and Churchill Press, 1928. 116 pp.

496. ───. *The Luminous Doctrine of the Spiritual Heart*. Boston, 1929. 197 pp.

497. ───. *Man--and His Counterpart--Woman*. Boston, 1930. 441 pp.

498. ───. *She, The Woman-Man*. Boston, 1935. 338 pp.

499. ───. *The Soul's First Student*. Boston, 1928. 93 pp.

500. ───. *The Spiral Road to God*. Boston, 1933. 170 pp.

501. Baphomet X°. *How to Contact Your Inner Teacher*. N.p., n.d. 17-page typescript.

502. Beth-Shin-Tau. *Magician's Desk Reference*. Berkeley, CA: B.S.T. Publishing, 1978.

503. *The Book of Perfection*. South Stukely, Que.: 93 Publishing, 1977. 117 pp.

504. Brennan, T. Casey. *The Revelation of the Damned*. Ann Arbor, MI: The Author, 1974. 10 pp.

505. Burland, C.A. *The Magical Arts*. New York: Horizon Press, 1966. 196 pp.

506. Clymer, R. Swinburne. *The Rose Cross Order*. Allentown, PA: Philosophical Publishing Co., 1916. 208 pp.

507. Culling, Louis. *Complete Magical Curriculum of the Secret Order G:.B:.G:.* St. Paul, MN: Llewellyn Publications, 1969. 127 pp.

508. ————. *A Manual of Sex Magick*. St. Paul, MN: Llewellyn Publications, 1971. 147 pp.

509. ————. *Occult Renaissance 1972-2000*. St. Paul, MN: Llewellyn Publications, 1972. 56 pp.

510. Damon, Alta, and Nemo. *Liber XIII*. Ramona, CA: Q.B.L.H., 1978. 84 pp.

511. Denning, Metita, and Osborne Phillips. *The Llewellyn Practical Guide to Astral Projection*. St. Paul, MN: Llewellyn Publications, 1979. 240 pp.

512. ————. *The Llewellyn Practical Guide to Creative Visualization*. St. Paul, MN: Llewellyn Publications, 1980. 225 pp.

513. ————. *The Llewellyn Practical Guide to Psychic Self-Defense and Well-Being*. St. Paul, MN: Llewellyn Publications, 1980. 253 pp.

514. ————. *The Magical Philosophy*. St. Paul, MN: Llewellyn Publications.
    I.   *Robe and Ring*, 1974. 192 pp.
    II. *The Sword and the Serpent*, 1975. 265 pp.
    III. *The Apparel of High Magick*, 1975. 176 pp.
    IV. *The Triumph of Light*, 1978. 250 pp.
    V.   *Mysteria Magica*, forthcoming.

515. *Document Number Two; Introductory Document.* Englewood, CO: The Order of the Lily and the Eagle, n.d. 18 pp.

516. Emmerettae. *The Book of Emmerettae.* Hamilton, Ont.: Acorn, 1980. 60 pp.

517. Feldman, Mark, and Ron Parshley. *Theorems of Occult Magick.* Methuen, MA: P-F Publications, 1971. Vols. I-IV.

518. Fleming, John. "Hoodoo You Trust? An Encounter with Chicago's Black Magic Theosophic Neo-Pythagorean Gnostic Master." *The Reader* (June 22, 1979) 3.

519. Fox, Jack D. "Magic: The Ancient Art of Mystery." *Coronet* 12,4 (April 1974) 12-15, 46.

520. Garrison, Omar. "Slain Scientist Priest in Black Magic Cult." *The Mirror* (Los Angeles) (June 20, 1952).

521. Gleadow, Rupert. *Magic and Divination.* Totowa, NJ: Rowman and Littlefield, 1976. 308 pp.

522. Grant, Kenneth. *Cults of the Shadow.* New York: Samuel Weiser, 1976. 244 pp.

523. ———. *The Magical Revival.* New York: Samuel Weiser, 1973. 244 pp.

524. ———. *Nightside of Eden.* London: Frederick Muller Limited, 1977. 304 pp.

525. Gray-Cobb, Geoff. "How to Make a Magic Mirror." *Fate* 25,10 (October 1972) 80-86.

526. Grossinger, Richard. *Book of the Cranberry Islands.* New York: Harper and Row Publishers, 1974. 299 pp.

527. Heflin, Lee. *The Island Dialogues.* San Francisco: Level Press, 1973. 169 pp.

528. Heidrick, Bill. *The Thirty-Two Emanations and the Path of Initiation.* N.p.: The Author, 1972. 22 pp.

529. Hinterberger, John. "Seasonal Guide to Witch Is Witch." *Seattle Times* (October 31, 1973) C1.

530. Kok, T.R. *Practical Elemental Magick*. N.p.: The
      Author, 1980. 12 pp.

531. Kulp, Thomas, and Radelle Kulp. *The Order of the Holy
      Grail: Ancient Wisdom for a New Age*. Richmond, VA:
      O.H.G., n.d. 9 pp.

532. Layne, Meade. *Retro Me or Psychic Self-Defense*. Vista,
      CA: Borderland Sciences Research Foundation, 1954.
      5th ed., 1976. 17 pp.

533. *Liber NV*. Berkeley, CA: O.T.O., n.d. 7 pp.

534. *Liber Rosh*. N.p.: O.T.O., n.d. 5 pp.

535. Luptak, Gene. "Husband-Wife Priest Team Lives Monastic
      Life on Farm." *Arizona Republic* (April 5, 1974).

536. *Membership Manual/Fraternity of the Restored Covenant*.
      Pasadena, CA: R.E.F. Inc., 1976. 57 pp.

537. Miller, Richard Alan. *The Magical and Ritual Use of
      Herbs*. Berkeley, CA: Organization for the Advance-
      ment of Knowledge, n.d. 144 pp.

538. Motta, Marcelo Ramos (Frater Parzival). *Manifesto*.
      Nashville, TN: Society Ordo Templi Orientis in America,
      1978. 6 pp.

539. ———. *Of the Political Aims of the O.T.O.* Nashville,
      TN: Society Ordo Templi Orientis in America, 1980.
      30 pp.

540. ———. *Thelemic Political Morality*. Nashville, TN:
      Society Ordo Templi Orientis in America, 1978. 8 pp.

541. Ophiel (pseudonym of Edmund Peach). *The Art and Prac-
      tice of Astral Projection*. New York: Samuel Weiser,
      1973. 116 pp.

542. ———. *The Art and Practice of Caballa Magic*. New
      York: Samuel Weiser, 1977. 152 pp.

543. ———. *The Art and Practice of Clairvoyance*. St.
      Paul, MN: Peach Publishing Co., 1969. 133 pp.

544. ———. *The Art and Practice of Talismanic Magic*. West
      Hollywood, CA: Peach Publishing Co., 1973. 139 pp.

545. O'Toole, Thomas J. "Practicing Witches Compete with Voodoo in New Orleans." *Chicago Sun-Times* (April 22, 1973).

546. Palmer, John Phillips. *Quit the Night and Seek the Day! An Invitation to Membership in the Bennu Phoenix Temple of the Golden Dawn.* N.p., 1975. 5 pp.

547. Parsons, John W. *The Book of Babalon.* N.p., n.d. 20-page typescript.

548. ———. *Magick, Gnosticism and the Witchcraft.* South Stukely, Que.: 93 Publishing, 1979. 37 pp.

549. *The Path of Light.* Philadelphia: The Fraternity of Light, 1974. 7 pp.

550. Pitney, Emmanuel Marpin, ed. *The Sacred Mysteries of R.O.T.A.* N.p.: Religious Education Foundation, 1974. 167 pp.

551. Randolph, Paschal Beverly. *Eulis.* Toledo, OH, 1896. Rpt. as *Eulis: Affectional Alchemy.* Quakertown, PA: The Confederation of Initiates, 1930. 230 pp.

552. ———. *The Grand Secret.* San Francisco, CA: Pilkinton & Randolph, 1861-62. 87 pp.

553. ———. *Magia Sexualis.* Paris: R. Felin, 1931. 218 pp.

554. Regardie, Israel. *The Art and Meaning of Magic.* Dallas, TX: Sangreal Foundation, 1964. 100 pp.

555. ———. *Ceremonial Magic.* Wellingborough, Northamptonshire: Aquarian Press, 1980. 127 pp.

556. ———. *Enochian Dictionary.* Dallas, TX: Sangreal Foundation, 1971.

557. ———. *The Eye in the Triangle.* St. Paul, MN: Llewellyn Publications, 1970. 517 pp.

558. ———. *Foundations of Practical Magic.* Wellingborough, Northamptonshire: Aquarian Press.

559. ———. *A Garden of Pomegranates*. London: Rider & Co.,
      1936. 160 pp. Rev. ed. St Paul, MN: Llewellyn Pub-
      lications, 1970. 160 pp.

560. ———, ed. *Gems from the Equinox*. St. Paul, MN:
      Llewellyn Publications, 1974. 1134 pp.

561. ———. *The Golden Dawn*. Chicago: Aries Press, 1937-
      40. 4 vols. Rpt. St. Paul, MN: Llewellyn Publica-
      tions, 1969. 1 vol.

562. ———. *How to Make and Use Talismans*. New York:
      Samuel Weiser, 1972. 63 pp.

563. ———. *Magic in East and West*. Dallas, TX: Sangreal
      Foundation, 1968.

564. ———. "Magic in East and West." *The Aries Quarterly*
      1,2 (June 1938) 9-16.

565. ———. *The Meaning of Magic*. Dallas, TX: Sangreal
      Foundation, 1964.

566. ———. *The Middle Pillar*. Chicago: Aries Press,
      1938. 154 pp. Rev. ed. St. Paul, MN: Llewellyn Pub-
      lications, 1970. 154 pp.

567. ———. *My Rosicrucian Adventure*. Chicago: Aries
      Press, 1936. 144 pp. Rev. ed. St. Paul, MN: Llewel-
      lyn Publications, 1971. 168 pp.

568. ———. *The Philosopher's Stone*. London: Rider & Co.,
      1938. 204 pp. Rev. ed. St. Paul, MN: Llewellyn
      Publications, 1970. 204 pp.

569. ———. *A Practical Guide to Geomanic Divination*.
      New York: Samuel Weiser, 1972. 64 pp.

570. ———. *Roll away the Stone*. St. Paul, MN: Llewellyn
      Publications, 1968. 241 pp.

571. ———. *The Tree of Life*. London: Rider & Co., 1932.
      284 pp. Rev. ed. New York: Samuel Weiser, 1971.
      284 pp.

572. ———. "Why I Wrote 'The Golden Dawn.'" *The Aries
      Quarterly* 1,1 (March 1938) 14-22.

573. Reynard. *Grand Knights of Dorset O.B.R.* Hamilton,
      Ont.: Acorn, n.d. 8 pp.

574. Russell, C.F. *Znuss Is Zness.* N.p.: The Author, 1970.
      3 vols.

575. Sandbach, John. *The Principles of Magic.* N.p.: The
      Author, 1979. 49 pp.

576. Saxon, Harry O. *The Master Key of Love.* Chicago: The
      Author, 1932. 127 pp.

577. *Sepher Yetzirah.* Berkeley, CA: Ordo Templi Orientis,
      1980. 31 pp.

578. Sommers, Robert. *The One True Magick.* Lakemont, GA:
      Turnhelm Press, 1976. 204 pp.

579. *Ssotbme: An Essay on Magic.* Surrey, Eng.: Nigel Grey-
      Turner, 1979. 96 pp.

580. Strabo, Mikhail. *The Magic Formula for Successful
      Prayer.* New York: Guidance House, 1943. 61 pp.

581. *Success in Candle Burning.* Pasadena, CA: The K Circle,
      1976. 17 pp.

582. Symon, Jon. *The Grimoreum Verum.* Hamilton, Ont.:
      Acorn, n.d. 48 pp.

583. ————. *The Sacred Magick of the Angels or Talismanic
      Intelligencer.* Hamilton, Ont.: Acorn, n.d. 83 pp.

584. ————. *The Stone Missal.* Hamilton, Ont.: Acorn, 1979.
      76 pp.

585. Tanith, Sor. "The O.T.O. in New York." *Sothis* (Sep-
      tember 1973) 67-70.

586. "To Know, In Order to Serve." N.p.: Ordo Templi Dianos,
      n.d. 2 pp.

587. Toups, Oneida. *Magick High and Low.* Jefferson, LA:
      Hope Publications, 1975. 162 pp.

588. *Vespers, with Services for the Administration of Holy
      Communion, Prime and Complin.* Phoenix, AZ: St.
      Thelema Press, 1972. 60 pp.

589. Wentler, William. *Fire Mist and Templars*. N.p.:
        Religious Education Foundation, 1974. 45 pp.

590. White, Nelson, and Anne White. *Secret Magick Revealed*.
        Pasadena, CA: Technology Group, 1979. 119 pp.

591. Zarathustra, Fra. *An Introduction to Magick*. Pasadena,
        CA: Labrys Press, 1972. 42 pp.

IV

WITCHCRAFT

A. WITCHCRAFT IN COLONIAL AMERICA

Settlers in the American Colonies in the 17th century brought
with them the folk magic of Europe, consisting largely of a
variety of low magic practices, the knowledge of which formed
the craft of the "Witch." They also brought with them the
popular ideas about Witches, their powers, and their connection with Satan.

Largely lost in the emphasis on Salem, the practice of
and concern with Witchcraft in the Colonial period was widespread. Trials occurred as far south as Virginia, and as
late as the 1720s. Trials occurred in New England for several
decades prior to the events of 1692. See Drake for a survey
of these trials.

The phenomenon described in this literature fits more
closely into the history of European Witchcraft than modern
Paganism and Witchcraft. Yet the connection with the modern
era, beyond the popular folklore about Salem, is real.

In at least some cases, the persons described as Witches
in the Colonial material accepted the label and image of
"Witch" and practiced various kinds of low magic. That the
trials stopped does not mean that the practice stopped.
Rather, the phenomenon moved underground to the edges of
urban life, or the less-populated rural areas. New immigrant
communities continually reinforced its presence. But after
the first quarter of the 18th century, the literature of the
period ignored it.

592. Bruce, Philip Alexander. *Institutional History of
      Virginia in the 17th Century.* Gloucester, MA: Peter
      Smith, 1964. I, pp. 278-89.

593. Burr, George Lincoln. *Narratives of the Witchcraft
      Cases, 1648-1706.* New York: Scribner's, 1914. 467 pp.

594. Davis, Richard Beale. "The Devil in Virginia in the
      Seventeenth Century." *The Virginia Magazine of His-
      tory and Biography* 65,2 (April 1957) 131-49.

595. Demos, John. "Underlying Themes in the Witchcraft of
      Seventeenth-Century New England." *American Historical
      Review* 75 (June 1970) 1311-26.

596. Douglas, Albert. "Ohio's Only Witchcraft Case." *Ohio
      Arch. & Hist. Society Publications* 33,2 (April 1924)
      205-14.

597. Drake, Frederick C. "Witchcraft in the American Colo-
      nies, 1647-62." *American Quarterly* 20 (Winter 1968)
      694-725.

598. Drake, Samuel Gardner. *Annals of Witchcraft in New
      England.* Boston: W.E. Woodward, 1869. 306 pp.
      Rpt. New York: B. Blom, 1967. 306 pp.

599. Folsom, Joseph Fulford. "Witches in New Jersey." *Pro-
      ceedings of the New Jersey Historical Society* 7,4
      (October 1922) 293-304.

600. James, E.W. "Witchcraft in Virginia." *William and Mary
      College Quarterly Historical Papers* 1,3 (January
      1893) 127-29.

601. James, Edward R. "Grace Sherwood--The Virginia Witch."
      William and Mary College Quarterly 3 (1894-95) 96-101,
      190-92, 242-45; 4 (1895) 18-22.

602. Kittredge, G.L. *Witchcraft in Old and New England.*
      New York: Russell & Russell, 1956. 641 pp.

603. Langden, Carolyn S. "The Case of Lydia Gilbert (Witch-
      craft in Connecticut)." *New England Galaxy* 5,3
      (Winter 1964).

604. Lyon, John. "Witchcraft in New York." *New-York His-
      torical Society Collections.* Publication Fund,
      Clarendon Papers, 1869.

605. Miller, William Marion. "How to Become a Witch."
      Journal of American Folklore 57 (October-December
      1944) 226.

606. Neill, Edward D. *Virginia Carolorum*. Albany, NY: Joel Munsell's Sons, 1886, pp. 239-40, 256-59.

607. Oliver, Betty. "Grace Sherwood of Princess Anne." *North Carolina Folklore* 10 (July 1962) 36-39.

608. Park, Francis Neal. "Witchcraft in Maryland." *Maryland Historical Magazine* 31,4 (December 1936) 271-98.

609. Riddell, William Renwick. "William Penn and Witchcraft." *Journal of the American Institute of Criminal Law and Criminology* 18 (1927) 11-16.

610. ————. "Witchcraft in Old New York." *Journal of the American Institute of Criminal Law and Criminology* 19 (1928) 252-56.

611. Steedman, Marguerite. "The Bewitched Ship." *Fate* 6,11 (November 1953) 71-73.

612. Winsor, Justin. "The Literature of Witchcraft in New England." *Proceedings of the American Antiquarian Society* n.s. 10 (October 1895) 371-73.

613. Worthen, Samuel Capp. "Witches in New Jersey and Elsewhere." *Proceedings of the New Jersey Historical Society* 8,2 (April 1923) 139-43.

B. SALEM

The trials of 1692 and the deaths of 19 individuals at Salem
Village (now Danvers), Massachusetts, were of monumental importance in both stopping trials for Witchcraft in the Western
world and in setting attitudes about Witchcraft for subsequent
generations. Prior to the trials, three groups, each holding
distinct opinions about Witchcraft, emerged. One group believed everything including the need to try and execute
Witches. A second group, which included Cotton Mather, believed in the existence of Witchcraft and abhorred it, but
quickly cooled to the idea of trials and denounced the use of
spectral evidence. Spectral evidence, which played a major
role at Salem, is defined as the unsubstantiated claims by
individuals that spectres (astral forms) of an accused Witch
haunted them. A third group did not believe in Witchcraft at
all.
    Prior to the trials, the first two groups were allies
against the latter, whom they termed "Sadducees." As the
trials progressed, the second group shifted its allegiance,
and Cotton Mather became a major force in stopping the trials.
After the trials, as the impact of their having executed so
many of their neighbors hit the colony, the third group's
opinions became dominant and, of course, came to be shared
by most historians and writers during the next two centuries.
They borrowed the term "hysteria" to explain this horrendous
event.
    The themes provoked by Salem have produced numerous books
and articles. In 1908 George F. Black of the New York Public
Library staff compiled and published a list of the works on
Salem and Colonial Witchcraft in the Library's periodical collection. This list is largely exhaustive of material to the
date of publication and is reprinted as Appendix I to this
volume.
    Below are the books and articles which have appeared since
Black's work along with a few items Black missed. Most of
this material merely continues the lines of thought established
firmly in previous centuries. Not to be missed, however, are
some new items published in the 1970s which offer a whole new
set of perspectives on Salem.

Hansen presented the evidence that in fact Witchcraft was being practiced by some of the accused and that the trials were given early credence by the discovery of magical artifacts in the home of Goodwife Nurse and Goode. Boyer and Nissenbaum have demonstrated the existence of a strong social schism within Salem Village. The pattern of accusers and victims followed a prior social division. Caporael offered observation on the possibility of psychedelic drugs finding their way into the Village food supply, a thesis refuted by Spanos and Gottlieb.

In spite of the volume of material already written, Salem still excites scholars and writers, and the definitive work has yet to be written.

614. Abernathy, Harold. "Did Witchcraft End at Salem?" *Occult* 4,3 (October 1973) 92-98, 109-10.

615. Baritz, Loren. *Witchcraft in America.* Saratoga Springs, NY: Empire State College, State University of New York, 1973. 32 pp.

616. Beard, George M. *Psychology of the Salem Witchcraft Excitement of 1692.* New York: G.P. Putnam's Sons, 1882.

617. *Bewitched in Salem, Massachusetts, Founded 1626.* Salem, MA: Tourist & Convention Division, Salem Chamber of Commerce, 1967. 52 pp.

618. Bonfonti, Leo. *The Witchcraft Hysteria of 1692.* Wakefield, MA: Pride Publications, 1971. 63 pp.

619. Booth, Sally Smith. *The Witches of Early America.* New York: Hastings House Publishers, 1975. 238 pp.

620. Boyer, Paul, and Stephen Nissenbaum. *Salem Possessed.* Cambridge, MA: Harvard University Press, 1974. 231 pp.

621. ————. *Salem-Village Witchcraft.* Belmont, CA: Wadsworth Publishing Company, Inc., 1972. 416 pp.

622. Bryn, Katherine. "The Sins of Salem." *Science Digest* 69,5 (May 1971) 29-31.

623. Burr, George H. "New England's Place in Witchcraft." *Proceedings of the American Antiquarian Society,*

new series 21 (1911). Rpt. Freeport, NY: Books for Libraries, 1971. 35 pp.

624. Caporael, Linnda R. "Ergotism: The Satan Loosed in Salem?" *Science* 192 (April 2, 1976) 21-26.

625. Caulfield, Ernest. "Pediatric Aspects of the Salem Witchcraft Tragedy." *American Journal for the Diseases of Children* 65 (1973) 788-802.

626. Danforth, Florence G. *New England Witchcraft*. New York: Pageant Press, 1965. 54 pp.

627. *The Diary of Samuel Sewall*, ed. Harvey Wish. New York: Capricorn Books, 1967. 189 pp.

628. Dickinson, Alice. *Salem Witchcraft Delusion, 1692*. New York: F. Watts, 1974. 64 pp.

629. Drake, Samuel Gardner. *The Witchcraft Delusion in New England*. Roxbury, MA: W.E. Woodward, 1866. 3 vols. Rpt. New York: B. Franklin, 1970. 3 vols.

630. Early, Eleanor. "Salem Is Still Hung Up on Witches." *Fate* 22,8 (August 1969) 36-41.

631. Fowler, Samuel P., ed. *Salem Witchcraft*. Salem, MA: H.P. Ives and A.A. Smith, 1867.

632. Gannon, Frederick Augustus. *A Brief History of Salem Witchcraft as Described by the Guide*. Salem, MA: Salem Books, 1963. 24 pp.

633. Goshko, John. "Salem Witches on LSD Trip in 1692, Study Concludes." *Chicago Sun-Times* (March 31, 1976) 32.

634. Guy, Don. "New Evidence Found of Witchcraft Hysteria." *Daily Evening Item* (Lynn, MA) (October 31, 1970).

635. Hansen, Chadwick. "The Metamorphosis of Tituba, or Why American Intellectuals Can't Tell an Indian Witch from a Negro." *New England Quarterly* 47,1 (March 1974) 3-12.

636. ————. *Witchcraft at Salem*. New York: George Braziller, Inc., 1969. Rpt. New York: New American Library, 1970. 318 pp.

637. Haraszti, Zolton. "Cotton Mather and Witchcraft Trials."
     More Books 15 (1940) 179+.

638. Henry, Stuart C. "Puritan Character in the Witchcraft
     Episode of Salem." In H. Shelton Smith, ed., *A Mis-
     cellany of American Christianity.* Durham, NC: Duke
     University Press, 1963, pp. 138-67.

639. Hoch, Edward D. "Something in Salem." *Exploring the
     Unknown* 5,2 (October 1964) 38-44.

640. Jackson, Shirley. *The Witchcraft of Salem Village.*
     New York: Random House, 1956. 176 pp.

641. Levin, David, ed. *What Happened in Salem?* Boston:
     Twayne Publishers, 1952. 198 pp. 2nd ed. New York:
     Harcourt, Brace & World, 1960. 238 pp.

642. ————. "Salem Witchcraft in Recent Fiction and Drama."
     New England Quarterly 28 (1955) 537-46.

643. Mather, Cotton. *The Wonders of the Invisible World.*
     Rpt. Amherst, WI: Amherst Press, n.d. 291 pp.

644. McKern, Sharon S. "They're Digging Up Witch Lore in
     Salem." *Science Digest* 69,5 (May 1971) 27-28, 32-34.

645. Murray, Jack. "Night Riders Keep Memory of Salem
     Atrocities Alive." *Probe the Unknown* 4,2 (March
     1976) 20-23, 59-60.

646. Nevins, Winfield S. *Witchcraft in Salem Village in
     1692.* Salem, MA: North Shore Publishing Company,
     1892. 272 pp.

647. Penneck, Rupert. *Witchcraft in New England.* Cambridge:
     Fenris-Wolf, 1976. 11 pp.

648. Perley, M.V.B. *A Short History of the Salem Village
     Witchcraft Trials.* Salem, MA: Perley Publishing
     Company, 1911. 76 pp.

649. Petry, Ann. *Tituba of Salem Village.* New York: Thomas
     Y. Crowell Company, 1964. 254 pp.

650. Poole, William E. *Memorial History of Boston.* Boston:
     Ticknor, 1881, vol. I, pp. 130-72.

651. Putnam, Allen. *Witchcraft in New England Explained by Modern Spiritualism.* Boston: Colby and Rich, 1880. 482 pp.

652. Ringel, Faye. "Colonial Witches: Our Early American Psychics." *ESP* 2 (January 1977) 26-28, 52-54.

653. Robbins, Peggy. "The Devil in Salem." *American History Illustrated* 6,8 (December 1971) 4-9.

654. Robotti, Frances Diane. *Chronicles of Old Salem.* New York: Bonanza Books, 1947. 129 pp.

655. Siegel, Benjamin. *Witch of Salem.* New York: Fawcett Publications, 1953. 170 pp.

656. Spanos, Nicolas P., and Jack Gottlieb. "Ergotism and the Salem Village Witch Trials." *Science* 194 (December 24, 1976) 1390-94.

657. Starkey, Marion Lena. *The Devil in Massachusetts.* New York: Time Incorporated, 1949. 344 pp.

658. ————. *A Tall Man from Boston.* New York: Crown Publishers, 1975. 46 pp.

659. ————. *The Visionary Girls.* Boston: Little, Brown, 1973. 176 pp.

660. Tapley, Charles Sutherland. *Rebecca Nurse.* Boston: Marshall Jones Company, 1930. 105 pp.

660a. Taylor, John M. *The Witchcraft Delusion in Colonial Connecticut 1647-1697.* New York: Burt Franklin, 1908. Rpt. 1971. 172 pp.

661. Thomas, M. Wynn. "Cotton Mather's *Wonders of the Invisible World*: Some Metamorphoses of Salem Witchcraft." In Sydney Angle, ed., *The Damned Art.* London: Routledge and Kegan Paul, 1977, pp. 202-26.

662. Upham, Charles W. *Salem Witchcraft with an Account of Salem Village and a History of Opinion on Witchcraft and Kindred Subjects.* Rpt. New York: Ungar, 1959. 2 vols.

663. Woodward, W.E., comp. *Records of Salem Witchcraft, Copied from the Original Documents.* New York: Burt Franklin, 1972. 2 vols.

C. POWWOW

To this day in Southeastern Pennsylvania the practice of powwowing or hexing exists. Powwow, a folk magic tradition very
similar to one brought from England, consists of low magic
formulae brought from Germany at the end of the 17th century.

The hexmeisters derive from a Theosophic-Rosicrucian group,
the "Chapter of Perfection," that flourished for several
decades beginning in 1692. They engaged in both high and low
magic. After the group dissolved, several members remained
in the area and passed along an oral magic tradition. The
story of the Chapter is told in Sachse and Melton.

The magic passed along from the Chapter and brought over
by 18th-century immigrants was compiled by Johann George
Hohman in *Der lange verborgene Freund* in 1819. An English
translation appeared in 1850 as *The Long Lost Friend*, and
this volume became the "Bible" of the hexmeisters.

The murders associated with the malevolent practice of
hexing in the 1920s had an effect similar to Salem for New
England, and provoked much writing, including a recent book
(Lewis). See also articles by Maxwell and Nichols.

The reality of modern hexing is described by Gandee.

664. Aurand, A. Monroe, Jr. *The Realness of Witchcraft in
        America*. Lancaster, PA: The Aurand Press, n.d.
        32 pp.

665. Bayard, S.P. "Witchcraft Magic and Spirits on the
        Border of Pennsylvania and West Virginia." *Journal
        of American Folklore* 51,199 (January-March 1938)
        47-59.

666. Crosby, John K. "Modern Witches of Pennsylvania."
        Journal of American Folklore 40,157 (1927) 304-9.

667. Frazier, Paul. "Some Lore of Hexing and Powwowing."
        Midwest Folklore 2 (1952) 101-7.

668. Gandee, Lee R. *Strange Experience*. Englewood Cliffs,
      NJ: Prentice-Hall, Inc., 1971. 355 pp.

669. ————. "'Using' to Heal in South Carolina." *Fate*
      14,3 (March 1961) 34-39.

670. ————. "The Witches of Fairfield, S.C." *Fate* 23,1
      (January 1970) 36-44.

671. Hark, Ann. *Hex Marks the Spot*. Philadelphia: J.B.
      Lippincott, 1938. 316 pp.

672. Heinzmann, Louis J. "Are Barn Signs Hex Marks?" *His-*
      torical Review of Berks County 12,1 (October 1946).

673. Hoffbower, Henry F. "Pennsylvania's Painted Prayers."
      Fate 18,10 (October 1965) 46-52.

674. ————. "You Can Be a Hex." *Fate* 21,2 (February 1968)
      92-98.

675. Hohman, Johann George. *Der lange verborgene Freund*.
      Reading, PA: n.p., 1819. 87 pp. Rpt. in English as
      The Long Lost Friend. Harrisburg, PA: n.p., 1850.
      72 pp.

676. ————. "The Long Hidden Friend." With introduction
      and notes by C.F. Brown. *Journal of American Folklore*
      17 (1904) 89-152.

677. Lewis, Arthur H. *Hex*. New York: Trident Press, 1967.
      255 pp. Rpt. New York: Pocket Books, 1970. 228 pp.

678. Maxwell, C.N.W. "The Pennsylvania Hex Murder." *Fate*
      2,1 (May 1949) 26-31.

679. Melton, J. Gordon. "Pioneers ... in Land, in Knowledge,
      in Astrology." *American Astrology* 41,10 (December
      1973) 18-21.

680. Nalesnyk, E. Linder. "Louisa: The Story of a Hex."
      Exploring the Unknown 5,2 (October 1964) 15-31.

681. Neifert, William W. "Witchcraft." *The Pennsylvania-*
      German 9,3 (March 1908).

682. Nichols, Dudley. "Witches Win in New York." *The Nation*
      128,3316 (January 23, 1929) 98-100.

683. Paxton, Henry D. *Where Pennsylvania History Began.*
Philadelphia, 1926. 248 pp.

684. Sachse, Julius Friedrich. *The German Pietists of
Provincial Pennsylvania.* Philadelphia: The Author,
1895. 504 pp.

685. Schultz, C.P. "The Kid's Powwow Healing." *Fate* 31,8
(August 1978) 61-62.

686. Shaner, Richard H. "Living Occult Practices in Dutch
Pennsylvania." *Pennsylvania Folklife* 12,3 (Fall
1961) 62-63.

687. ————. "Recollections of Witchcraft in the Oley Hills."
Pennsylvania Folklife 21, supp. (1972) 39-43.

688. Shoemaker, Alfred L. *Hex Signs.* Lancaster, PA: Photo
Arts Press, 1974. 16 pp.

689. Shoemaker, Henry Wharton. *The Origin and Language of
Central Pennsylvania Witchcraft.* Reading, PA: Eagle
Press, 1927. 23 pp.

690- Numbers deleted.
 699.

700. Tortora, Vincent R. "Pennsylvania Dutch Powwow Healing." *Fate* 9,2 (February 1926) 41-45.

701. Westkott, Marcia. "Powwowing in Berks County." *Pennsylvania Folklife* 19,2 (Winter 1969-70) 2-9.

702. "Witchcraft Murders." *Literary Digest* (January 5, 1929)
19-20.

703. Yoder, Don. "Twenty Questions on Powwowing." *Pennsylvania Folklife* 17,4 (Summer 1967).

704. ————. "Witch Tales from Adams County." *Pennsylvania
Folklife* 12,4 (Summer 1962) 29-37.

705. Zook, Jacob, and Jane Zook. *Hexology.* Paradise, PA:
The Authors, 1962. 16 pp.

D. PRE-MODERN WITCHCRAFT

From the time of the last of the Witchcraft trials until the
early 20th century, only scant evidence of the existence of
Witches in America remains. That evidence comes from the accounts of early ethnologists, folklorists, and local historians (particularly at the county level). These accounts
paint a consistent picture.

In rural America, for the past two centuries, existed
individuals who were both called Witches and accepted the
designation. They operated a system of low "magic" centering
on charms, spells, potions, healings, blessings, and cursing.
Their practices were consistent with such practices in Europe.
The techniques were passed orally from generation to generation.

Most Witches of whom records have survived were women
either never married or widowed. There is some indication
that "Witch" is a term given to women living alone. The
possible acceptance of the term by women who wished to remain unmarried might be a fruitful area of inquiry for feminist
scholars.

The Witches' neighbors ascribed both respect and fear to
Witchcraft and those who practiced it. The general public
had inherited the worldview tying Witchcraft to Satanism and,
while generally accepting a live-and-let-live policy, viewed
Witches as comrades of Satan's internal majesty and practitioners of black arts.

No records have survived of Witchcraft groups or of
Witches practicing anything similar to modern Pagan rituals.
No theology is present, though a sophisticated demonology
and angelology appear. No sign of Mother Goddess worship is
manifest. Hence it seems that modern Wicca and Paganism are
not a continuation of the folk Witchcraft except as it has
absorbed some of its low magic practices, and modern Witches
seem to have learned their low magic from the literature
(particularly Vance Randolph) rather than directly from the
few surviving rural Witches.

Within this section the works of Vance Randolph are most
important, but the other folklorists cannot be ignored. The

booklets by Riva, Rose (a pseudonym), and the White Witch Doctor represent recent attempts to compile the low magic of the rural folk Witchcraft tradition and make it accessible to the modern Pagan community.

Welsh's article on the trial in Omaha highlights the variety of folk magic brought to the United States by ethnic immigrants, in this case Italian.

706. Baily, Henry D.B. *Local Tales and Historical Sketches*. Fishkill Landing, NJ: John W. Spaight, 1874, pp. 132-36.

707. Bowles, John E. "People Still Believe in Witches." *Search* 22 (July 1957) 12-15.

708. Brittan, Emma Hardinge, ed. *Art Magic*. New York: The Author, 1876. 467 pp.

709. Combs, Josiah Henry. "Sympathetic Magic in the Kentucky Mountains: Some Curious Folk Survivals." *Journal of American Folklore* 27,105 (July-September 1917) 328-30.

710. Cross, Tom Peete. "Witchcraft in North Carolina." *Studies in Philology* 16,3 (July 1919) 217-49.

711. ————. *Witchcraft in North Carolina*. Chapel Hill: University of North Carolina Press, 1919. Rpt. Norwood, PA: Norwood Editions, 1976. 287 pp.

712. Davis, Hubert J. *The Silver Bullet and Other American Witch Stories*. Middle Village, NY: Jonathan David Publishing, 1975. 231 pp.

713. Erwin, Milo. *The History of Williamson County*. Marion, IL: Herrin News, 1976. 283 pp.

714. Fair, London. "When We Encountered Witchcraft." *Fate* 8,10 (October 1955) 88-91.

715. Forbes, Esther. *A Mirror for Witches*. Boston: Houghton Mifflin Company, 1928. 214 pp.

716. Gunn, John H. "Witchcraft in Illinois." *Magazine of American History* 14,5 (1885) 458-63.

717. Harris, Jesse W. "Some Southern Illinois Witch Lore." *Southern Folklore Quarterly* 10,3 (September 1946) 183-190.

718. Harvey, Gerald. *The Secret Lore of Witchcraft*. Girard,
      KS: Haldeman-Julius Publications, 1946. 23 pp.

719. Hyatt, Harry Middleton. *Folklore from Adams County,
      Illinois*. New York: Memoirs of the Alma Egan Hyatt
      Foundation, 1935, pp. 455-545.

720. Kenyon, Theda. *Witches Still Live*. New York: Ives
      Washburn, 1929. 379 pp.

721. Laidlaw, William K. "Albany County Witch Lore." *New
      York Folklore Quarterly* 2,1 (February 1946) 60-62.

722. Le Breton, John. *White Magic*. Philadelphia: Macrae-
      Smith Company, n.d. 100 pp.

723. LeGros, George Cardinal. "The Witch of Calhoun County."
      Search 29 (November 1958) 21-24, 34.

724. Martin, Frances Louise. "I Practiced Black Magic."
      Fate 9,10 (October 1956) 15-18.

725. Miller, William Marion. "How to Catch a Witch." *Southern
      Folklore Quarterly* 10,13 (September 1946) 199.

726. Minor, Marz. "Witch Woman Destroys Midwestern Town."
      Beyond 2,15 (November 1969) 59-64.

727. Morgan, Fred T. *Unharrie Magic*. Durham, NC: Moore
      Publishing Company, 1974. 215 pp.

728. Newley, Joanne. "White Witch Reveals Magic Spells."
      National Examiner (January 13, 1981) 13.

729. Overton, Marion F. "Long Island Witchcraft." *Long
      Island Forum* 14,10 (October 1951).

730. Owens, Ethel. "Witchcraft in the Cumberlands." *Kentucky
      Folklore Record* 11,4 (October-December 1965) 76-77.

731. Randolph, Vance. *Ozark Superstitions*. New York: Colum-
      bia Press, 1947. 367 pp. Rpt. as *Ozark Magic and
      Folklore*. New York: Dover Publications, 1964. 367 pp.

732. ———. "The Witch on Bradshaw Mountain." *University
      Review* 2,4 (Summer 1936) 203-6.

733. ————. "A Witch Trial in Carroll County." *Arkansas Historical Quarterly* (September 1952) 89-90.

734. Raskin, Joseph, and Edith Raskin. *Ghosts and Witches Aplenty; More Tales Our Settlers Told*. New York: Lothrop, Lee and Shepard Co., 1973. 128 pp.

735. Riva, Anna. *Candle Burning Magic*. Toluca Lake, CA: International Imports, 1980. 96 pp.

736. Rose, Donna. *Love Spells*. Hialeah, FL: Mi-World Publishing Co., n.d. 27 pp.

737. ————. *The Magic of Herbs*. Hialeah, FL: Mi-World Publishing Co., 1978. 27 pp.

738. ————. *The Magic of Oils*. Hialeah, FL: Mi-World Publishing Co., 1978. 32 pp.

739. ————. *Money Spells*. Hialeah, FL: Mi-World Publishing Co., 1978. 24 pp.

740. ————. *Tarot*. Hialeah, FL: Mi-World Publishing Co., n.d. 15 pp.

741. ————. *Unhexing and Jinx Removing Spells*. Hialeah, FL: Mi-World Publishing Co., 1978. 28 pp.

742. Schul, Bill D. "The Link." *Probe the Unknown* 1,6 (December 1973) 34-39.

743. Seabrook, William. *Witchcraft: Its Power in the World Today*. New York: Harcourt, Brace & Co., Inc., 1940. 387 pp.

744. Seip, Elizabeth Eloud. "Witch-Finding in Western Maryland." *Journal of American Folklore* 47 (1934) 39-44.

745. Skinner, Charles M. *Myths and Legends of Our Own Land*. Philadelphia: Lippincott, 1896. 2 vols.

746. Speare, Eva A. *New Hampshire Folk Tales*. Plymouth, NH, 1964, pp. 139-61.

747. Tyler, Sarah. "Our Friendly Neighborhood Witch." *Fate* 17,11 (November 1964) 86-89.

748. Webb, Wheaton P. "Witches in the Cooper Country." *New York Folklore Quarterly* 1,1 (February 1945) 5-20.

749. Welsh, Roger. "Omaha's Witch Trial." *Sunday World Herald Magazine of the Midlands* (September 20, 1970) 22.

750. White Witch Doctor. *The Use of Voodoo Potions*. New York: Abrahadabra, Inc., 1980. 31 pp.

751. ————. *Voodoo Love Secrets*. New York: Abrahadabra, Inc., 1980. 32 pp.

752. Whittemore, James O. "The Witch's Curse." *New England Magazine* 27 (September 1902) 111-13.

753. "The Witch of Clarkstown." *York State Tradition* 28,2 (1974) 28-30.

754. "Witchcraft Still Earning Millions." *Literary Digest* (October 31, 1936) 7-8.

755. Wright, Elbee. *Book of Legendary Spells*. Minneapolis, MN: Marlar Publishing Co., 1968. 226 pp.

E. GERALD B. GARDNER

The modern movement of Witchcraft (or Wicca) and Paganism
continues only in small measure any tradition from previous
centuries. It developed its beliefs, worship, and structure
more from books on Ancient and Medieval Witchcraft and Paganism
than on the encounter with existing practitioners at the time
of its emergence.

By the 1940s a large body of material had appeared des-
cribing ancient Paganism, Witchcraft, magic, and polytheism.
Some evidence exists that a few groups calling themselves
Witches existed prior to World War I. But only after World
War II did Witch covens appear in any number.

The literature of this section documents the emergence
of the new Witchcraft and Pagan movement in England. The
crucial event was the publication in 1954 of Gerald Gardner's
Witchcraft Today. This book for the first time proclaimed
the existence of Witchcraft covens, broadly described their
beliefs and structure, and established Gardner as the person
to contact by future Wiccans.

Of course others, most notably Margaret Murray, paved
the way for Gardner's reformation. Murray, an Egyptologist,
wandered into folklore studies and in her *The Witch-cult in
Western Europe* (1921) asserted the idea that Wicca was a Pre-
Christian survival of Pagan religion. She described the
religion as a polytheistic fertility cult that met as thirteen-
member covens for the eight great sabbats and lesser eshats.

Bracelin describes Gardner's life and the sources for many
of his particular practices such as nudity. Raymond and Rosemary Buckland, Gardner's first American disciples, through
their writings and the numerous articles about them in the
popular press, spread Gardnerian Witchcraft across the United
States. In recent years, the Bucklands divorced, and Raymond
has developed a new system which he calls Saxon Wicca.

Alexander Saunders developed an early variation on Gardner's practices (Alexandrian Wicca) which has become popular
though not to the degree of Gardner's. Saunders' work is
described fully by Farrar and Johns. His own lectures on
Witchcraft, which had circulated only in typescript, were

recently published. Like the Bucklands, Saunders and his wife Maxine have been divorced; Maxine has since written a bitter denunciation of her former husband.

Mary Nesnick, an Alexandrian priestess, is but one of several Gardnerian and Alexandrian leaders to develop their own variations on the Gardnerian theme. She calls her system Algard.

Aidan Kelly, one of the founders of a Gardnerian-like Pagan group in California, the New Reformed Orthodox Order of the Golden Dawn, has offered the most mature reflection on the Gardnerian tradition from the point of view of a practitioner. His work has done much to define the work of Gardner as the creator rather than transmitter of modern Wicca.

756. *The Alex Sanders Lectures.* New York: Magical Childe, Inc., 1980. 52 pp.

757. "Born to Be a Witch." *Impact* 1,3, pp. 5-7.

758. Bracelin, Jack L. *Gerald Gardner, Witch.* London: Octagon Press, 1960. 224 pp.

759. Buckland, Raymond. *Anatomy of the Occult.* New York: Samuel Weiser, 1977. 151 pp.

760. ————. *Ancient and Modern Witchcraft: The Truth about Witchcraft by a High Priest.* New York: Castle Books, 1970.

761. ————. *Candle Spells & Rituals.* N.p.: Acrowley Publications, n.d. 62 pp.

762. ————. *Here Is the Occult.* New York: House of Collectibles, Inc., 1974. 143 pp.

763. ————. "I Live with a Witch." *Beyond* 1,2 (October 1968) 106-13.

764. ————. *The Magick of Chant-o-Matics.* West Nyack, NY: Parker Publishing Company, 1978. 227 pp.

765. ————. *A Pocket Guide to the Supernatural.* New York: Ace Books, 1969. 189 pp.

766. ————. *Practical Candle Burning.* St. Paul, MN: Llewellyn Publications, 1972. 153 pp.

767. ————. *The Tree: The Complete Book of Saxon Witch-craft*. New York: Samuel Weiser, 1974. 158 pp.

768. ————. *Witchcraft from the Inside*. St. Paul, MN: Llewellyn Publications, 1971. 140 pp.

769. ————. *Witchcraft: Ancient & Modern*. New York: H.C. Publishers, 1970. 192 pp.

770. ————. *Witchcraft ... the Religion*. New York: The Buckland Museum of Witchcraft & Magick, 1966. 24 pp.

771. Farrar, Stewart. *What Witches Do*. New York: Coward, McCann & Geoghegan, Inc., 1971. 211 pp.

772. Gardner, Gerald B. *High Magic's Aid*. London: Michael Houghton, 1949. 351 pp.

773. ————. *The Meaning of Witchcraft*. London: Aquarian Press, 1959. 283 pp.

774. ————. *The Museum of Magic and Witchcraft*. Castletown, Isle of Man: Castletown Press, n.d. 23 pp.

775. ————. *Witchcraft Today*. London: Rider, 1954. Rev. ed. London: Jarrolds, 1968. 192 pp.

776. Graves, Robert. "Witches in 1964." *Virginia Quarterly Review* 40 (1964) 550-59.

777. Grunder, Hartnett. "Witchcraft Coven Photographed in Secret Rituals." *Beyond* 2,12 (August 1969) 83-92.

778. Hoffman, Lisa. "The Witch Next Door." *New York Sunday News* (October 27, 1968).

779. Johns, June. *King of the Witches*. New York: Coward-McCann, Inc., 1969. 155 pp.

780. Kelly, Aidan. *The Rebirth of Witchcraft; Traditions and Creativity in the Gardnerian Reform*. The Author, 1977. 336 pp.

781. McGraw, Walter J. "World's Only Museum of Witchcraft." *Fate* 22,3 (March 1969) 88-97.

782. Nesnick, Mary, and Mary Smith. *Witchcraft Fact Book*. N.p., 1972. 18 pp.

783. Murray, Margaret A. *The God of the Witches*. London:
      Faber & Faber, 1931. 212 pp.

784. ————. *The Witch-cult in Western Europe*. Oxford:
      Clarendon Press, 1921. 303 pp.

785. "Old Pagan Cult Discovered to Be Active in London."
      Birmingham News (Alabama) (June 1, 1959).

786. Saunders, Maxine. "Naked and Afraid, I Am Made a Queen
      Witch at the Altar of Evil." *News of the World*
      (April 6, 1975) 3.

787. "Self-Styled Witch Takes Own Life." *The Wichita Eagle*
      (August 5, 1974).

788. Wall, Don. "Psychologist Wears Witch's Hat." *Wichita
      Eagle* (November 17, 1973) 1,5A.

F. MODERN BRITISH WICCA

From 1954 until Gardner's death, his movement spread rapidly, but since his death numerous variations have appeared. Below are cited a selection of materials produced by the British progeny of Gardner and circulating in America. The writings of the Crowthers and Valiente have circulated freely among American Witches. The Isis movement of Olivia Robertson has several American affiliate groups. Marian Green remains a major writer and publisher of Wiccan literature in England.

789. *A.D.I.C. Prayer Book*. London: Spook Enterprises, 1973. 53 pp.

790. Crowther, Arnold, and Patricia Crowther. *The Secrets of Ancient Witchcraft*. Secaucus, NJ: University Books, 1974. 218 pp.

791. Crowther, Patricia. *Witch Blood*. New York: H.C. Publishers, 1973. Rpt. New York: House of Collectibles, 1974. 190 pp.

792. ———, and Arnold Crowther. *The Witches Speak*. Douglas, Isle of Man: Athol Publications, 1965. 151 pp. Rpt. New York: Samuel Weiser, 1976. 145 pp.

793. Durdin-Robertson, Lawrence. *The Goddesses of India, Tibet, China and Japan*. Enniscorthy, Eire: Cesara Publications, 1976. 532 pp.

794. ———. *The Goddesses of Chaldaea, Syria and Egypt*. Enniscorthy, Eire: Cesara Publications, 1975. 440 pp.

795. Green, Marian. *Magic in Principle and Practice*. London: Marian Green, 1979. 50 pp.

796. ———. *The Paths of Magic*. London: Marian Green, 1980. 36 pp.

797. Maxwell, C.N.W. "The Black Art." *Fate* 1,3 (Fall 1948)
      62-68.

798. Robertson, Olivia. *The Call of Isis*. Enniscorthy,
      Eire: Cesara Publications, 1975. 126 pp.

799. ———. *The Isis Wedding Rite*. Enniscorthy, Eire:
      Cesara Publications, 1975. 16 pp.

800. ———. *Ordination of a Priestess*. Enniscorthy, Eire:
      Cesara Publications, n.d. 16 pp.

801. ———. *Rite of Rebirth*. Enniscorthy, Eire: Cesara
      Publications, 1977. 20 pp.

802. ———, and Lord Strathloch, eds. *The Fellowship of
      Isis: Directory for 1980*. Enniscorthy, Eire: Cesara
      Publications, 1979. 52 pp.

803. Valiente, Doreen. *An ABC of Witchcraft Past & Present*.
      New York: St. Martin's Press, 1973. 416 pp.

804. ———. *Natural Magic*. New York: St. Martin's Press,
      1975. 184 pp.

805. ———. *Where Witchcraft Lives*. London: Aquarian
      Press, 1962. 112 pp.

806. ———. *Witchcraft for Tomorrow*. New York: St. Martin's
      Press, 1978. 205 pp.

807. ———. "Witches Out of Hiding." *Fate* 17,6 (June 1964)
      79-88.

808. A Witch. *The Devil's Prayerbook*. London: Mayflower,
      1975. 93 pp.

809. "Witchcraft in Europe Today." *Flash News Illustrated*
      1,2 (1964) 15-17.

G. DIRECTORIES

In the early 1970s the *Green Egg* and the *W.I.C.A. Newsletter* began to publish directories and lists of contacts for Pagans and Witches who wanted to know of others in their neighborhoods or wanted to affiliate with a larger group. Living on the very edge of culture as Pagans do, many potential members find such directories vital in locating others of their kind. The bulletin boards of occult bookstores are the only significant alternative.

The small directories by the *New Broom* and *Nemeton* appeared first. They were joined by Ken Ward's, which focused more on ritual magic groups. Ward's supplements have regularly expanded and updated his original list. Two much larger and detailed guides by Rhuddlwm Gawr and Selena Fox have recently appeared and currently serve most Pagans. Fox, one of the leaders of Circle Wicca, publishes several national periodicals whose mailing list constitutes the largest Wicca/Pagan network in the United States.

The *Q Directory* is the British equivalent of the Circle Directory.

810. Fox, Selena. *Circle Guide to Wicca & Pagan Resources.* Madison, WI: Circle Publications, 1979. 113 pp. Rev. ed. 1980. 133 pp.

811. Gawr, Rhuddlwm. *Pagan/Occult/New Age Directory.* Atlanta: Pagan Grove Press, 1978. 38 pp. Supplement, Autumn 1978. 18 pp. Rev. ed. Athens, GA: Pagan Grove Press, 1980. 43 pp.

812. *Nemeton Directory.* Oakland, CA: Nemeton, 1973. 16 pp.

813. *The New Broom's Directory of Contacts.* N.p., n.d. 8 pp.

814. *The Q Directory, 1980-81.* London: Pallas-Aquariana, 1980. 117 pp.

815. Ward, Ken. *Occult Directory*. Saskatoon, Saskatchewan:
      The Author, 1973. 17 pp. Supplements semi-annually.

H. MODERN WICCA IN AMERICA

Witchcraft emerged in the 1960s as a new religion in the American context, and this section attempts an exhaustive listing of the material that the American Wicca community has produced about its life, teachings, and experience, as well as that written about it by others.

Among the many items cited below, Margot Adler's *Drawing Down the Moon* stands in a class by itself. Adler, both a professional journalist and a Wiccan priestess, spent several years travelling the country, interviewing Wiccan and Pagan leaders, and working her way through a mass of material. As a result, her book has received both the approval of non-Pagans for its clear presentation of the Pagan world and of Witches and Pagans for its factual and sympathetic treatment. It is "must" reading for students of the field and stands in stark contrast to the fly-by-night and error-filled books by Hans Holzer.

Other surveys of Witchcraft worthy of attention include Roberts and Weinstein. Farren writes as a Roman Catholic convert to Wicca and offers a lucid exposition of belief and practice. Buczynski, Cunningham, Graves, Selene, and Taylor offer basic expositions of Wicca but write from one tradition rather than as representatives of the entire movement.

Among the items found below produced by Witches and their group are autobiographies (Gawr and Sherwood), ritual books (Aima, the Dixons, Haldane, Mestel [965-966], and Lady Sheba), and magic books (Cunningham, Dey, the Dixons, Grammary, Huson [913], Jacobs [917], Jeanne, Leek [931], Morrison, Norling, Osiris, Riva, Seleneicthon, and Worth). Discussions of herbs and herbology, a topic much broader than its use by Witches, but of significance to them for the working of low magic, is found in Aima, Huson, Jacobs (916), Mestel (965), and Riva (989).

A large number of books on the general theme of "Witchcraft in America today" appeared in the 1970s, many only in paperback editions. Though generally sympathetic, they vary widely in quality. As a whole they treat the subject with little depth and should be checked with material published

by Witches and/or Pagans before one relies too heavily upon
them. The titles by Ebon, Fritscher, Haining, Hershman,
Kriss, Schurmacher, Frank Smith, Suzy Smith, and Wallace fit
into this category. Of course much of the material in this
chapter consists of magazine and newspaper articles written
by journalists who had only brief contact with a particular
Witch or coven.

Several Witches have written widely about the Craft and
their work within it. Sybil Leek is the most famous, especially among the general public. No attempt at a complete
listing of her writings was attempted here; many, such as
her vast astrology and divinatory writings, bear only tan-
gentially on the subject of Witchcraft. Her *Diary of a Witch*
and *Complete Art of Witchcraft* represent Lady Sybil at her
best as a Witch. See also the collection by Hilken.

Leo Martello, an activist Witch who lives in Manhattan,
has written a number of pamphlets as well as several substantive books, the best of which--*Witchcraft: The Old Religion*--
would be on the most-recommended booklists of Wiccan materials.
His earlier *Weird Ways of Witchcraft* was for many years the
only readily available, sizable exposition of modern Wiccan
life.

The Frosts, Gavin and Yvonne, head one of the larger Wiccan
bodies, the Church and School of Wicca, headquartered in New
Bern, North Carolina. Two books--*Witchcraft, The Way of
Serenity* and *The Witch's Bible*--explain their particular view
of Wicca. Controversy has swirled around the Frosts since
the early 1970s as Wiccans attacked their position on homosexuality, the role of the Mother Goddess, and the "preten-
sion" of *The Witch's Bible* to speak for all Witches.

No less controversial in the early 1970s, Louise Huebner
became famous as the official Witch of Los Angeles. She was
criticized by most Pagans as unrepresentative of Witchcraft
as a whole.

Among issues that excited the Pagan community, homosexuality
had few equals. Unfortunately most items produced by this controversy appear in articles in Pagan magazines, the indexing
of which was beyond the scope of this bibliography. One book
representative of the gay wing of Paganism has appeared.
Evans considers the confluence of Witchhunting, the persecution
of homosexuals, and modern Paganism. While his style is highly
polemic and his historical work questionable, he presents
important data for review within the wider context of Wiccan
issues.

Evans's work raises not only homosexual issues but the
question of the Christian opposition to Witchcraft. Numerous
tracts and pamphlets and even books have appeared in response
to what Christians see as an occult explosion. As a whole

this material has been put aside for another possible volume.
It rarely treats modern Paganism in a manner that offers factual material on the Pagan movement or mature reflection on
the impact of modern Wicca. Starke's article is an exception.
    However, one element of the Christian attack on Paganism
deserves attention, the John Todd affair. John Todd (aka Lance
Collins) emerged in the 1970s as an ex-Witch turned Christian.
His outlandish claims and the numerous contradictions in his
story have led even the conservative Christian press to with-
draw support and condemn him. See Hicks & Lewis' book for
the most substantive reporting of the whole affair. Other
items include Abercrombie, Beculhimer, Miller, Nichols, Plowman, and Rubinton.

816. Abercrombie, Sharon. "That Old Black Magic--'It's Worse
        than Heroin Addiction.'" *Citizen-Journal* (Columbus,
        OH) (May 11, 1974) 4.

817. Abragail and Valaria. *How to Become a Sensuous Witch*.
        New York: Paperback Library, 1971. 155 pp.

818. Adler, Margot. *Drawing Down the Moon*. New York: Viking
        Press, 1979. 455 pp.

819. Aima. *Ritual Book of Herbal Spells*. Los Angeles:
        Hermetic Science Center, 1970.

820. Alderman, Clifford Lindsey. *Witchcraft in America*.
        New York: Julian Messner, 1974. 191 pp.

821. *A.U.M./The Sacred Word*. Glendale, OR: First Temple of
        Tiphareth, 1975. 5 pp.

822. Barreiro, José. "Witchcraft." *Minnesota Daily* (October
        11, 1973) 9-12.

823. *Basics of Magic: Handbook*. Wheatridge, CO: Church of
        the Seven Arrows. I, 47 pp., 1979; II, 47 pp., 1980.

824. Beculhimer, Marvin. "Who Holds the Future? A Look at
        the Message of John Todd." *Contact* 27 (January 1980)
        12-15.

825. Benninghoff, Mary. "An Afternoon in the Uncanny."
        Beyond Reality 22 (September-October 1976) 20-22,
        56.

826. Bidart, Gay-Darlene. *The Naked Witch*. New York: Pin-
      nacle Books, 1965. 212 pp.

827. Bonewits, Philip Emmons Isaac. "Which Witch Is Which?"
      Fate 29,8 (August 1976) 69-75.

828. *The Book of Laws*. Des Moines, IA: Coven of the Mirror,
      1977. 25 pp.

829. Bowman, James H. "Good Witch of the South." *Mystique*
      1 (April 1973) 18-20, 48.

830. Brissenden, Constance. "That Old White Magic." *McLeans
      Magazine* (February 18, 1980) 52-53.

831. Brunswick, N. "Witchcraft U.S.A." *Beyond Reality* 1,1
      (October-November 1972) 25-26.

832. Bryant, James. "Pretty Modern 'Witch' Keeps Cauldron
      Boiling." *St. Louis Post-Dispatch* (July 31, 1970)
      1, 4.

833. Buczynski, Edmund M. *Witchcraft Fact Book*. New York:
      Abrahadabra, n.d. 20 pp. Rpt. as *Witchcraft Fact
      Book, 1974*. Brooklyn Heights, NY: Earth Religion
      Supplies, 1973. 23 pp.

834. Canavan, Kathy. "Occult Dealing in Yardley." *Bucks
      County (PA) Courier Times* (September 28, 1973).

835. Carlson, John. "Halloween No Joke for Iowa City
      Witch." *The Gazette* (Cedar Rapids) (October 29,
      1978) 1B.

836. Carter, Carl. "Increase Seen in Pagan Religions and
      Witchcraft." *The Birmingham News* (May 30, 1980) 3B.

837. Chappell, Helen. *The Waxing Moon*. New York: Links,
      1974. 214 pp.

838. Choyke, Bill. "Helen Miller: A Witch or Just Misunder-
      stood?" *The News-Sun* (Waukegan, IL) (July 24, 1973)
      1B.

839. Christianson, Penny. "Everything You Always Wanted to
      Know about Witches ... but Were Too Scared to Ask."
      San Fernando Valley Magazine 21,10 (September 1979)
      36-39, 78-79.

840. *Circle Wicca: Witchcraft in the Aquarian Age.* Madison,
      WI: Circle, n.d. 16 pp.

841. *Circle's Practical Guide to Meditation.* Madison, WI:
      Circle, 1976. 7 pp.

842. Cohen, Daniel. "Witches in Our Midst." *Science Digest*
      69 (June 1971) 22-27.

843. Cunningham, Sara. *Candle Magic.* Hollywood, CA:
      Phoenix House, 1974. 40 pp.

844. ————. *Questions and Answers on Wicca Craft.* Wolf
      Creek, OR: Stonehenge Farm, 1974. 27 pp.

845. Dart, John. "Earth Religions Prepare for Allhallows
      Eve." *Los Angeles Times* (October 31, 1979) 3, 25.

846. Dew, Joan. "Witches: Religion or Big Business?"
      Coronet 12,4 (April 1974) 16-20, 107-9.

847. Dey, Charmaine. *The Magic Candle.* Las Vegas, NV:
      Bell, Book and Candle, 1979. 62 pp.

848. Dickson, Larry. "Witchcraft: Magic or Religion?"
      Beyond Reality 1,3 (March 1973) 28-30, 46.

849. DiPalo, James. "American Witches and the I.R.S."
      Other Dimensions 1974 1 (1974) 38-39, 92-94.

850. Dixon, Jo, and James Dixon. *The Color Book: Ritual,
      Charms, and Enchantments.* Denver: Castle Rising,
      1978. 86 pp.

851. Downey, Tab. "Valley of Witchcraft." *Men in Conflict*
      2,7 (February 1966) 12, 40-41.

852. Dugan, Donald S. "Old Religion Story Done with New
      Television Style." *Waukesha Post* (Wisconsin) (October
      17, 1979) A8.

853. Dykstra, Dirk. *Love Charms.* N.p.: Ravenswood Press,
      1974. 13 pp.

854. Ebon, Martin. "America's Most Popular Witch: Sybil
      Leek." *Probe the Unknown* 3,3 (June 1975) 32-33.

855. ———, ed. *Witchcraft Today*. New York: New American
      Library, 1971. 144 pp.

856. Eddison, Robert. "A Night with Today's Witches."
      Weekend 32 (1966).

857. Eklund, Christopher. "Witches Jim Alan and Selena Fox
      Let Their Cauldron Bubble with Minimal Toil and
      Trouble." *People* (November 5, 1979) 47-58.

858. Elridge, Marcia. "A Meeting of Witches." *Atlanta
      Gazette* (May 27, 1979) 5-6.

859. Evans, Arthur. *Witchcraft and the Gay Counterculture*.
      Boston: Fag Rag Books, 1978. 180 pp.

860. Farren, David. *Living with Magic*. New York: Simon and
      Schuster, 1974. 319 pp.

861. ———. *The Return of Magic*. New York: Harper & Row,
      1972. 118 pp.

862. ———. *Sex and Magic*. New York: Simon and Schuster,
      1975. 191 pp.

863. Fitzgerald, Arlene J. *"Everything You Always Wanted
      to Know about Sorcery ... but Were Afraid...."* New
      York: Manor Books, 1973. 190 pp.

864. Fleesor, Lucinda. "Witches." *Boston Globe* (August 19,
      1973).

865. Freiberg, Warren. "The Witches Hold a Convention."
      Coq 1,2 (February 1974) 62-63, 88-90.

866. Fritscher, John. *Popular Witchcraft; Straight from the
      Witch's Mouth*. Bowling Green, KY: Bowling Green
      University Press, 1972. 130 pp.

867. Frost, Gavin. *Witchcraft: The Way to Serenity*. St.
      Charles, MO: School of Wicca, n.d. 28 pp.

868. ———, and Yvonne Frost. *The Magic Power of Witch-
      craft*. West Nyack, NY: Parker Publishing Company,
      1976. 203 pp.

869. ———. *Meta-Psychometry: Key to Power and Abundance*.
      West Nyack, NY: Parker Publishing Company, 1978. 241
      pp.

870. ⸺. *Power Secrets from a Sorcerer's Private Magnum Arcanum.* West Nyack, NY: Parker Publishing Company, 1980. 217 pp.

871. ⸺. *The Witches' Bible.* Los Angeles: Nash Publishing Co., 1972. Rpt. New York: Berkley Publishing Company, 1972. 310 pp.

872. ⸺. *A Witch's Guide to Life.* Cottonwood, AZ: Esoteric Publications, 1978. 136 pp.

873. Frye, Rod. "Discovering Witchcraft." *Beyond Reality* 15 (June 1975) 32-35, 50.

874. Gawr, Rhuddlwn, with Marcy Edwards. *The Quest.* Smyrna, GA: Pagan Grove Press, 1979. 182 pp.

875. Geist, Bill. "Modern Witches Trade Pointed Hats for Pantsuits." *Suburban Trib* (Chicago) (July 20, 1979) 2.

876. Gentile, Don. "How a Setauket Divorcee Runs a Coven of Witches." *New York Sunday News* (March 7, 1976).

877. Giles, Carl H., and Barbara Ann Williams. *Bewitching Jewelry.* New York: A.S. Barnes and Company, 1976. 159 pp.

878. Glass, Justine. *Witchcraft, The Sixth Sense.* No. Hollywood, CA: Wilshire Book Company, 1965. 203 pp.

879. "The Good Witch of the West." *Life* (April 10, 1970) 59-61.

880. Goranson, Mark. "Occult No Game to Local Witches." *Daily Iowan* (November 27, 1978) 5.

881. Graham, Arthur. "I Joined a Wild Witchcraft-Passion Cult." *Men* 17,8 (August 1968) 40-41, 66-71, 73.

882. Grammary, Ann. *The Witch's Workbook.* New York: Pocket Books, 1973. 270 pp.

883. Graves, Robert. "Witches in 1964." *Virginia Quarterly Review* 40 (1964) 550-59.

884. Graves, Samuel R. *Witchcraft: The Osirian Order.* The Osirian Order, n.d. 140 pp.

885. Greeley, Andrew. "There's a New-Time Religion on
      Campus." *New York Times Magazine* (June 1, 1969)
      14-28.

886. Griffin, Jean Latz. "Which Witch Do You Believe In?"
      Suburban Trib (Chicago) (October 31, 1977) 3, 6.

887. Gundella. *The Werewolf of Grosse Pointe and Other
      Stories*. Detroit, MI: Earsight Products, 1976. 81 pp.

888. Gunther, Max. "Behind the Boom in Witchcraft." *True*
      51,401 (October 1970) 46-50.

889. Haining, Peter. *The Anatomy of Witchcraft*. New York:
      Taplinger Publishing Co., 1972. 212 pp.

890. ————. *The Warlock's Book*. New Hyde Park, NY: Univer-
      sity Books, Inc., 1971. 110 pp.

891. ————. *The Witchcraft Papers*. Secaucus, NJ: University
      Books, 1974. 240 pp.

892. Haldane, Claudia, and the People of Holy Earth. *The
      Sabbats*. Jamaica Plain, MA: The People of Holy
      Earth. 24 pp.

893. Hammond, Ruth. "With Secret Rituals, Oaths and Dances,
      Local Witches Practice Their Ancient Craft." *Min-
      neapolis Tribune* (May 10, 1980) 18-28.

894. Hanna, Pat. "Gavin, Yvonne Mix Happy Witch Brew."
      Boulder Daily Camera (July 29, 1972).

895. Heagney, John. "Tarot Tells Tale of Future with a
      Shuffle of the Deck." *Bucks County (PA) Courier
      Times* (June 10, 1976).

896. Herrmann, Pat. "Nature Cultists Gather at Stanton."
      The Democrat (Flemington, NJ) (June 19, 1975).

897. Hershberger, Barbara, and Hersh Hershberger. *The Book
      of Gera*. N.p.: The Authors, n.d. 24 pp.

898. Hershman, Florence. *Witchcraft U.S.A.* New York: Tower
      Publications, Inc., 1971. 156 pp.

899. Hicks, Darryl E., and David A. Lewis. *The Todd Phenom-
      enon*. Harrison, AK: New Leaf Press, 1979. 160 pp.

900. Hilken, Glen A., ed. *The Best of Sybil Leek*. New York: Pocket Library, 1974. 253 pp.

901. Hill, Dave. "Witches, Warlocks, Astrologers, Palm Readers, Mystics." *Sun* (Minneapolis) (June 22, 1976) 5-6.

902. Hoeller, Stephen A. "Beware! Witches at Work!" *Exploring the Unknown* 2,6 (February 1962) 8-19.

903. Holman, Nancy. "Orenda: Practices of a Modern Day Springfield Witch." *Springfield Magazine* 2,6 (November 1980) 44-46.

904. Holzer, Hans. *Heather: Confessions of a Witch*. New York: Mason and Lipscomb Publishers, 1975. 226 pp.

905. ————. *Pagans and Witches*. New York: Manor Books, 1978. 219 pp.

906. ————. *The Truth about Witchcraft*. Garden City, NY: Doubleday, 1969. 230 pp.

907. ————. *Wicca: The Way of the Witches*. New York: Manor Books, 1979. 235 pp.

908. ————. *The Witchcraft Report*. New York: Ace Books, 1973. 222 pp.

909. Huebner, Louise. *Never Strike a Happy Medium*. Los Angeles: Nash Publishing, 1970. 334 pp.

910. ————. *Power Through Witchcraft*. New York: Bantam Books, 1971. 183 pp.

911. ————. *Your Lucky Numbers*. Kansas City, MO: Springbook Editions, 1972. 26 pp.

912. Huson, Paul. *Mastering Herbalism*. New York: Stein and Day, 1974. 371 pp.

913. ————. *Mastering Witchcraft*. New York: G.P. Putnam's Sons, 1970. 154 pp.

914. Hyman, Tom. "Space Age Witches." *Saga* 31,6 (March 1966) 50-53, 92-96.

915. "Interview: Sybil Leek." *Psychic* 1,3 (October-November 1969) 4-7, 26-32.

916. Jacobs, Dorothy. *A Witch's Guide to Gardening.* New
      York: Taplinger, 1964. 117 pp.

917. ———. *Cures and Curses.* New York: Taplinger, 1967.
      144 pp.

918. Jeanne. *Magick and Ceremonies.* New York: Lancer Books,
      1972. 176 pp.

919. Joiner, Robert L. "Jet Set Witches ... Not Broom
      Riders." *St. Louis Post-Dispatch* (March 14, 1972)
      1, 70.

920. Joseph, Greg. "In the Temple of the Occult, There's
      No Mighty Me." *Pasadena (CA) Union* (July 12, 1972)
      A1-2.

921. Kenyon, Richard L. "City's Witches Hope to Dispel Old
      Fears." *Milwaukee Journal* (August 19, 1978) 4.

922. Klemesrud, Judy. "6 Witches and Channel 13 Auction
      Turn Out for a Full-Moon Ceremony." *New York Times*
      (September 2, 1976).

923. Kotula, Denise. "Witchcraft: The Wiccan Faith." *Minne-
      sota Daily* (October 31, 1979) 9-11.

924. Kriss, Marika. *Witchcraft Past and Present for the
      Millions.* Los Angeles: Sherbourne Press, 1970. Rpt.
      New York: Award Books, 1970. 155 pp.

925. Krochmal, Pat. "Some Are Bewitched." *Suburban Week*
      (Chicago) (September 10-11, 1975) N3.

926. Lacy, Edward F. "Witchcraft Texas Style." *East Village
      Other* (April 1-15, 1966).

927. LaJoie, Raymond A. "Ted Raboum--New England Warlock."
      Fate 24,3 (March 1970) 38-46.

928. Lavender, Curtis. *Confessions of a Warlock.* New York:
      Lancer Books, 1970. 190 pp.

929. Lawrence, Lynda. *The Weekend Warlock.* Chatsworth, CA:
      Books for Better Living, 1974. 160 pp.

930. ———. *The Weekend Witch.* Chatsworth, CA: Books for
      Better Living.

931. Leek, Sybil. *Cast Your Own Spell*. New York: Bee-Line Books, 1970. 156 pp.

932. ———. *Complete Art of Witchcraft*. New York: World Publishing Company, 1971. 205 pp.

933. ———. *Diary of a Witch*. Englewood Cliffs, NJ: Prentice-Hall, Inc., 1968. 187 pp.

934. ———. *A Fool and a Tree*. Sidcup, Kent: Lambarde Press, 1964. 138 pp.

935. ———. *My Life in Astrology*. Englewood Cliffs, NJ: Prentice-Hall, Inc., 1972. 205 pp.

936. ———. *Mr. Hotfoot Jackson*. London: Frederick Muller, 1965. 75 pp.

937. ———. *Phrenology*. London: Collier-Macmillan, Ltd., 1970. 154 pp.

938. ———. *The Sybil Leek Book of Fortune Telling*. New York: Collier Books, 1969. 144 pp.

939. ———. *Sybil Leek's Book of Curses*. Englewood Cliffs, NJ: Prentice-Hall, Inc., 1975. 159 pp.

940. ———. *Sybil Leek's Book of the Curious and the Occult*. New York: Ballantine Books, 1976. 181 pp.

941. ———. *Telepathy*. New York: Collier Books, 1971. 160 pp.

942. ———. "Witchcraft in America." *Argosy* 281,2 (February 1975) 70-75.

943. Leininger, Madeline. "Witchcraft Practices and Psycho-cultural Therapy with Urban U.S. Families." *Human Organization* 32,1 (Spring 1973) 74-82.

944. Lewis, Sharon. "The Tools of Witchcraft." *Cosmos* (October 1969) 6.

945. Lightman, Herb A. "Filming 'Isis' among the Witches or 'I Don' Wanna Get Turned into No Frog!'" *American Cinematographer* (February 1972) 1570-73, 1596-1602.

946. Lloyd, Susannah Miller. "The Occult Revival: Witch-
      craft in the Contemporary United States." Columbia,
      MO: University of Missouri, Ph.D. dissertation, 1978.

947. Lyons, Delphine. *Everyday Witchcraft.* New York: Dell
      Purse Books, 1972. 64 pp.

948. McFerran, Douglass. "Witchcraft: The Truth about the
      Old Religion." *Listening* 9,3 (Autumn 1974) 105-11.

949. McKenna, Peter. "Witches: Not All Toil and Trouble."
      Islip News (New York) (February 19, 1976).

950. Mallowe, Mike. "That New Black Magic." *Philadelphia*
      67,10 (October 1976) 141-45, 210-15.

951. Manning, Al G. "E.S.P. Lab." *Cosmos* 11,11 (1971)
      30-33.

952. ————. *Helping Yourself with White Witchcraft.* West
      Nyack, NY: Parker Publishing Company, 1972. 226 pp.

953. ————. "How to See and Use Your Aura." *Cosmos* 7
      (December 1972) 20-23.

954. Martello, Leo L. *Black Magic/Satanism/Voodoo.* New
      York: H.C. Publishers, Inc., 1972. 192 pp.

955. ————. "Early Traditions of the Old Religion."
      Occult 5,3 (October 1974) 54-57, 102-3.

956. ————. *How to Prevent Psychic Blackmail.* New York:
      Hero Press, 1966. Rpt. New York: Samuel Weiser, 1975.
      192 pp.

957. ————. *1000 Witchcraft Questions Answered.* New York:
      Hero Press, 1973.

958. ————. *Weird Ways of Witchcraft.* New York: H.C. Pub-
      lishers, 1969. 224 pp.

959. ————. *What It Means to Be a Witch.* New York: The
      Author, n.d. 28 pp.

960. ————. "Witchcraft: A Way of Life." *Aquarian Agent*
      1,11 (November 1970) 5, 15.

961. ———. *Witchcraft: The Old Religion.* Secaucus, NJ: University Books, n.d. 287 pp.

962. ———. *Witches' Liberation and Guide to Covens.* New York: Hero Press, 1972.

963. ———. "Witches' Liberation or a True Witch Fights Back." *Occult* 2,4 (December 1971) 9-17, 91-94.

964. Meara and Wolfe. "Witches Talk Back." *Psychic Reporter* 1,10 (November 1975) 1, 7.

965. Mestel, Sherry, ed. *Earth Rites: I, Herbal Remedies.* Brooklyn, NY: Earth Rites Press, 1978. 83 pp.

966. ———, ed. *Earth Rites: II, Rituals.* Brooklyn, NY: Earth Rites Press, 1978. 121 pp.

967. Miller, Elliot. "John Todd: Dividing the Brethren." *The Maranatha Letter* 2,2 (November 1978) 10.

968. Moore, Martin. *Sex and Modern Witchcraft.* Los Angeles: Echelon Book Publishers, 1969. 160 pp.

969. Morrison, Sarah Lloyd. *The Modern Witch's Spellbook.* Secaucus, NJ: Lyle Stuart, Inc., 1971. 246 pp.

970. Morrow, Darrell. "Effectiveness of Psychologist Hurt by Witch Story, Witnesses Contend." *Wichita Eagle* (March 1, 1974).

971. Newsom, Ted. "Witchcraft." *Valley News* (San Fernando Valley, CA) (October 26, 1980) 6, 7, 20.

972. Nichols, Woodrow. "Profiles in Witchcraft: John Todd and the Illuminati." *The Pergamum Fifth Column* 1,2 (Spring 1979) 5-12.

973. Norling, Rita. *Rituals and Magic for Perfect Living.* West Nyack, NY: Parker Publishing Company, 1974. 212 pp.

974. Osirus. *Potions and Spells of Witchcraft.* San Francisco: JBT Marketing, 1970.

975. O'Sullivan, Gerry. "The Urban Cauldron." *Point Magazine* 9,2 (October 1979) 3-4, 16.

976. *Pagan Sexism?* N.p.: The Witching Well Education and
      Research Center, 1980. 6 pp.

977. *The Pagan Way and the Old Religion.* Smyrna, GA: Atlanta
      Pagan Way, 1977. 7 pp.

978. Paulson, Kathryn. *The Complete Book of Magic and Witch-
      craft.* New York: New American Library, 1970. 158 pp.

979. Pepper, Elizabeth, and John Wilcox. *Witches All.* New
      York: Grosset and Dunlap, 1977. 127 pp.

980. Pearson, Ann. "You Too Can Be a Witch." *Cosmopolitan*
      (July 1965) 18-20.

981. Picone, Patricia. "Occult Expert in Bucks Says Witches
      Are Not Evil." *Bucks County (PA) Courier Times*
      (October 29, 1974).

982. Plowman, Edward E. "The Legend(s) of John Todd."
      Christianity Today (February 2, 1979) 38-42.

983. *"Real* Old Time Religion." *Anakreon* 6 (Beltane 9980/
      May 1, 1980) 1-10.

984. "Religion Changes Seen in Aquarian Age." *St. Paul
      Dispatch* (September 15, 1973).

985. Richler, Mordecai. "Witches Brew." *Playboy* (July
      1974) 9-92, 120, 122, 164-65.

986. "The Rise of Neo-Paganism." *Destiny Bulletin* (Fall
      1979) 1-2.

987. Riva, Anna. *Candle Burning Magic.* Toluca Lake, CA:
      International Imports, 1980. 96 pp.

988. ———. *Golden Secrets of Mystic Oils.* Toluca Lake,
      CA: International Imports, 1978. 64 pp.

989. ———. *The Modern Herbal Spellbook.* Toluca Lake, CA:
      International Imports, 1974. 64 pp.

990. ———. *Spellcraft, Hexcraft and Witchcraft.* Toluca
      Lake, CA: International Imports, 1977. 64 pp.

991. Roberts, Susan. *Witches U.S.A.* New York: Dell Pub-
      lishing Company, 1971. 264 pp. Rev. ed. Hollywood,
      CA: Phoenix House, 1974. 318 pp.

992. Rubinton, Noel. "Zionsville Baptists Prepare for Final War with Witches." *Indianapolis Star* (July 4, 1978) 1, 14.

993. *Rune-Sticks: An Age-Old Method of Divination.* N.p.: The First Temple of the Craft of W.I.C.A., 1959. 13 pp.

994. Samuel, Jack, comp. *Around the Psychic World with Dame Sybil Leek....* N.p., n.d. 24 pp.

995. Schafer, Ed. "Witches 'Heal' with Penicillin, Nude Dancing." *Kansas City Star* (August 6, 1975) 6A.

996. Schurmacher, Emile C. *Witchcraft in America Today.* New York: Paperback Library, 1970. 176 pp.

997. Selene. *About Witchcraft.* N.p., n.d. Ms., 8 pp.

998. Seleneicthon. *Applied Magick.* N.p., n.d. 27 pp.

999. ————. *Spokes of the Wheel.* N.p., 1979. 49 pp.

1000. Sevarg, Luba. *The Do-It-Yourself Witchcraft Guide.* New York: Award Books, 1971. 155 pp.

1001. Sharp, Daisy. "Ancient Tarot Cards Haven't Lost Appeal in Modern World." *Sunday Times Advertiser* (Trenton, NJ) (September 16, 1973).

1002. Sheba, Lady. *Book of Shadows.* St. Paul, MN: Llewellyn Publications, 1973. 155 pp.

1003. ————. *The Grimoire of Lady Sheba.* St. Paul, MN: Llewellyn Publications, 1972. 219 pp. 2nd ed. 1974. 236 pp.

1004. ————. *Witch.* St. Paul, MN: Llewellyn Publications, 1973. 111 pp.

1005. ————. *The Witches' Workbook.* New York: Zebra Books, 1975. 192 pp.

1006. Sherwood, Debbie. *The Story of a Happy Witch.* New York: Lancer Books, 1973. 192 pp.

1007. Shirota, Jon. "Which Witch Is Which?" *Probe the Unknown* 1,1 (December 1972) 24-29.

1008. Simbro, William. "In D.M.—a Witches' Coven." *Des Moines Tribune* (October 27, 1977) 1-2.

1009. Simor, George. "Witchcraft Alive and Well and Living on Long Island." *Paumonok, the Magazine of Long Island Living* 1,1 (June 1973).

1010. Simpson, Damien. "The Unknown Power of Witchcraft." *Cosmos* (October 1969) 4-5.

1011. Slagle, Alton. "A Couple of Witches in an Explosive Texas Situation." *San Francisco Sunday Examiner & Chronicle* (August 26, 1979) 7B.

1012. Smith, Robert T. "The Rise of the Occult." *Minneapolis Tribune Picture Magazine* (December 17, 1972) 14-19.

1013. ————. "The Way of Wicca." *Minneapolis Tribune Picture Magazine* (December 17, 1972) 4-9.

1014. ————. "Witches Stir Brew under Full Moon." *Minneapolis Tribune* (September 6, 1971) 1A-4A.

1015. Smith, Suzy. *Today's Witches.* Englewood Cliffs, NJ: Prentice-Hall, 1970. 180 pp.

1016. Smyth, Frank. *Modern Witchcraft.* N.p.: Castle Books, 1970. 125 pp. Rpt. New York: Harper & Row Publishers, 1973. 127 pp.

1017. Starkes, M. Thomas. "Witchcraft: Twentieth Century Revival." In *B.O.O.K. (Beliefs of Other Kinds).* Atlanta, GA: Home Mission Board/Southern Baptist Convention, n.d., pp. 108-11.

1018. Stowers, Carlton. "Panhandle Witchcraft." *Dallas Morning News* (November 6, 1977) 1A, 22A.

1019. Strauch, Art. "Hometown Witch." *Fate* 17,9 (September 1964) 43-49.

1020. Taylor, Barney C. (Eli). *The First Book of Wisdom.* N.p., 1973. 35 pp.

1021. ————. *The Second Book of Wisdom.* N.p., n.d. 126 pp.

1022. Thomas, Ed. "Witchcraft: Suburbia's Latest Sex Gim-
          mick." *Man's Illustrated* 10,3 (June 1972) 20-23,
          54, 56, 58.

1023. Thomas, Veronica. "The Witches of 1966." *Atlantic
          Monthly* 218 (September 1966) 119-25.

1024. Tonn, Martin. "What Is Your WQ? (Witchcraft Quotient)."
          Coronet 12,4 (April 1974) 6-7, 154.

1025. Town, Sandra. "How to Detect a Genuine Witch."
          National Spotlite (December 1976).

1026. Trent, Bill. "There Are Some Weird Things Going On in
          Toronto." *Weekend* (Toronto) (March 15, 1969).

1027. *The Truth about Witchcraft.* Watertown, NY: Starrcraft-
          Moonstar, n.d. 11 pp.

1028. Truzzi, Marcello. *Caldron Cookery.* New York: Meredith
          Press, 1969. 115 pp.

1029. Vachon, Brian. "Witches Are Rising." *Look* (August 24,
          1971) 40-44.

1030. Wallace, C.H. *Witchcraft in the World Today.* New
          York: Award Books, 1967. 191 pp.

1031. Weinstein, Marion. *Positive Magic.* New York: Pocket
          Books, 1978. 299 pp.

1032. "Welcome ... to a Witches' Wedding!" *Midnight Globe*
          (Rouses Point, NY) (January 17, 1978) 40-41.

1033. Weschcke, Carl L. *The Science of Feeling Fine.* St.
          Paul, MN: Chester-Kent, 1954. 194 pp.

1034. West, Robert H. "Some Popular Literature of Witchcraft
          Since 1969." *The Review of Politics* 37,4 (October
          1975) 547-56.

1035. "Wiccan Believers to Mark Spring Festival This Week."
          The Milwaukee Journal (April 26, 1980) 5.

1036. Williams, Wentworth. "Witches Beware!" *Beyond* 2,11
          (July 1969) 68-78.

1037.   Wilson, Robert Anton.   "The Witches Are Coming."   *Gallery* [issue unknown].

1038.   Wisby, Gary.   "A Spell Sealed Bookshop Deal."   *Chicago Sun-Times* (November 18, 1970) 16.

1039.   *Witchcraft: An Introduction.*   Minneapolis, MN: Mental Science Institute, n.d.   16 pp.

1040.   *Witchcraft: The Way of Wisdom.*   Chicago Heights, IL: First Temple of the Craft, n.d.   4-page tract.

1041.   "Witches Ride Tonight."   *Capital Times* (Madison, WI) (October 31, 1975) 5.

1042.   Witt, Robin.   "A Pagan Renaissance? Sacramento Witches See Their Ranks Swell."   *Sacramento Bee* (April 26, 1980) B5.

1043.   Wolfe.   "An Insider's Look at Witchcraft."   *Psychic Reporter* (July 1976) 7-9.

1044.   Woodside, Jeani.   "My Co-Workers Branded Me ... Navy Witch."   *Fate* 29,7 (July 1976) 53-55.

1045.   Worley, Elizabeth.   "The Wooing of Wicca."   *Atlanta* (December 1979) 62-64.

1046.   Worth, Valerie.   *The Crone's Book of Words.*   St. Paul, MN: Llewellyn Publications, 1971.   155 pp.

1047.   Zalasin, Paul.   *Witchcraft.*   Hempstead, NY: Gemini International Press, 1979.   97 pp.

1048.   Zientora, Bob, and Michael Carson.   "Seances Part of New 'Psychic' Fulfillment."   *The Herald* (Libertyville, (IL) (June 21, 1972).

1049-   Numbers deleted.
1059

I. FEMINIST WICCA

First becoming audible in the mid-1970s, voices advocating
Witchcraft as a women's religion began to be heard in the
feminist movement and then through Morgan McFarland and Z.
Budapest in the larger Wiccan movement. The feminists provoked much controversy in both camps. Some feminists viewed
the Witches as too extreme. The Witches resented the separatist tendencies seen in all-female covens, and many rejected
the tie between the feminists and lesbians. Both were seen
to significantly redefine the balance between male and female
so central to Wiccan thought.

Within the feminist community, the Witches exist at one
end of a spectrum that includes Christians who talk of God in
the feminine, to Goddess worshippers who do not keep regular
festivals, to Goddess worshippers who keep seasonal festivals
but shun the label Witch, to those who claim the title. Only
the latter are represented in this set of books and articles.
Morgan McFarland and Z. Budapest were the first, and their
writings are essential to understanding the movement.

As the 1970s gave way to a new decade other voices arose--
Deborah Bender, Chris Carol, Carol Christ, Naomi Goldenberg,
Robin Morgan, Merlin Stone, and most recently Starhawk.

Increasingly the feminist controversy within the Wiccan
community is losing its steam as a live-and-let-live policy
has become dominant.

Rosemary Ruether raises issues with the Wiccan feminists
on another front. She speaks as a Christian theologian and
questions their viability to guide the feminist movement.

1060. Adler, Margot. "Ending Our Poverty: A Workshop in
          Music, Chants & Shouts." *Womanspirit* 2,8 (Summer
          Solstice 1976) 32-33.

1061. Amber. "Personal Shrines for Women." *Womanspirit* 25
          (Fall Equinox 1980) 10.

1062. ————. "Wiccan Altars." *Womanspirit* 25 (Fall Equinox
          1980) 9-10.

1063. Beardwoman, Helen. "Lesbianism and Witchcraft." *Woman-
       spirit* 2,8 (Summer Solstice 1976) 90.

1064. Bender, Deborah. "How to Keep Your Coven, Circle or
       Grove Healthy and Growing." *Womanspirit* 6,21 (Fall
       1979) 59.

1065. ————. "Spells and Ethics." *Womanspirit* 5,20 (Summer
       1979) 54-55.

1066. Brown, Dennise C. "Feminist and Witch." *Womanspirit*
       6,21 (Fall 1979) 59.

1067. Budapest, Zsuzsanna Emese. "Christian Feminist vs.
       Goddess Movement." *Womanspirit* 6,24 (Summer Solstice
       1980) 26-27.

1068. ————. *The Feminist Book of Lights & Shadows.* Venice,
       CA: Luna Publications, 1976. 127 pp.

1069. ————. *The Holy Book of Women's Mysteries, Part 1.*
       Los Angeles: Susan B. Anthony Coven, No. 1, 1979.
       136 pp.

1070. ————. "Masika!" *Womanspirit* 13 (Fall 1977) 33-36.

1071. ————. "My Salem in L.A." *Womanspirit* 2,5 (Fall
       Equinox 1975) 8.

1072. ————. "Politics of Women's Religions." *Bread &
       Roses* 2,3 (Autumn 1980) 26, 28-29.

1073. ————. "Requiem for Masika." *Womanspirit* 6,22 (Win-
       ter 1979) 24-25.

1074. ————. *The Rise of the Fates.* Los Angeles: Susan B.
       Anthony Coven, No. 1, 1976. 91 pp.

1075. ————. *Selene: The Most Famous Bull-leaper on Earth.*
       Baltimore, MD: Diana Press, 1976. 52 pp.

1076. ————. "Witch Is to Woman as Womb Is to Birth."
       Quest 2,1 (Summer 1975) 50-56.

1077. Carol, Chris. "Celebrating a Total Eclipse of the
       Sun." *Womanspirit* 5,19 (Spring 1978) 23.

1078. ————. "A Midsummer Night's Celebration." *Womanspirit* 6,24 (Summer Solstice 1980) 2.

1079. Christ, Carol P. "Another Response to 'A Religion for Women.'" *Womanspirit* 6,25 (Fall Equinox 1980) 14.

1080. ————, and Judith Plaskow. *Womanspirit Rising.* San Francisco: Harper & Row, 1979. 287 pp.

1081. "Feminism & Witchcraft?" *Womanspirit* 5,20 (Summer 1979) 61.

1082. Forfreedom, Ann. *Mythology, Religion and Woman's Heritage.* Sacramento, CA: Sacramento City Unified School District, n.d. 80 pp.

1083. ————, and Julie Ann, eds. *Book of the Goddess.* Sacramento, CA: The Temple of the Goddess Within, 1980. 346 pp.

1084. Fox, Selena. "Moon Mirror Magick." *Womanspirit* 6,23 (Spring 1980) 60-61.

1085. ————. "Wicca: Channeling the Goddess Within." *Bread & Roses* 2,3 (Autumn 1980) 24-29.

1086. Gauthier, Xavière. "Why Witches." *Bread & Roses* 2,3 (Autumn 1980) 35-37.

1087. Gearhart, Sally. *The Feminist Tarot.* Venice, CA: Pandora's Box, 1976. 82 pp.

1088. Gidlow, Elsa. "Ella Young: Druidess." *Womanspirit* 10 (Winter 1976) 11-13.

1089. Goldenberg, Naomi R. *Changing of the Gods.* Boston: Beacon Press, 1979. 152 pp.

1090. ————. "To Spin a New Vision." *Womanspirit* 6,24 (Summer Solstice 1980) 30.

1091. *The Great Goddess.* Special issue of *Heresies* (New York: Heresies Collective), Spring 1978. 136 pp.

1092. Harvey, Steve. "'Witch' to Go on Trial." *Los Angeles Times* (April 10, 1975).

1093. Herron, Patricia. *The Spinning Cross*. San Francisco,
       CA: Patricia Herron, 1977. 26 pp.

1094. Janz, M.L. *Unwholly Woman*. N.p.: Calligraphics, n.d.
       36 pp.

1095. Kenyon, Richard L. "Religions Doomed, Feminist Says."
       Milwaukee Journal (February 23, 1980) 5.

1096. Lesh, Cheri. *Ancient Women: With Truth if Not with
       Praise*. N.p., n.d. 2-page flyer.

1097. ————. *Feminist Spiritual Alternatives*. N.p., n.d.
       2-page flyer.

1098. ————. *Witchcraft: Taking Control of One's Life*.
       N.p., n.d. 2-page flyer.

1099. McFarland, Morgan. "Into the Silent Land: Women's
       Hidden History." *Womanspirit* 2,8 (Summer Solstice
       1976) 48-49.

1100. ————. "Witchcraft: The Art of Remembering." *Quest*
       1,4 (Spring 1975) 41-48.

1101. Maior, Ursa. "Starting Covens, Groves and Circles."
       Womanspirit 2,8 (Summer Solstice 1976) 91.

1102. Mari, Seagull. "My Own Witchcraft." *Womanspirit* 5,17
       (Fall 1978) 21.

1103. Mariechild, Diane. *Womancraft*. Boston: The Author,
       1976. 46 pp.

1104. Mars, Dina Acosta. "Wommon Chant." *Spectrum* 1,4
       (February 1979).

1105. Morgan, Robin. *Going Too Far*. New York: Vintage
       Books, 1978. 334 pp.

1106. Morgana, Ardurne, and Boreas. *Footsteps on a Dianic
       Path*. N.p.: Coven of Morgana, n.d. 4 pp.

1107. Morning Glory, and Ohoyo Osh Ghishba. "Lament of the
       Witch." *Womanspirit* 6,23 (September 1980) 24.

1108. Morning Glory, and Otter G'Zell. *Who on Earth Is the
       Goddess?* Berkeley, CA: Covenant of the Goddess, n.d.
       7-page tract.

1109. Oak. "My Vision of a Coven." *Womanspirit* 9 (Fall 1976) 4.

1110. Potts, Billie. *A New Women's Tarot*. Woodstock, NY: Elf and Dragons Press, 1977. Rev. ed. 1978. 54 pp.

1111. "Responses to 'Matriarchy.'" *Womanspirit* 6,22 (Winter 1979) 46-49.

1112. Roberts, Mark. "Effeminism, Witchcraft, and Goddess Worship." *Double-F: A Magazine of Effeminism* 3 (Winter 1975-76) 26-35.

1113. ————. *An Introduction to Dianic Witchcraft*. Dallas, TX: The Mother Grove, n.d. 71 pp.

1114. Ruether, Rosemary. "A Religion for Women." *Womanspirit* 6,24 (Summer Solstice 1980) 22-25.

1115. Rush, Anne Kent. *Moon Moon*. Berkeley, CA: Moon Books, 1976. 415 pp.

1116. St. Clair, David. "Los Angeles Witch-Hunt 1975." *Fate* 28,9 (September 1975) 77-83.

1117. Seagull. "A Pagan Calendar." *Womanspirit* 9 (Fall 1976) 3.

1118. Sena. "Samhain--All Hallow's Eve." *Womanspirit* 1 (Autumn Equinox 1974) 45.

1119. Sisters of the Owl. "Covenant of the Sisters of the Owl." *Womanspirit* 2,5 (Fall Equinox 1975) 28-30.

1120. Starhawk. "The Goddess of Witchcraft." *Anima* 5,2 (Spring 1979) 125-29.

1121. ————. *The Spiral Dance*. San Francisco: Harper & Row, 1979. 218 pp.

1122. Stone, Merlin. *Ancient Mirrors of Womanhood, I*. New York: New Sybilline Books, 1979. 213 pp.

1123. ————. *When God Was a Woman*. New York: Harcourt Brace Jovanovich, 1976. 265 pp.

1124. Weinstein, Marion. *Earth Magic*. New York: Earth Magic Productions, 1980. 48 pp.

1125. "Witch Trial." *Womanspirit* 1,4 (Summer Solstice 1975)
       51.

1126. "The Witch's Altar." *Womanspirit* 5,17 (Fall 1978)
       23-24.

1127. "Women Libbers Go Pagan." *Christian Inquirer* (August
       1978).

1128. Wyoming, Anona D.   "One Woman's Witch." *Womanspirit*
       6,21 (Fall 1979) 58.

J. SONGBOOKS AND POETRY

The Pagan movement naturally finds expression in song and verse and has quickly produced a wide variety of its own music and poetry. *Circle Magick Songs* has been the most widely circulated. Two volumes, Chris Carol's *Silver Wheel--Trice Thirteen Songs* and the Wings of Vanthi Coven's *Songs of Love and Pleasure*, have a feminist orientation.

Victor Anderson, a teacher of many California Witches, wrote *Thorns of the Blood Rose*, a set of poems reflective of his Wicca life.

1129. Alan, Jim, and Selena Fox. *Circle Magick Songs.* Madison, WI: Circle Publications, 1977. 60 pp.

1130. Anderson, Victor. *Thorns of the Blood Rose.* San Leandro, CA: Cora Anderson, 1970. 106 pp.

1131. Carol, Chris. *Silver Wheel--Trice Thirteen Songs.* Portland, OR: The Author, 1979. 36 pp.

1132. House of Ravenwood. *Ravenwood Songbook.* N.p.: Ravenwood Press, 1980. 24 pp.

1133. Martello, Leo Louis. *Curses in Verses.* New York: Hero Press, 1971. 32 pp.

1134. *Neandir, Lady of the Flame.* N.p.: Victoria Lynn Ganger, 1979. 15 pp.

1135. *Nine Apples.* Colorado Springs, CO: Artemisia Press, 1979. 87 pp.

1136. Pendderwen, Gwydion. *The Rites of Summer.* Redwood Valley, CA: Nemeton, 1980. 17 pp.

1137. *Songs for the Old Religion.* Oakland, CA: Nemeton, 1972. 16 pp.

1138.   *Songs of Love and Pleasure*.   N.p.: Wings of Vanthi
        Coven, 1975.   15 pp.

1139.   Wayne, Phillip, and Cynthia A. McQuillin.   *Crystal
        Visions*.   Seal Beach, CA: The Authors, 1980.   24 pp.

1140.   *Wheel of the Year*.   Redwood City, CA: Nemeton, 1979.
        48 pp.

1141.   *Whispering Pines*.   N.p.: Pine Grove, 1979.   19 pp.

1142.   *Witches' Revival*.   Oakland, CA: Nemeton.

K. CALENDARS

1143.   *Astrological Calendar*. St. Paul, MN: Llewellyn Pub-
        lications. Issued annually.

1143a. Beguin, Rebecca. *The Crane Dance and 1980 Lunar Calen-
        dar*. The Author, 1979.

1143b. Clement, Carol, and Z. Budapest. *1977: A Year and a
        Day Calendar*. Baltimore: Diana Press, 1976. 16 pp.

1143c. *The Druids Calendar 1979*. Dobbs Ferry, NY: Cahill &
        Company, 1978.

1144.   Edwards, C. Taliesen. *The Pagan-Craft Calendar Appoint-
        ment Book and Almanack: March 1976 to March 1977*.
        Oakland, CA: Wordsmith Press, 1976. 62 pp.

1145.   *Lunar Phases*. Watertown, MA: Snake and Snake Produc-
        tions, 1981.

1146.   *Lunatics*. Baltimore, MD: Suidya Stone, 1981.

1147.   Maynard, Jim. *Celestial Influences*. Ashland, OR:
        Quicksilver Production. Published annually.

1148.   Passmore, Nancy F.W. *The Lunar Calendar*. Boston:
        Luna Press. Issued annually since 1977.

1149.   *A Witches' Calendar*. Hialeah, FL: Mi-World Publishing
        Company. Issued annually since 1979.

1150.   *The Witches' Calendar*. W.A. Noel. Issued annually
        since 1971.

V

NEO-PAGANISM

A. PAGANISM

The line between Pagan and Witch is vague in the extreme, but
within the larger Neo-Pagan community many individuals consider themselves Pagans but not Witches. Most follow ancient
traditions other than those of Western and Southern Europe.
They are Norse, Greek, and Egyptian. Some call themselves
Druids, a non-Wiccan tradition of the British Isles.

Others, such as Tim Zell and the Church of All Worlds, are
decidedly modern and eclectic. These Neo-Pagan groups combine
modern ideas and forms, including insights from science fiction, with materials drawn from the scope of ancient Pagan
tradition.

The materials cited below, with the exception of the
several items documenting Gleb Botkin's Church of Aphrodite,
are the product of modern Paganism or reflections upon it.
The Norse, Druid, Egyptian, and Illuminati/Discordian materials
have been separated into their own sections. Fred Adams, Ed
Fitch, and Tim Zell are the three names most often heard when
the origins of modern Paganism are discussed. Fred Adams
founded Fereferia (described by Ellwood), first of the modern
Pagan groups. Ed Fitch wrote some of the rituals of the
Pagan Way, one of the early, loosely related groups which at
one time had groves in a number of cities. Fitch's original
rituals were published in the *Book of Pagan Rituals*.

Tim Zell, founder of the Church of All Worlds, formerly
the largest Neo-Pagan group in this country, published the
Green Egg, the most influential Pagan journal until 1976.
He is one of the most articulate spokespersons for Neo-Pagan
causes.

David Miller has written a sophisticated contemporary
defense of Neo-Pagan theology, and his book circulates widely
through the Pagan community though he himself does not identify with the groups. Houston Roberts, better known by his
Pagan name, Cyprian, has begun the process of producing a Pagan

theology. Gorham had attempted an early Pagan theology, but
his text, privately published prior to the time most Pagans
joined the movement, has had little circulation among modern
Pagan leaders.

Most attempts to describe the modern Pagan community are
limited to the magazine articles and newspaper feature items
cited below. The one exception, Holzer's 1972 book, abounds
in errors reflective of his sloppy data collection and hasty
writing.

1151. *About the Aquarian Anti-Defamation League, Inc.*
       Minneapolis, MN: AADL, n.d. 6-page tract.

1152. Adams, Frederick C. *The Henge: Land Sky Love Temple.*
       Altadena, CA: Fereferia, 1969. 6 pp.

1153. —————. *Hesperian Life: The Maiden Way.* Altadena,
       CA: Fereferia, 1970. 26 pp.

1154. Adams, James E. "The New Religions Creating Tax
       Exemption Cases." *St. Louis Post Dispatch* (April 7,
       1972).

1155. Andrius. *A Child's Wish Book.* Minneapolis, MN:
       The Rowen Tree, 1979. 17 pp.

1156. *Andrius Book.* Minneapolis, MN: The Unicorn, n.d.
       9 pp.

1157. Asherah, and Allen H. Greenfield. *The Al-Asherah
       Philosophy of Ecstatic Dance (The New Belly Dance
       Book).* Tampa, FL: Hermetic Educational Institute,
       n.d. 35 pp.

1158. Bella, Rick. "Witchcraft Isn't Hags and Broomsticks."
       Springfield (OR) News (October 27, 1976) 1A, 3A.

1159. Beyerl, Paul W. *The Holy Books of the Devas.* Minnea-
       polis, MN: The Rowen Tree, 1980. 48 pp.

1160. *A Book of Pagan Rituals.* Brooklyn, NY: Earth Religion
       Supplies, n.d. 61 pp. Rev. ed. New York: Samuel
       Weiser, 1978. 142 pp.

1161. *The Book of Shadow and Substance.* N.p.: Owlexandrian
       Multimedia/Hermetic Educational Institute, n.d.
       7 pp.

1162. Bowman, James. "Love Those Witches." *Chicago Daily News* (February 18, 1971).

1163. Breslin, Jack. "Harvest Rites Unite 'Ordinary Folks.'" *The Daily Freeman* (Kingston, NY) (October 8, 1979) 1, 5.

1164. ————. "Pagans Meet by Moonlight in Rosendale." *The Daily Freeman* (Kingston, NY) (October 5, 1979) 1, 5.

1165. Butler, Patrick. "It's That Old Time Religion on Wellington Avenue." *Lerner Skyline Newspapers* (Chicago) (January 22, 1974).

1166. Carter, Carl. "Witches Gather in Georgia, Claim Their Craft Widespread." *Birmingham News* (June 30, 1980) 9B.

1167. Castleberry, Brett. "Let Nothing You Dismay." *Spectrum* (Tallahassee, FL) 13 (Yule 1979).

1168. Chew, Willa C. *The Goddess Faith*. Hicksville, NY: Exposition Press, 1977. 222 pp.

1169. *Church of All Worlds: Is It Really a Church?* N.p., n.d. 29 pp.

1170. "Church of Aphrodite." *Newsweek* (November 27, 1939) 32.

1171. "Church of Aphrodite, Goddess of Love, Is Chartered in New York." *Life* (December 4, 1939) 101.

1172. Clark, Carolyn, and Tim Zell. *If You're a Woman ... Can You Be a Christian?* St. Louis, MO: Church of All Worlds, n.d. 8-page tract.

1173. Cole, Donna, and Herman Enderle. *The Pagan Way, Volume I*. Chicago: n.p., 1971.

1174. Daniels, Mary. "Witch Hunt." *Chicago Tribune* (July 26, 1970).

1175. Dawson, Johnny. *A Look Back at Pan-Pagan Festival 1980*. Fountain, FL: Natural Science Church, 1980. 8 pp.

1176. *Delphic Paganism: The Worship of the True Gods of*
       Nature and Man. Baldwin Park, CA: The Delphic
       Fellowship, n.d.   8 pp.

1177. *The Do-It-Yourself Past-Life Recall Exercise Book.*
       Stillwater, OK: Thales Microuniversity Press, 1976.
       27 pp.

1178. Ellwood, Robert S. "Notes on a Neopagan Religious
       Group in America." *History of Religions* (August
       1971) 125-39.

1179. *Embers: Visions of the Transition.* Stillwater, OK:
       Thales Microuniversity Press, 1976.   27 pp.

1180. Fairgrove, Rowan, comp. *A Handbook of Botanical In-*
       censes. Tallahassee, FL: The Author, n.d.   15 pp.

1181. *Fereferia; From the Magic Maiden, a Love Culture for*
       Wilderness. N.p., n.d.   5 pp.

1182. Gilbert, Andrea. "Witch Wants to Stir Up New Image
       for Old Belief." *Seattle Times* (October 13, 1974)
       H10.

1183. Good, Sandy. *A Book.* Harrisburg, PA: The Neo American
       Church, 1974.   141 pp.

1184. Gorham, Melvin. *The Pagan Bible.* Portland, OR:
       Buifords & Mort, 1967.   296 pp.

1185. Gray, David C. *Book of the Phoenix: A Way of Living.*
       Miami Springs, FL: Neo-Animist Church, 1978.   49 pp.

1186. Gross, R. *Thoughts.* Chicago: Temple of the Pagan Way,
       n.d.   8 pp.

1187. Gruen, John. *The New Bohemia.* New York: Grosset &
       Dunlap, 1966, pp. 49-60.

1188. Haldane, Claudia. *Introducing Deboran Reform Witch-*
       craft: An Aquarian-Age Tradition. Concord, MA: The
       Author, n.d.   4-page typescript.

1189. Holzer, Hans. *The New Pagans.* Garden City, NY:
       Doubleday & Company, Inc., 1972.   197 pp.

1190. Humphrey, Christopher C. *Whole-Earth Inner Space*.
      Stillwater, OK: Thales Microuniversity Press, 1973.
      220 pp.

1191. *If Not You, Who?* St. Louis: Church of All Worlds, n.d.
      6-page tract.

1192. Kabouter, Jomo. *Varying Currents: The Woody Doctrine
      Applied to Minzey*. Berkeley, CA: Committee on
      Religious Cannabis, 1973. 51 pp.

1193. Kelly, Tom. *Pagan Musings*. Berkeley, CA: Pentalpha,
      n.d. 7-page tract.

1194. *The Kerista Village Handbook*. San Francisco: Kerista
      Consciousness Church, 1979. 16 pp.

1195. Kulp, Thomas, and Radelle Kulp. *The Order of the Holy
      Grail: Ancient Wisdom for a New Age*. N.p., n.d.
      9-page typescript.

1196. *The Lazy Nickels Action Philosophy*. Los Angeles:
      Buffalo Ghost Dance Productions, n.d. 16 pp.

1197. *The Lazy Nickels: General Information*. Los Angeles:
      Buffalo Ghost Dance Productions, n.d. 12 pp.

1198. Miller, David L. *The New Polytheism*. New York:
      Harper & Row, 1974. 86 pp.

1199. Minerva (E. Soiret). *Parthenon West: The Parthenonian
      Tradition*. Richton Park, IL: Parthenon West, 1977.
      3 pp.

1200. ———. *Reflective Analysis*. Richton Park, IL:
      Parthenon West, n.d. 5 pp.

1201. Pagan Pathfinders. *Book of God Evocations*. London:
      Pallas-Aquariana, n.d. 27 pp.

1202. *The Pagan Way: An Introduction to Paganism*. Philadel-
      phia, PA: The Pagan Way, n.d. 8 pp.

1203. *The Pagan Way and the Old Religion*. Smyrna, GA:
      Atlanta Pagan Way, 1977. 7 pp.

1204. Poppy, John. *Why We Need a New Religion*. St. Louis:
      Church of All Worlds, n.d. 8-page tract.

1205.   "Preaching Pan, Isis and Om." *Time* (August 6, 1979)
        83.

1206.   *Prospectus.* San Francisco: Shrine of Sothis, n.d.
        12 pp.

1207.   *The Purposes of the Church of the New Essenes.* Pasca-
        goula, MS: Church of the New Essenes, n.d.   4-page
        tract.

1208.   Roberts, Houston. *A Brief Assessment of NeoPagan
        Theology.* Nashville, TN: The Author, 1980. 16 pp.

1209.   Ross, Lilla. "Pagans Dance Under Solstice." *Florida
        Times Union* (Jacksonville) (June 28, 1980) Al, A6.

1210.   Sender, Ramon, and Alicia Bay Laurel. *Being of the
        Sun.* New York: Harper & Row, 1973.

1211.   Sigl, Susan T. *Between Worlds ... Fragments of a
        Faceted Crystal.* N.p.: The Author, 1980.   30 pp.

1212.   Stowe, Caryl, and Murray Winter. *Witchcraft.* Gary,
        IN: Woods Park Pagan Temple, n.d. 5-page typescript.

1213.   "10 Seized in Hippie Cult Raid at Pagan Church." *St.
        Louis Post-Dispatch* (August 6, 1970) 3A.

1214.   *Topocosmic Mandala of the Sacred Land Sky Love Year.*
        Altadena, CA: Fereferia, 1969.   3 pp.

1215.   *Uranus.* Chicago: Uranus, n.d.   7 pp.

1216.   *The Venusian Church: Information.* Seattle, WA: The
        Venusian Church, n.d.   3-page tract.

1217.   Wagstaff, Beverly. "Witches' Sabbath." *Oregon Life*
        (October 30, 1976) 1A, 3A.

1218.   *The Way of the Sun to the Fire.* Stillwater, OK: Thales
        Microuniversity Press, 1979.   27 pp.

1219.   Wille, Lois. "Myths and Reality in World of Witches."
        Chicago Daily News (March 3-4, 1973) 3-4.

1220.   "Witchcraft P.R." *Christianity Today* (December 6,
        1974) 27.

1221. *Wizard*. Stillwater, OK: Thales Microuniversity Press, 1976. 27 pp.

1222. Zakatarious. *The Secret of the Golden Calf*. Berkeley, CA: House of Zwillingsbruder Press, 1974. 80 pp.

1223. Zell, Tim. *Cataclysm and Consciousness: From the Golden Age to the Age of Iron*. Redwood Valley, CA: The Author, 1977. 47 pp.

1224. ————. *The Gods of Nature; The Nature of Gods*. St. Louis: Church of All Worlds, n.d. 7 pp.

1225. ————. *An Old Religion for a New Age: Neo-Paganism*. St. Louis: Church of All Worlds, n.d. 8-page tract.

1226. ————. *Neo-Paganism and the Church of All Worlds: Some Questions and Answers*. St. Louis: Church of All Worlds, n.d. 8-page tract.

1227. ————. *What on Earth Is the Church of All Worlds?* St. Louis: Church of All Worlds, n.d. 6-page tract.

1228. Ziomek, Jon. "Witch Business--No Goblins Here." *Chicago Sun-Times* (October 31, 1971).

B. EGYPTIAN PAGANISM

Ancient Egypt runs as a thread of influence through the whole
occult community, and several groups, drawing on the massive
research on Egyptian magic and religion, were among the first
to respond to the magical revival. The material below concerns three groups: the Church of Eternal Source in Southern
California; an independent temple headed by Rosemary Clark in
suburban Chicago (see Brown and Frisbie); and the Egyptian
Church founded by James Neruda and Charles Renslow of Chicago,
who produced a number of tracts relating their teachings.

1229. Brown, Steve. "Suburban Home Becomes Temple for Wor-
         ship of Egypt Sun God." *Chicago Sun-Times* (June 25-
         26, 1977) 5.

1230. Butler, Patrick. "Ancient Egyptian Gods Come to
         Chicago." *Fate* 27,3 (March 1974) 84-92.

1231. *Catechism of the Egyptian Holy Church*. N.p., n.d.
         5-page ditto.

1232. Colburn, Marcia Froelke. "Is Gary Nepon the Great Gay
         Hope of Chicago?" *The Reader* 7,22 (March 3, 1978)
         1, 20-24.

1233. *Congregation Universal Enlightenment*. Chicago: Egyptian
         Holy Church, n.d. 7 pp.

1234. *Egyptian Brothers of the Resurrection*. Chicago: Egyptian
         Holy Church, n.d. 3-page tract.

1235. *Falcon-Spirit of the Sun*. Chicago: Egyptian Holy Church,
         n.d. 3-page tract.

1236. *Four Major Holy Days of the Church*. Chicago: Egyptian
         Holy Church of Ihknaten, n.d. 2-page tract.

1237. Frisbie, Tom. "She Peers into Egypt's Ancient Secrets."
      Suburban Week (Chicago) (September 16, 1976) 3.

1238. *History of the Egyptian Holy Church.* N.p., n.d. 7-page
      ditto.

1239. *Life in Abundance.* Chicago: Egyptian Holy Church, n.d.
      3-page tract.

1240. Neruda, James. *Buckle of Isis.* Chicago: Egyptian
      Holy Church, n.d. 3-page tract.

1241. *Our Modern Practice of the Ancient Egyptian Religion.*
      Burbank, CA: Church of the Eternal Source, 1974.
      12 pp.

1242. *The Pentagram.* Chicago: Egyptian Holy Church of
      America, n.d. 3-page tract.

1243. *Pristine Egyptian Orthodox Church.* Chicago: Pristine
      Egyptian Orthodox Church, n.d. 3-page tract.

1244. Renslow, Charles. *The Divine Liturgy of the Two Lands.*
      N.p., n.d. 24 pp.

1245. *Secrets of Ancient Egypt.* Chicago: Egyptian Holy
      Church, n.d. 3-page tract.

1246. Stewardson, Jack. "Cult Branch Is Founded." *The
      Standard-Times* (New Bedford, MA) (July 1, 1972).

1247. *War Is Immoral.* Chicago: Egyptian Holy Church, n.d.
      3-page tract.

1248. *What Is an "Egyptian?"* Chicago: Egyptian Holy Church,
      n.d. 3-page tract.

C. NORSE PAGANISM

The Norse Pagans have been the source of endless controversy
within Paganism. While Paganism as a movement represents
Western and Northern European-Americans searching for their
pre-Christian roots, many Norse Pagans have gone far beyond a
mere identification with ancient Vikings. They have advocated
racial superiority, and some have openly identified with
Neo-Nazi groups.

The convergence of Norse and Neo-Nazi movements led to a
series of angry letters in the old *Green Egg* and helped keep
Norse Pagan participation in the larger movement much lower
than it might have been otherwise.

The main literature of Norse Paganism has been in periodicals (see Section IX-A). The items below are the only books
and articles which have appeared to date.

1249. Herdegen, Lance J. "A Viking Celebration, 1977-Style."
       Chicago Sun-Times (September 30, 1977).

1250. Howard, Michael. *The Magic of the Runes*. New York:
       Samuel Weiser, 1980. 96 pp.

1251. Hundingsbani, Helgi. *Odin*. Red Wing, MN: Viking Horse,
       1978. 154 pp.

1252. *Introduction; Prospectus and Inquiry*. New Haven, CT:
       New Haven Pagan Community, 1977. 6 pp.

1253. McNallen, Stephen A. *What Is the Norse Religion?* Tur-
       lock, CA: The Author, n.d. 5-page tract.

1254. Redmond, Jeffery R. *"Viking" Hoaxes in North America*.
       New York: Carlton Press, 1979. 64 pp.

1255. *Wisdom from the Edda*. Toronto: The Odinist Movement,
       n.d. 15 pp.

D. DRUIDS

To speak of Druids in England calls up images of ancient priests and their modern counterparts who annually gather at Stonehenge to salute the rising sun on June 21. In America, Druids are a completely different reality.

Created in 1964 as a religion to protest compulsory chapel services at Carleton College in Northfield, Minnesota, the Reformed Druids of North America have grown into a national body, and the writings they produced have grown into a substantial book, *The Druid Chronicles (Evolved)*.

1256. Adcock, Joe. "Your Neighbor May Be One: Those 2,500 Druids in Philadelphia." *The Evening Bulletin* (June 11, 1971) 3.

1257. Bastasz, Bob. "Druids Keep Spirit of Stonehenge." *Carletonian* (Northfield, MN) (October 10, 1968) 1.

1258. Broad, Sally. "Arch Druid Fisher Tells Newman Club of Druid Philosophy." *Carletonian* (Northfield, MN) (January 22, 1964) 1, 4.

1259. Carr, Gary. "Druid Service Chills Observer, Is Huge Success for Faithful." *Carletonian* (Northfield, MN) (November 6, 1963).

1260. *The Druid Chronicles (Evolved)*. Berkeley, CA: Berkeley Drunemetom Press, 1976. 202 pp.

1261. *The Druid Chronicles; Reformed*. N.p.: Carleton Drynemetum Press, 1964. 25 pp.

1262. Gibson, Richard. "In the Light of the Full Moon...." *Minneapolis Star* (September 26, 1972) 1C.

1263. Maughan, T. "The Druid Order." *Beyond Reality* 13 (January-February 1975) 24-26, 46-48.

1264.   Nelson, Norman E.   "Carleton Stonehenge: Reformed Druids
        Partake of Waters, Invoke Earth-Mother."   *Carletonian*
        (Northfield, MN) (May 28, 1963) 2.

1265.   O'Donnell, Franklin.   "Give Me That Old Time Religion."
        New West (March 24, 1980) 83-85.

1266.   *Order of Worship, Reformed.*   N.p.: Carleton Drynemetom
        Press, 1966.   14 pp.

1267.   Sheridan, Jack.   "Druidism in Chicago."   *Fate* 3,1 (Jan-
        uary 1950) 80-85.

1268.   *The Song of the Earth.*   N.p.: Reformed Druids of North
        America, 1964.   8 pp.

1269.   Wallace, Kevin.   "Druids Emerge in S.F."   *San Francisco
        Chronicle* (November 3, 1975) 2.

1270.   *What Is Reformed Druidism?*   N.p.: Reformed Druids of
        North America, 1964.   8 pp.

E. THE DISCORDIANS AND ILLUMINATI

Robert Anton Wilson has united two themes within the Pagan movement. The Discordians, worshippers of Eris, the goddess of chaos, believe that the disorder in the universe is more metaphysically real than the order. The original Illuminati, a secret conspiratorial order in 18th-century Germany, symbolizes most clearly the conspiratorial and paranoid vision of life.

The Illuminati and Discordian literature included in the list below varies between the farcical and fictional and the straight and serious. Between the lines of it all is a peculiar Pagan vision.

1271. Hill, Greg (Malaclypse the Younger). *Principia Discordia or How I Found the Goddess and What I Did to Her When I Found Her*. 4th ed., San Francisco: Rip-Off Press, 1970. 75 pp. 5th ed., Mason, MI: Loompanics Unlimited, 1979. 91 pp.

1272. Shea, Robert, and Robert Anton Wilson. *Illuminatus*. New York: Dell, 1975. I. *The Eye in the Pyramid*, 304 pp.; II. *The Golden Apple*, 272 pp.; III. *Leviathan*, 253 pp.

1273. Wilgus, Neal. *The Illuminoids*. New York: Pocket Books, 1978. 256 pp.

1274. Wilson, Robert Anton. *Cosmic Trigger*. Berkeley, CA: And/Or Press, 1977. 269 pp.

1275. ————. *The Illuminati Papers*. Berkeley, CA: And/Or Press, 1980. 150 pp.

1276. ————. *Schrodinger's Cat*. New York: Pocket Books, 1979. 256 pp.

VI

AFRO-AMERICAN MAGICAL RELIGIONS

A. VOODOO

Few words are used so loosely in describing magical phenomena
as Voodoo. Oftentimes, in both popular conversation and the
mass media, "Voodoo" means a kind of malevolent evil power
which some people supposedly can turn on others. The use
derives from old B-movies. The second misuse of the term,
common to journalists, identifies Voodoo with any number of
Latin American magical religions and Southern black folk magic.
Unfortunately this confusion of terms carries over into the
scholarly literature, especially the psychiatric material.

Properly speaking, *Voodoo* (Voodun) is the magical religion
brought to the United States from Haiti. It originated in
Africa, primarily among the Ibo, and developed an overlay of
French Roman Catholicism (see Desmangles [1293] for a discussion of the relationship). The major deities include Damballah, the serpent.

Three main types of material make up this section. First,
some books describe Haitian Voodoo in its home context. Bach
and Seabrook provide popular anecdotal introductions. For
more in-depth material see Gilford, Leyburn, Metraux, and
Rigaud. Denning and Phillips give an appraisal of what they
feel are paranormal phenomena at Voodoo services.

Second, Voodoo in New Orleans began in the early 1800s as
French slave owners attempted to escape the effects of the
black freedom movement in Haiti. During the 19th century,
the city became known for its Voodoo services, both public
and private, and for its Voodoo queen, Marie Laveau. For an
understanding of New Orleans Voodoo, begin with Tallant and
Touchstone, then proceed to Asbury, Fossier, Jackson, King,
and Saxon, each of whom adds information to the others.

Third, chroniclers have largely ignored Voodoo, which has
silently spread across the United States in the past two
decades. While not nearly as large as its cousin, Santeria,
it can now be found in most urban complexes where Haitian

immigrants have settled. No books have appeared, but the articles by Arboo, Beckley, Devine, Fenley, LeBlanc, Singer, and Snow, taken together, offer some perspective.

Finally, we come to the important but confusing works of James Haskins. Haskins' two books are almost the only surveys of the practices of magic in the contemporary American black community, hence providing much source material not found elsewhere. Unfortunately, Haskins confuses and mixes the various types of magic, mainly the Caribbean types, with hoodoo (see below) and must be used with extreme care. The same confusion arises in the Pelton article (1321).

1277. Arboo, Madam. "What 'Voodoo' Really Is." *Exploring the Unknown* 4,6 (April 1964) 6-19.

1278. Asbury, Herbert. *The French Quarter.* New York: Alfred A. Knopf, 1936, pp. 254-83.

1279. Bach, Marcus. "The Medium and the Voodoo Priest." *Fate* 25,8-9; I (August 1972) 46-51; II (September 1952) 90-97.

1280. ————. *Strange Altars.* Indianapolis: Bobbs-Merrill Company, 1952. 254 pp.

1281. ————. "Voodoo Fire Walking in Haiti." *Fate* 13,8 (August 1960) 27-33.

1282. Beam, Maurice. "Voodoo in America." In *Cults of America.* New York: Macfadden-Bartell, 1964, pp. 112-27.

1283. Beckley, Timothy. "Voodoo Next Door: Tampering with the Psychic Forces." *ESP* 2,2 (March 1977) 36-38, 59-62.

1284. *Black and White Magic Attributed to Marie Laveau.* N.p., n.d. 40 pp.

1285. Cassidy, Hugh J.B., with Edward Wakin. "Saturday Night Voodoo: Sunday Morning Mass." *U.S. Catholic* 43,7 (July 1978) 35-38.

1286. Cocke, Ed. "Voodoo." *New Orleans Magazine* 4 (January 1970) 50-53.

1287. Culin, Stewart. "Reports Concerning Voodooism."
        Journal of American Folklore 2 (1889) 232-33.

1288. d'Argent, Jacques. *Voodoo*. Los Angeles: Sherbourne
        Press, 1970. 160 pp.

1289. Davis, Frank. "For Fear of Gris-Gris!" *Probe the
        Unknown* 1,4 (August 1973) 27-31.

1290. Dayhoof, Eleanore. "Voodoo ... Death Beside the
        Hearth." *Fate* 21,10 (October 1968) 61-65.

1291. Denning, Melita, and Osborne Phillips. *Voudoun Fire*.
        St. Paul, MN: Llewellyn Publications, 1980. 182 pp.

1292. Desmangles, Leslie G. "Androgeneity of the Principle
        of Crossroads in Vodun: Symbiosis of Legbaand St.
        Peter in Haiti." A paper for the Society for the
        Scientific Study of Religion, San Antonio, Texas,
        October 1979. 19 pp.

1293. ————. "The Vodun Way of Death: Cultural Symbiosis
        of Roman Catholicism and Vodun in Haiti." *The
        Journal of Religious Thought* 36,1 (Spring-Summer
        1979) 5-20.

1294. Devine, John W. "Voodoo--New Menace to American Cities."
        Beyond 2,13 (September 1969) 42-46.

1295. Diederich, Bernard, and Al Burt. *Papa Doc*. New York:
        Avon Books, 1970. 350 pp.

1296. Fenley, Bob. "Who Do? Voo Doo!" *Dallas Times-Herald
        Magazine* (December 4, 1966) 34-37.

1297. Fossier, Albert A. *New Orleans--The Glamour Period
        1800-1840*. New Orleans: Pelican Publishing Company,
        1957. 378 pp.

1298. Gilfond, Henry. *Voodoo: Its Origins and Practices*.
        New York: Franklin Watts, 1976. 114 pp.

1299. Haskins, James. *Voodoo and Hoodoo*. New York: Stein
        and Day, 1978. 226 pp.

1300. ————. *Witchcraft, Mysticism and Magic in the Black
        World*. Garden City, NY: Doubleday & Company, 1974.
        156 pp.

1301. Hearn, L. "The Scenes of Cable's Romances." *Century Illustrated Monthly Magazine* 27 (November 1885) 45+.

1302. Hildebrand, Norb. "The Gods of Voodoo." *Fate* 6,8 (August 1953) 12-21.

1303. Holdredge, Helen. *Mammy Pleasant.* New York: G.P. Putnam's Sons, 1953. 311 pp.

1304. ————. *Mammy Pleasant's Partner.* New York: G.P. Putnam's Sons, 1954. 300 pp.

1305. *Information.* New York: The Chamber of Holy Voodoo, n.d. 12 pp.

1306. Jackson, Joy J. *New Orleans in the Gilded Age.* New Orleans: L.S.U. Press, 1968, pp. 256-57.

1307. Kelley, George M. "New Orleans Devil Worship." *Fate* 9,8 (August 1956) 16-20.

1308. Kennedy, L. "Vodu and Vodun." *Journal of American Folklore* 3 (1890) 241.

1309. King, Grace. *New Orleans: The Place and the People.* New York: Macmillan, 1928, pp. 340-42.

1310. ————. *Fabulous New Orleans.* New York: The Century Co., 1928, pp. 237-46, 309-22.

1311. Lafarque, André. "Louisiana Linguistic and Folklore." *Louisiana Historical Quarterly* 24,3 (July 1941) 751-52.

1312. "Lawyer by Day, Voodoo Dancer by Nightfall." *Jet* (February 22, 1979).

1313. LeBlanc, Rena Dictor. "Voodoo Priests Are Nice People ... but Would You Want One Living Next Door?" *Probe the Unknown* 2,4 (Fall 1974) 20-22.

1314. Leyburn, James G. *The Haitian People.* New Haven: Yale University Press, 1966, pp. 131-65.

1315. Martinez, Raymond J. *Marie Laveau, Voodoo Queen, and Folk Tales along the Mississippi.* Jefferson, LA: Hope Publications, 1956. 96 pp.

1316. Métraux, Alfred. *Voodoo in Haiti*. London: Andre Deutsch, 1959. 400 pp. Rpt. London: Sphere Books, 1974. 368 pp.

1317. Morand, Paul. *Black Magic*. New York: Viking Press, 1929. 218 pp.

1318. Moutray, Eva Martin. "Haitian Voodoo in Louisiana." *Fate* 23,4 (April 1970) 85-88.

1319. Newell, W.W. "Reports of Voodoo Worship in Haiti and Louisiana." *Journal of American Folklore* 2 (1889) 41-47.

1320. Pelton, Robert W. *The Complete Book of Voodoo*. New York: G.P. Putnam's Sons, 1972. 254 pp.

1321. ———. "Voodoo--American Style." *Occult* 4,4 (January 1974) 18-23, 107-8.

1322. ———. "Voodoo--an Orgy Ritual." *Occult* 4,4 (January 1975) 54-58.

1323. ———. *Voodoo Charms and Talismans*. New York: Drake Publishing Co., 1973. 219 pp.

1324. ———. *Voodoo Secrets from A to Z*. South Brunswick, NJ: A.S. Barnes, 1973. 138 pp.

1325. ———. *Voodoo Signs and Omens*. South Brunswick, NJ: A.S. Barnes, 1974. 284 pp.

1326. Prose, Francine. *Marie Laveau*. New York: Berkley Publishing Corp., 1977. 342 pp.

1327. Reed, Ishmael. "Voodoo in New Orleans." *Oui* 6,1 (January 1977) 124-31.

1328. Rigaud, Milo. *Secrets of Voodoo*. New York: Pocket Books, 1971. 214 pp.

1329. Riva, Anna. *Voodoo Handbook of Cult Secrets*. No. Hollywood, CA: Spencer International, 1968. 48 pp.

1330. Saxon, Lyle. *Fabulous New Orleans*. New York: The Century Co., 1928, pp. 237-46, 309-28.

1331. ————. "Voodoo." *New Republic* (March 23, 1927) 35-59.

1332. Seabrook, W.B. *The Magic Island.* New York: Harcourt,
       Brace and Company, 1929. 336 pp.

1333. Number deleted.

1334. Singer, Dale. "Voodoo Shop Owner Keeps the Faith."
       Chicago Daily News (September 19, 1977).

1335. Snow, Loudell F. "I Was Born Just Exactly with the
       Gift: An Interview with a Voodoo Practitioner."
       Journal of American Folklore 86,341 (July-September
       1973) 272-81.

1336. Stahl, Annie Lee West. "Free Negro in Ante-Bellum
       Louisiana." *Louisiana Historical Quarterly* 25,2
       (April 1962) 366-68.

1337. Stanton, Herb. "Voodoo Worked at Midnight." *Fate*
       27,12 (December 1974) 74-76.

1338. Tallant, Robert. *Voodoo in New Orleans.* New York:
       Macmillan, 1946. Rpt. New York: Collier Books,
       1965. 252 pp.

1339. Tegarden, J.B. Hollis. "Voodooism." Chicago: University
       of Chicago M.A. Thesis, 1924 (Dept. of Practical
       Theology).

1340. Touchstone, Blake. "Voodoo in New Orleans." *Louisiana
       History* 13,4 (Fall 1972) 371-86.

1341. "Voodooism." *Literary Digest* (January 2, 1938) 29.

1342. Warner, Charles Dudley. "A Voodoo Dance." *Harper's
       Weekly* (June 25, 1887). Rpt. in *Studies in the
       South and West.* New York: Harper, 1889, pp. 64-74.

1343. Webb, Julie Yvonne. "Louisiana Voodoo and Supersti-
       tions Related to Health." *HSMHA Health Report* 86
       (1971) 291-99.

B. SANTERIA

Voodoo's cousin originated in West Africa among the Yoruba.
It has an overlay of Spanish Catholicism, but is usually
referred to as the Chango (or Shango) Cult from its principal
deity, a god of fire and stone. Santeria, a name given it
because of the popular identification of the Yoruban gods
with Catholic saints, arrived in America only in recent
decades, but can now be found in most urban centers with a
Spanish-speaking population.

By far the best survey of Santeria, both as a system and
as a religion present in America, can be found in Gonzalez-
Wippler. Bascom and Gleason (1353) describe the faith in
more general terms. The bulk of the articles, many somewhat
amusing, present pictures of Santeria as it manifests itself
in American cities as seen through the eyes of reporters who
view it as an alien phenomenon, and tend to agree with
Fabricio that "Santeria is a Wild Faith."

1344. Barker, Dennis. "Inside the Spanish Santeria." *ESP*
       1,4 (November 1976) 26-28, 51-53.

1345. Bascom, William. *Shango in the New World.* Austin:
       University of Texas, African and Afro-American Re-
       search Institute, 1972. 23 pp.

1346. ————. *The Yoruba of Southwestern Nigeria.* New
       York: Holt, Rinehart and Winston, 1969. 118 pp.

1347. "Cuddly Pets Are Brutally Murdered by Cult Members."
       Midnight/Globe (Rouses Point, NY) (November 29, 1979) 4.

1348. de Lama, George. "Cuban Spiritualism a Mix of God,
       Saints, Magic." *Chicago Tribune* (September 21, 1978).

1349. Fabricio, Robert. "Santeria Is a Wild Faith." *Floridian*
       (Miami) (July 1, 1973) 19, 22, 23.

1350. ———. "Santeria: Voodoo or Religion?" *Coronet* 12,4
       (April 1974) 8-11, 124-30.

1351. Garcia, Raquel. "Healed by a Santeria." *Fate* 27,4
       (April 1974) 77-79.

1352. Gastman, Floria. "Las Botanicas." *Beyond Reality*
       14 (March-April 1975) 46-49.

1353. Gleason, Judith. *A Recitation of Ifa, Oracle of the
       Yoruba.* New York: Grossman Publishers, 1973.   338
       pp.

1354. ———. *Santeria, Bronx.* New York: Atheneum, 1975.
       223 pp.

1355. Gonzalez-Wippler, Migene. *Santeria.* New York: The
       Julian Press, 1973.   181 pp.

1356. Heffernan, Bill. "Bloody Voodoo Cult Terrorizing N.J.
       Town." *National Enquirer* (August 21, 1979).

1357. *Let Us Pray; Ask Divine Blessing.* Brooklyn, N.Y.:
       E. Davis, n.d.   48 pp.

1358. *Let Us Pray; Sea Queen; 28 Favorite Prayers.* Bronx,
       NY: Original Products Co., n.d.   31 pp.

1359. Longworth, R.C. "Voodoo." *Chicago Tribune Magazine*
       (April 2, 1978) 52-62.

1360. Moreau, John Adam. "Successful Smell of Superstition."
       Chicago Sun-Times (November 10, 1969) 46.

1361. Murphy, Joseph M. "Afro-American Religion and Oracles:
       Santeria in Cuba." A paper for the Society for the
       Scientific Study of Religion, San Antonio, Texas,
       October 1979.   14 pp.

1362. Rose, Donna. *Santeria.* Hialeah, FL: Mi-World Publish-
       ing Co., 1980.   44 pp.

1363. Sullivan, Ronald. "Putting a Hex on Voodoo." *New
       York Times Magazine* (November 11, 1962).

1364. Suro, Roberto. "This Is Voodoo: Drums, Dances and
       Saints." *Chicago Sun-Times* (November 9, 1976) 8.

1365. "Voodoo Can Be Best Medicine for Refugees." *Chicago
       Sun-Times* (August 17, 1980) 19.

C. HOODOO

Frequently confused with Voodoo, even in scholarly literature, the practices of the Southern conjure man, usually called *hoodoo*, continued the folk magic not of Africa but of England. Whitten's important article thoroughly distinguished conjure man practice from its African counterparts. Protestant slave owners, less tolerant of African religion than Roman Catholics, took more thorough steps to obliterate the native magical practices, which were replaced with European ones.

Folklorists, in collecting material in the South, extensively documented hoodoo practice both from talking to and observing conjure men and recording the reflections about them in the community in which they worked. See Botkin, Dorson, Owen, and Puckett especially.

Hurston holds a unique place among those scholars who have written on black people's magic. Her work was largely ignored when it appeared, and only in recent years has it been appreciated for the monumental contribution it makes.

McTeer, the retired sheriff of Beaufort County, South Carolina, included in his folksy memoirs a lengthy section describing his long-term relationship with the chief hoodoo practitioner of his county. His account vividly illustrates how hoodoo works on a practical level.

Psychiatrists working in hospitals serving the American black community encounter hoodoo frequently among patients claiming to have been healed by magic or bewitched. The articles by Canon, Cappannari, Golden, Jordan, Kimball, Kuna, Manduro, Mathis, Michaelson, Snell, Tiling, and Wintrob constitute a set of materials describing the doctor's experiences and include numerous case histories.

1366. Allsopp, Fred W. "Voodooism in Little Rock." In *Folklore of Romantic Arkansas.* N.p.: The Grolier Society, 1931, pp. 182-83.

1367. Botkin, B.A. *A Treasury of Southern Folklore.* New York: Crown Publishers, 1949, pp. 527-47.

1368. Canon, W. "Voodoo Death." *Psychosomatic Medicine* 19
       (1957) 182-90.

1369. Cappannari, Stephen C., et al. "Voodoo in the General
       Hospital: A Case of Hexing and Regional Euleritis."
       Journal of the American Medical Association 237
       (1975) 938-40.

1370. Cole, Henry. "Voodoo in Chicago." *Fate* 19,10 (October
       1966) 89-95.

1371. "Concerning Negro Sorcery in the United States."
       Journal of American Folklore 3 (1890) 281-87.

1372. Dorson, Richard M. *Buying the Wind*. Chicago: Univer-
       sity of Chicago Press, 1964, pp. 55-64, 111-17,
       267-70, 314-22.

1373. ————. *Negro Folktales in Michigan*. Cambridge, MA:
       Harvard University Press, 1956, pp. 100-19, 137-54.

1374. ————. *Negro Tales from Pine Bluff, Arkansas and
       Calvin, Michigan*. Bloomington: Indiana University
       Press, 1958, pp. 206-9.

1375. Fortier, Alcee. "Customs and Superstitions in Louisia-
       na." *Journal of American Folklore* 1 (1888) 136-40.

1376. Golden, M.D. "Voodoo in Africa and the U.S." *American
       Journal of Psychiatry* 134 (1977) 1425-27.

1377. Hall, J.A. "Negro Conjuring and Tricking." *Journal
       of American Folklore* 10 (1897) 241-43.

1378. Hurston, Zora Neale. *Mules and Men*. Philadelphia:
       J.B. Lippincott, 1935. Rpt. New York: Harper & Row,
       1970. 343 pp.

1379. Number deleted.

1380. Jordan, Wilvert C. "Voodoo Medicine." In Richard A.
       Williams, ed., *Textbook of Black-Related Disease*.
       New York: McGraw-Hill, 1975, pp. 715-38.

1381. Kimball, C. "A Case of Pseudocyesis Caused by 'Roots.'"
       American Journal of Obstetrics and Gynecology 107
       (1970) 801-3.

1382. Kuna, Ralph R. "Hoodoo: The Indigenous Medicine Psychiatry of the Black American." *Mankind Quarterly* 18,2 (October-December 1977) 137-51.

1383. McLean, Patricia S. "Conjure Doctors in Eastern North Carolina." *North Carolina Folklore* 20,1 (February 1972) 21-29.

1384. McTeer, J.E. *High Sheriff of the Low Country.* Beaufort, SC: Beaufort Book Company, Inc., 1970. 101 pp.

1385. Manduro, Reynaldo J. "Hoodoo Possession in San Francisco." *Ethos* 3 (1975) 424-27.

1386. Mathis, J. "A Sophisticated Version of Voodoo Death." *Psychosomatic Medicine* 26 (1964) 104-7.

1387. Michaelson, Mike. "Can a 'Root Doctor' Actually Put a Hex on or Is It All a Great Put-on?" *Today's Health* 5 (March 1972) 39.

1388. Minor, Mary Y. "How to Keep Off Witches." *Journal of American Folklore* 11 (1898) 76.

1389. Mitchell, Faith. *Hoodoo Medicine: Sea Islands Herbal Remedies.* N.p.: Reed, Cannon & Johnson, 1978. 108 pp.

1390. Owens, Mary Alicia. "Among the Voodoos." In *The International Folklore Congress.* London: Strand, 1892.

1391. ————. *Voodoo Tales as Told Among the Negroes of the Southwest.* New York: Putnam, 1893. 310 pp.

1392. Peck, Mrs. M.S. "Voodooism in Tennessee." *Atlantic Monthly* 64 (September 1889) 376-80.

1393. Pendleton, Louis. "Notes on Negro Folklore and Witchcraft in the South." *Journal of American Folklore* 3 (1890) 201-7.

1394. Puckett, Niles. *Folk Beliefs of the Southern Negro.* Chapel Hill: University of North Carolina Press, 1926. 644 pp. Rpt. as *The Magic and Folk Beliefs of the Southern Negro.* New York: Dover Publications, 1969. 644 pp.

1395.   Snell, John E.   "Hypnosis in the Treatment of the
        'Hexed' Patient."   *American Journal of Psychiatry*
        124 (1967) 311-16.

1396.   Steiner, Roland.   "Observations on the Practice of
        Conjuring in Georgia."   *Journal of American Folklore*
        14 (1901) 173-80.

1397.   Thanet, O.   "Plantation Life in Arkansas."   *Atlantic
        Monthly* 68 (July 1891) 37-38.

1398.   Tiling, David.   "Voodoo, Root Work and Medicine."
        Psychosomatic Medicine 26 (1967) 483-90.

1399.   Whitten, Norman E.   "Contemporary Patterns of Malign
        Occultism among Negroes in North Carolina."   *Journal
        of American Folklore* 75,298 (October-December 1962)
        311-25.

1400.   Wiltse, H.M.   "A Hoodoo Charm."   *Journal of American
        Folklore* 13 (1900) 212.

1401.   Wintrob, Ronald M.   "The Influence of Others: Witch-
        craft and Rootwork as Explanation of Behavior Dis-
        turbances."   *Journal of Nervous and Mental Disease*
        156 (1973) 318-26.

D. MACUMBA

Macumba, the Brazilian cousin of Voodoo and Santeria, has made little impact as yet on the United States. Only one center, described by Interollo, has been located. This situation is likely to change, if for no other reason than the attraction of some non-Brazilians for Macumba (see Gregor). These titles are, however, included here so that the interested student may be able to understand Macumba as differentiated from Voodoo and Santeria.

1402. Bramly, Serge. *Macumba; The Teachings of Maria-Jose, Mother of the Gods*. New York: St. Martin's Press, 1977. 214 pp.

1403. Gregor, Paul. *Magic & Sex = Religion (?)*. London: P. Sebescen, 1980. 200 pp.

1404. Interollo, Lisa. "Long Island's 'Spiritist' Advisers Market Supernatural Cure-Alls." *Sunday Advocate* (Baton Rouge, LA) (October 8, 1978) 4D.

1405. Langguth, A.J. *Macumba*. New York: Harper & Row, 1975. 273 pp.

1406. McGregor, Pedro. *The Moon and Two Mountains*. London: Souvenir Press, 1966. 238 pp.

1407. St. Clair, David. *Drum & Candle*. Garden City, NY: Doubleday & Company, 1971. 255 pp.

E. THE YORUBANS OF SOUTH CAROLINA

In 1973 a group of black people from New York City's Harlem section moved to Beaufort County, South Carolina, and established a settlement modeled on a traditional Nigerian village. King Efuntala presides over the village, which has become a major black religious center in the South. Efuntala first encountered Santeria in Cuba, but then travelled to Nigeria to learn of life and religion first-hand. Religion there differs little from Santeria, but no identification of the Yoruban deities with Christian saints occurs.

Besides the two pamphlets produced by the community (Adefumni and Canet), all of the items are feature newspaper and magazine articles written by reporters who visited the kingdom of Oyo-tungi, as Efuntala and his followers call it.

1408.   Adefumni, Baba Oseijeman. *Ancestors of the Afro-Americans; Vol. I, The Akan*. Long Island City, NY: Aims of Modzawe, 1973. 28 pp.

1409.   Ayres, D. Drummond. "Voodoo Kingdom Home to 35 Harlem Dropouts." *New York Times* (December 21, 1973).

1410.   Brooks, Amanda. "Ikomojade." *Lakeside* 3 (Fall 1977) 3-5, 24.

1411.   Canet, Carlos. *Oyotunji*. Miami, FL: Editorial AIP, n.d. 14 pp.

1412.   Greene, Daniel St. Albin. "Voodoo? Yes, a Few Do." *National Observer* (November 29, 1975) 1, 20.

1413.   "The New Yorubans." *Newsweek* (December 24, 1973) 20.

1414.   Sneed, Michael. "'Only King in U.S.' Contented in His Voodoo Village." *Chicago Tribune* (December 28, 1980) 6.

1415.   Sympson, Ron. "There's Something Strange in Them Thar Hills." *Probe the Unknown* 2,5 (Winter 1974) 27-35.

VII

KAHUNA

After the overthrow of the ancient Hawaiian faith in 1819, the kahuna practices seemed destined to disappear except as a topic of interest to historians and archaeologists. Only slowly were the sacred centers--the heiaus--brought under protection, and only in recent years have huna practitioners become public.

In the early 20th century one man, Max Freedom Long, went to Hawaii and spent many years learning about huna. He returned to California and began to write of his experiences and correlate what he had discovered with Western occult teachings. His work, now institutionalized in the Huna Research Associates, was a major force behind the revival of huna teaching in the 1970s.

This revival has led to the production of a number of studies of huna (Rodman, Gutmanis, Stone, and Westervelt), but more importantly to Hawaiians claiming to teach and practice huna religion. Enid Hoffman leads a huna magic group in Connecticut.

1416. Barrère, Dorothy B. *The Kumuhonua Legends*. Honolulu: Bernice P. Bishop Museum, 1969. 47 pp.

1417. Gutmanis, June. *Kahuna La'au Lapa'au*. Honolulu: Island Heritage Limited, 1979. 144 pp.

1418. Hillinger, Charles. "In Hawaii All Signs Point to Kahuna." *Chicago Sun-Times* (August 5, 1973).

1419. Hiroa, Te Rangi. *Arts and Crafts of Hawaii; X. Religion*. Honolulu: Bernice P. Bishop Museum Special Publication 45, 1964. 585 pp.

1420. Hoffman, Enid. *Huna: A Beginner's Guide*. Gloucester, MA: Para Research, 1976. 118 pp.

1421. Kamakau, Samuel Manaiakalani. *Ka Po'e Kahiko; The People of Old*. Honolulu: Bishop Museum Press, 1964. 165 pp.

1422. ————. *The Works of the People of Old*. Honolulu:
      Bishop Museum Press, 1976. 170 pp.

1423. Long, Max Freedom. *Growing into Light*. Vista, CA:
      Huna Research Publications, 1955. 177 pp.

1424. ————. *The Huna Code in Religions*. Santa Monica,
      CA: DeVorss, 1965. 366 pp.

1425. ————. *Introduction to Huna*. Sedona, AZ: Esoteric
      Publications, 1975. 79 pp.

1426. ————. *The Secret Science at Work*. Vista, CA: Huna
      Research Publications, 1953. 343 pp.

1427. ————. *The Secret Science Behind the Miracles*.
      Vista, CA: Huna Research Publications, 1948. Second
      ed. 1954. 408 pp.

1428. ————. *Self-Suggestion*. Vista, CA: Huna Research
      Publications, 1958. 117 pp.

1429. ————. *Short Talks on Huna*. Cape Girardeau, MO:
      Huna Press, 1978. 107 pp.

1430. McBride, L.R. *The Kahuna: Versatile Mystics of Old
      Hawaii*. Hilo, HI: The Petroglyph Press, n.d.
      68 pp.

1431. Melville, Leinani. *Children of the Rainbow*. Wheaton,
      IL: Theosophical Publishing House, 1969. 183 pp.

1432. Pumara, Hazel J. Diaz. "Hawaiian Kahunas Who Can
      Pray a Man to Death." *Occult* 4,2 (July 1973) 97-106.

1433. Rodman, Julius Scammon. *The Kahuna Sorcerers of
      Hawaii*. Hicksville, NY: Exposition Press, 1979.
      399 pp.

1434. Shen, Yao. "Hawaiian Kahuna Saved My Life." *Fate*
      29,7 (July 1976) 63-68.

1435. Steiger, Brad. *Secrets of Kahuna Magic*. New York:
      Award Books, 1971. 157 pp.

1436. Stone, Margaret. *Supernatural Hawaii*. Honolulu:
      Tongg Publishing Co., 1979. 38 pp.

1437. Westervelt, William D. *Hawaiian Historical Legends.*
Rutland, VT: Charles E. Tuttle Company, 1977.
218 pp.

1438. Wilkerson, Clark. *Cosmic Wisdom; Mental Expansion
Course.* Playa del Rey, CA: Cosmic Wisdom, n.d.
6 vols.

1439. ————. *Hawaiian Magic.* Playa del Rey, CA: Institute
of Cosmic Wisdom, 1968. 242 pp.

VIII
BRUJA

Similar to hoodoo, *bruja* is the folk magic of the Mexican Southwest. It derives its particular spells and practices from the various Indian tribes as well as the Spanish, and thus differs slightly from place to place. Brujas are feared in many places as workers of malevolent magic (see Borino, Galvin & Ludwig, Starr, and Vega) and often are seen in opposition to the healers, the *curanderos*. Simmons and Middleton provide the better sources on bruja and related phenomena. Most of the articles below describe the brief encounter of the author with a single bruja or curandero and are, as such, limited in both information and perspective. Cordova, Dodson, McNeil, and Steagall speak from their expertise as folklorists.

1440. Borino, Bob. "Witches Terrorize Texas." *Midnight/ Globe* (Rouses Point, NY) (February 5, 1980) 44.

1441. Bowke, John G. "Superstitions of the Rio Grande." *Journal of American Folklore* 7,25 (April 1894) 142-46.

1442. Chavez, Tibo J. "Early Witchcraft in New Mexico." *El Palacio* 77 (1970) 7-9.

1443. Cordova, Gabriel. "Black and White Magic on the Texas-Mexican Border." In Mody C. Boatwright, W.M. Hudson, and Allen Maxwell, eds., *Folk Travelers*. Austin: Texas Folklore Society, 1953, pp. 195-99.

1444. Daniels, Mary. "Witchcraft Got Me a Husband." *Fate* 25,10 (October 1972) 40-45.

1445. Dodson, Ruth. "Don Pedrito Jaramillo: The Curandero of Los Olmos." In Wilson M. Miller, ed., *The Healer of Los Olmos and Other Mexican Lore*. Austin: Texas Folklore Society, 1951, pp. 9ff.

1446. Evans, Wick. "Witchcraft 1958." *Fate* 11,12 (December
       1958) 75-78.

1447. Galvin, James A.V., and Arnold M. Ludwig. "A Case of
       Witchcraft." *Journal of Nervous and Mental Disease*
       133 (1961) 161-68.

1448. Holden, William Curry. *Teresita*. Owing Mills, MD:
       Stemmer House, 1978. 232 pp.

1449. Hurt, Wesley R., Jr. "Witchcraft in New Mexico."
       El Palacio 47 (April 1940) 73-83.

1450. Kiev, Ari. *Curanderismo*. New York: Free Press, 1968.
       207 pp.

1451. "Lasting Power of Hex." *Fate* 21,4 (April 1968) 92.

1452. McNeil, Brownie. "Curanderos of South Texas." In
       M.C. Boatwright, W.M. Hudson, and Allen Maxwell, eds.,
       And Horns on the Toads. Dallas, TX: SMU Press, 1959,
       pp. 32-44.

1453. Middleton, John, ed. *Magic, Witchcraft, and Curing*.
       Austin: University of Texas Press, 1967. 346 pp.

1454. Padilla, Floy. "Witch Stories from Tapia Azul and
       Tres Fulgores." *New Mexico Folk Lore Record* 6
       (1951-52) 11-19.

1455. Rosnek, Carl E., ed. "Southwest Witchcraft." Special
       issue of *El Palacio* 80,2 (September 1974). 52 pp.

1456. Simmons, Marc. *Witchcraft in the Southwest*. Flag-
       staff, AZ: Northland Press, 1974. 184 pp.

1457. Starr, Bill. "Mexicans Lynch Another Witch." *Fate*
       21,7 (July 1968) 88-91.

1458. ————. "Red Carpet for a Texas Witch." *Fate* 20,8
       (August 1967) 29-33.

1459. ————. "Witchcraft Pays Off Along the Rio Grande."
       Fate 24,12 (December 1971) 78-84.

1460. Steagall, Archie. "The Voodoo Man of the Brazos." In
       Dobie, Boatwright, and Ransom, eds., *Texas Stomping*

Grounds. Austin: Texas Folklore Society, 1941, pp. 113-14.

1461. Vega, Antonio. "I Fought Off a Witch Attack." *Fate* 30,1 (January 1977) 65-68.

1462. "Witchcraft Found in Southwest." *San Jose Mercury* (December 16, 1963) 24.

1463. Zubryn, Emil. "The Case of the Cackling Housewife." *Fate* 23,2 (February 1970) 40-42.

IX

PERIODICALS

A. AMERICAN PERIODICALS

Because of the dispersion of the magical religious community
into many small, unconnected groups, the periodicals which
circulate within the movement perform a vital function in
tying the individual leaders and groups together. Most of
the periodicals are small newsletters with a circulation in
the hundreds. Most are subsidized by the editor/publisher
and have lasted or will last only for four or five issues;
the energy needed to keep them going is more than amateur
publishers are aware of when they begin.

No attempt has been made to categorize the periodicals
as has been done with the non-periodical material. Though
some fall neatly into specific categories, most are of a
more general thrust and contain material on Paganism, Witchcraft, and the broader issues of magical religion and the
occult. The index on page 231 provides a listing of those
periodicals most associated with a particular emphasis.

With each periodical is given--where known--the name of
any sponsoring group, current address, and the frequency of
issue. *Where no current address is given, the periodical is
defunct*. No attempt was made to include the date of the
first issue, as it was impossible to establish this for most
of the periodicals which circulate on an extremely informal
basis.

Most Pagan periodicals carry little more than brief
announcements and occasional short articles by members of
the sponsoring group. A few, however, have attempted to be
substantive Pagan journals which have regularly carried
articles of general interest on Pagan thought, new ritual
material, and/or columns by major Pagan writers. *Gnostica*
consistently presented the most substantive articles and
was, until its unfortunate demise, the only major commercial
Pagan/magical periodical. Only slightly less influential,

the *Green Egg* became notorious for its letters column, which
would often run for over 20 pages.

The major periodicals historically (i.e., among those now
defunct) are *Azoth, Earth Religion News, The Hidden Path,
Nemeton, Occult Digest,* and *Pagan.* Among current periodicals,
the most important include the several issued by Circle, and
*The Cincinnati Journal of Ceremonial Magick, The Covenant of
the Goddess Newsletter, Crystal Well, Georgian Newsletter,
Korythalia, Newaeon Newsletter, O.T.O. Newsletter, Runestone,
Seventh Ray, Sword of Dyrnwyn, Themis, The White Light,* and
the *Witches' Almanac.*

1. *A.A.D.L. News.* Aquarian Anti-Defamation League, Minnea-
    polis, MN. Issued bi-monthly.

2. *Adytum News Notes.* Builders of the Adytum, Los Angeles,
    CA. Issued quarterly.

3. *Alexandrian Newsletter.* See *Algard Newsletter.*

4. *Algard Newsletter* (formerly *Alexandrian Newsletter*).
    New York, NY. Issued irregularly.

5. *American Norseman.* American Norse Social Organization,
    4213 W. Grace, Chicago, IL 60613. Issued monthly.

6. *Ancient Illuminated Seers of Bavaria.* Ancient Illuminated
    Seers of Bavaria, Box 650, Blacksburg, VA 24060.
    Issued irregularly.

7. *Anthony Egan's Newsletter.* New York, NY. Issued irregu-
    larly.

8. *Aries Quarterly.* Aries Press, Chicago, IL. Issued
    quarterly.

9. *The Arman Journal.* Church of Arman Dawn, Box 1184,
    Costa Mesa, CA 92626. Issued quarterly.

10. *At the Sacred Source of Teutonic Strength.* Runic
    Society, Milwaukee, WI. Issued bi-annually.

11. *At the Sacred Source of Teutonic Strength.* Ludendorff
    Study Group, Box 3235, Wichita, KS 67201. Issued 3
    times per year.

12. *Atlan Annals*. Church of All Worlds, St. Louis, MO. Issued irregularly.

13. *Azoth*. Azoth Publishing Company, Cooperstown, NY. Issued bi-monthly.

14. *The Bard*. Annwn Temple of Gwynfyd, c/o Ralph & Irene Hill, 4332 N. Longview #1, Phoenix, AZ 85014.

15. *The Benton Harbor Rat-Weasel*. L'Imprime de la Journalisme Jaune, 1891 D Union St. #1D, Benton Harbor, MI 49022.

16. *The Black Dwarf*. Lazy Nichels, Los Angeles, CA.

17. *Black Lite*. The Pagan Way, Hollywood, FL. Issued irregularly; superseded by the *Enchanted Cauldron*.

18. *Boreas*. Oak, Ash and Thorn, Box 1182, New Haven, CT 06505. Issued 8 times per year.

19. *Bulletin*. Huna Research Associates, Box 875, Vista, CA.

20. *Castle Rising Newsletter*. Castle Rising, 1730 Wazee Street, Denver, CO 80202. Issued monthly.

21. *Cauldron*. Madrakara, Box 82, Occidental, CA 95465. Issued quarterly.

22. *Cauldron's Link*. Fane of Dawn, Afton, MO.

23. *Changing Times*. Chameleon Club, Box 174, Perry, OH 44081.

24. *Church of All Worlds Membership Newsletter*. Evanston, IL. Only one issue appeared.

25. *Church of Eternal Source Newsletter*. Burbank, CA 91505.

26. *Cincinnati Journal of Ceremonial Magick*. Conquering Child Publishing Co., Box 1343, Cincinnati, OH 45201. Issued annually.

27. *Circle Network News*. Circle, Box 9013, Madison, WI 53715. Issued quarterly.

28. *Circle News*. Circle, Box 9013, Madison, WI 53715. Issued monthly.

29. *The Coming of the Sun*. Stillwater, OK. Only one issue known.

30. *Coven Publications*. Coven Publications, Central City, MO. Only one issue appeared.

31. *Covenant of the Goddess Newsletter*. c/o Alison Harlow, Box 3716, Stanford, CA 94305. Issued 13 times per year at the full moon.

32. *Craft News Brews*. Coven of the Mirror, Des Moines, IA. Issued irregularly.

33. *Cross Quarters*. Temple of Rebirth. W. Milford, CT.

34. *Crossroads*. Athanor Fellowship, Box 464, Allston, MA 02134. Issued quarterly.

35. *Crossroads*. Our Lady of Enchantment, 1087 Lehigh Valley Circle, Danville, CA 94526.

36. *Crystal City Festival*. Earth Star Temple, Chicago, IL. Issued 8 times per year.

37. *Crystal Well*. Labrys Foundation, Box 3145, Seal Beach, CA 90740. Issued quarterly.

38. *Crystal Well*. Philadelphia. Prior to 7,2 known as *Waxing Moon*.

39. *Dagon*. Brooklyn, NY. Issued bi-weekly.

40. *The Diagonal Relationship*. Arthur D. Hlavaty, 250 Goligni Avenue, New Rochelle, NY 10801.

41. *Earth Notes*. Earth Church of Amarqi, 11345 Prospect Drive, Bridgeton, MO 63044. Issued monthly.

42. *Earth Religion News*. Brooklyn, NY. Issued irregularly.

43. *Einherjar*. Runic Society, Milwaukee, WI. Issued 3 times per year.

44. *The Elvenstone*. Oaken Moon Pagan Association, 242 Brent-borough-on-Broadmeade, Sheridan, OR 97378. Issued quarterly.

45. *The Emerald Star*. Society of the Emerald Star, Box 547, East Greenwich, RI 02818. Issued quarterly.

46. *Enchanted Cauldron*. Hollywood Coven, Hollywood, FL. Issued irregularly; supersedes *Black Lite*.

47. *Enchantments*. c/o Our Lady of Enchantment, Box 69, New Bern, NC 28560. Issued quarterly.

48. *EON*. Order of the Lily and the Eagle, Englewood, CO. Issued quarterly.

49. *E.S.P. Laboratory Newsletter*. E.S.P. Laboratory, 7559 Santa Monica Blvd., Los Angeles, CA 90046. Issued monthly.

50. *Florida Aquarian*. N. Miami Beach, FL. Issued monthly.

51. *The Folk*. 14800 E. Fairgrove Ave., Valenda, CA 91744. Issued 8 times per year.

52. *Forever Forests Newsletter*. Church of All Worlds, Forever Forests, Box 212, Redwood, CA 95470.

53. *Georgian Newsletter*. Church of Wicca of Bakersfield, 1908 Verde Street, Bakersfield, CA 93304. Issued monthly.

54. *Gnostic Review*. Giordanisti Press, Chicago, IL. Issued bi-annually.

55. *Gnostica*. Llewellyn Publications, St. Paul, MN. Issued bi-monthly.

56. *Green Egg*. Church of All Worlds, St. Louis, MO. Issued 8 times per year.

57. *The Gryphon*. Church of Eternal Light, 909 Reinli, Austin, TX 78751. Issued bi-monthly.

58. *The Harp*. The Seekers, Dallas, TX.

59. *Harvest*. Box 278, South Farmington, MA 01701. Issued 8 times per year.

60. *The Hidden Path*. Louisville, KY. Issued 8 times per year.

61. *Homebrew*. Box 6, Berkeley, CA 94704. Issued quarterly.

62. *Huna Newsletter*. Kahanahou Hawaiian Foundation, Box 1639, Kealakekua, HI 96750. Issued quarterly.

63. *The Hyperborean Times*. Box 2251, Peachtree City, GA 30269.

64. *In the Continuum*. College of Thelema, Box 2043, Dublin, CA 44566. Issued bi-monthly.

64a. *International Journal of the Tantrik Order*. Tantrik Order in America, New York, NY.

65. *Iris*. Iris Publications, Chicago, IL.

66. *Jerseynet*. Box 130, Ramsey, NJ 07446. Issued irregularly.

67. *Julian Review*. The Delphic Fellowship, Baldwin Park, CA.

68. *Kaaba*. Ra Hoor Khuit Lodge-O.T.O., Box 6018, Teall Avenue Station, Syracuse, NY 13217. Issued bi-annually.

69. *K.A.M. Newsletter*. Keepers of the Ancient Mysteries Lady Ayeisha, Box 922, Columbia, MO 21044. Issued bi-annually.

70. *Khabs*. Hyattsville, MD. Only one issue known.

71. *Korythalia*. Feraferia, Box 41363, Eagle Rock, CA 90041. Issued irregularly.

72. *Labyrinthos*. Rite Ancien et Primitif de Memphis-Misraim, Chicago, IL.

73. *Lakes Nest Monster, Chicago*. Lakes Nest Church of All Worlds, Chicago, IL. Issued irregularly.

74. *Lapwing*. New York, NY.

75. *The Living Unicorn*. Fellowship of the Living Unicorn, Box 48, Calpella, CA 95418. Issued 8 times per year.

76. *Lunar Letter*. Ninefold Muse Ltd., c/o Monica Yohann, 2008 South 31 Street, Milwaukee, WI 53215. Issued monthly.

77. *Magical Unicorn Messenger*. Temple of Wicca, Box 1302, Findlay, OH 45840. Issued 8 times per year.

78. *Mailing List*. Coven of the Mirror, Des Moines, IA. Issued irregularly.

79. *Mandragore*. Grove of the Star and the Snake, Box 3504, Grand Central Station, New York, NY 10017. Issued irregularly.

80. *Mands Best Friend*. Collective of Young Pagans, New York, NY.

81. *Medicine Wheel*. Delphian Coven, Lauder, NY. Issued 8 times per year.

82. *Meta-Earth News, San Francisco*. Chalice of Wisdom Collective, Louise T. Michaelson, San Francisco, CA. Issued monthly; formerly known as *Chalice of Ecstasy*.

83. *Mezla*. Ordo Templi Orientis, Box 177, Niagara Square Station, Buffalo, NY 14201. Issued irregularly.

84. *Moonstone*. Grove of the Unicorn, 34 Don Juan Circle, Chamblee, GA 30341. Issued 8 times per year.

85. *Moontides*. Dallas, TX.

86. *Mythos*. Church of All Worlds, St. Louis, MO. Issued quarterly; only 5 issues appeared.

87. *Nemeton*. Nemeton Fellowship, Oakland, CA. Only 3 issues appeared.

88. *Nemeton Newsletter*. Nemeton Fellowship, Oakland, CA. Issued bi-monthly.

89. *New Broom*. Dallas, TX. Issued quarterly.

90. *New Dimensions*. St. Paul, MN, and Toddington, Gloucestershire, Eng.; Llewellyn Publishing and Helios Book Service. Issued bi-monthly.

91. *New Haven Pagan Community Bulletin*. Box 1882, New Haven, CT 06505. Issued irregularly.

92. *Newaeon Newsletter*. Temple of Thelema, Pittsburgh, PA. Issued bi-monthly.

93. *News from Golgonooza*. Church of the Blake Recital,
     Millsfield, OH. Issued monthly.

94. *Newsletter*. Starwise Society, Cleveland, OH.

95. *Ninth Way*. Michael Hurley, Bloomington, IL. Issued
     irregularly.

96. *Northwind News*. People of Holy Earth, Jamaica Plain,
     MA. Issued quarterly.

97. *Occult Americana*. Painesville, OH. Issued bi-monthly.

98. *Occult Digest*. Chicago, IL. Issued monthly, 1925-1941.

99. *Occult Digest*. Chicago, IL. Issued monthly; Volume I
     (1971) issued as *Occult Observer*.

100. *The Odinist*. Box 1647, Crystal River, FL. Issued 8
     times per year.

101. *Old Gods and New Devils*. Santa Barbara, CA. Issued
     monthly.

102. *The Oracle of Thoth*. Box 281, Bronx, NY 10462. Issued
     quarterly.

103. *The Oriflamme*. Society for the Propagation of Religious
     Truth, 603 Tenth Avenue, 5 RN, New York, NY 10036.
     Issued quarterly.

104. *O.T.O. Newsletter*. Ordo Templi Orientis, P.O. Box 2303,
     Berkeley, CA 94702. Issued quarterly.

105. *The Owl*. Covenant of the Ancient Way, Box 161672,
     Sacramento, CA 95816. Issued bi-monthly.

106. *Owlet*. Pittsburgh, PA. Issued 8 times per year.

107. *Oyez*. Heru-Ra-Ha Lodge-O.T.O., Box 3111, Newport Beach,
     CA 92663. Issued quarterly.

108. *Pagan*. Church of All Worlds, St. Louis, MO. Issued 8
     times per year.

109. *Pagan Circles*. c/o Circle, Box 9013, Madison, WI 53715.
     Issued 8 times per year.

110. *Pagan Paths*. c/o First Fellowship of Neo-Pagans, Box
     12415, San Francisco, CA 94112. Issued irregularly.

111. *Pagan Press*. Berkeley, CA. Only one issue known.

112. *Pagan Renaissance*. Castle Rising, Aurora, CO. Issued
     quarterly.

113. *Pagan Spirit Alliance Newsletter*. c/o Circle, Box 9013,
     Madison, WI 53715. Issued irregularly.

114. *Pagan Tongue*. Temple of the Golden Calf, Berkeley, CA.

115. *Pagana*. Pagan/Witchcraft Sig of Mensa, 4130 Aper
     Drive #5, San Jose, CA 95117. Issued quarterly.

116. *Patterns of Form*. Morgan Delt Cabal of the Paratheo-
     Anametamystikhood of the Eris Esoteric, Irvington,
     NJ. Only one issue known.

117. *Pegasus Express*. 4701 Lyons Road, Box 159, Pompano
     Beach, FL 33067. Issued 8 times per year.

118. *Pentalpha Journal*. Pentalpha, 921 Colorado Avenue,
     Palo Alto, CA 94303. Issued quarterly; formerly
     Druid Chronicler and *Pentalpha Journal & Druid
     Chronicler*.

119. *The Phoenix Rose*. Temple of the Phoenix Rose, 63 E. Col-
     lege Avenue, Yardley, PA 19067. Issued 8 times per
     year.

120. *Pioneer*. 225 E. Utah, Fairfield, CA 94533.

121. *Psychic Eye & WICA Newsletter*. Toledo, OH.

122. *Revival*. Coven of the Mirror, Des Moines, IA. Issued
     8 times per year.

123. *Robin Hood's Barn*. Witchcraft/Occult/Pagan Special
     Interest Group, American Mensa Limited, Ramsey, NY.
     Issued quarterly.

124. *Rose Runes*. Pittsburgh, PA 15221. Issued 8 times per
     year.

125. *Runes*. Box 9513, North Hollywood, CA 91609. Issued 8
     times per year.

126. *Runestone.* Asatru Free Assembly, 3440 Village Avenue, Dennair, CA 95316. Issued quarterly.

127. *Runic Society Bulletin.* Runic Society, Box 2811, Milwaukee, WI. Issued monthly.

128. *St. John's Bread.* Los Altos, CA 94022.

129. *Seax Wica Voys.* School of Seax Wicca, Box 5149, Virginia Beach, VA 23455. Issued quarterly.

130. *The Seven Whistlers.* c/o G.W. Holmes, Box 234, Chula Vista, CA 92011. Issued quarterly.

131. *Seventh Ray.* Church of Hermetic Sciences, Box 3341, Pasadena, CA 91103. Issued quarterly.

132. *The Shadow's Edge.* Box 1172, National City, CA 92050.

133. *Silver Ankh.* Sierra Vista, AZ. Issued 8 times per year.

134. *Still Waters.* Box 9154, Denver, CO 80209. Issued quarterly.

135. *The Summoner.* Milwaukee Temple of the Wiccan Rede, Milwaukee, WI. Issued monthly.

136. *Survival.* Church and School of Wicca, Box 1502, New Bern, NC 28560. Issued irregularly.

137. *Sword of Dyrnwyn.* Church of Y Tylwyth Teg, Box 4152, Athens, GA 30602. Issued 8 times per year.

138. *Tamlacht.* Linden, NJ. Issued 3 times per year.

139. *Temple of the Elder Gods Newsletter.* Temple of the Elder Gods, Sunland, CA. Issued monthly.

140. *Thelema.* Box 267, Denville, NJ 07834.

141. *Themis.* Susan B. Anthony, Coven No. 1, Box 42121, Los Angeles, CA 90042. Issued quarterly.

142. *Thunderbow.* Church of the Seven Arrows, 4381 Hoyt Street, #103, Wheatridge, CO 80033. Issued monthly.

143. *Tiphareth.* Earthstar Association, Chicago, IL.

144. *Touchstone*. Council of American Witches, Minneapolis,
     MN. Issued irregularly.

145. *The Truth*. Natural Science Church, Box 142, Fountain,
     FL 32438.

146. *Tsunami!* Church of the Latter Day Surf, Box 131, Bend,
     AZ 97701. Issued quarterly.

147. *Unicorn*. Box 8814, Minneapolis, MN 55408. Issued 8
     times per year.

148. *Unicorn Gardens*. Unicorn Circle, Box 45061, Dallas,
     TX 75245. Issued irregularly.

149. *The Unicorn Speaks*. Chattanooga, TN. Issued monthly.

150. *Valkrie*. Runic Society, Box 19858, Milwaukee, WI.
     Issued quarterly.

151. *VOR TRU*. 511 W. Panorama Rd., Apt. F86, Tucson, AZ 85704.
     Issued quarterly.

152. *The Voyage of the Dawntreader*. c/o Children of the Dawn,
     1017 Dartmouth, N.E., Albuquerque, NM 87106.

153. *Waxing Moon*. Order of 1734, Sunland, CA.

154. *Which Way? Witch Way*. 1640 N.W. 3 St., Deerfield Beach,
     FL 33441. Issued monthly.

155. *The White Light*. The Light of Truth Church, Box 3125,
     Pasadena, CA 91103. Issued quarterly.

156. *WICA Newsletter*. Witches International Craft Associates,
     New York, NY. Issued irregularly.

157. *Wicca Times*. Miami Pagan Grove, N. Miami, FL. Issued
     quarterly.

158. *The Wise Woman*. Temple of the Goddess Within, Box 19241,
     Sacramento, CA 95819. Issued quarterly.

159. *Witchcraft Digest*. Witches International Craft Asso-
     ciates, New York, NY. Issued annually; only two
     issues appeared.

160. *Witches' Almanac*. Elizabeth Pepper, John Wilcox, New
      York, NY. Issued annually.

161. *Witches Newsletter*. Salem, MA. Issued bi-monthly.

162. *Witches Trine*. New Reformed Orthodox Order of the Golden
      Dawn, Oakland, CA. Issued quarterly.

163. *Witch's Broomstick*. Lawton, OK. Issued semi-annually;
      only 2 issues appeared.

164. *The Wiz*. c/o Interlight Trading Co., 608 Summer St.,
      Kalamazoo, MI 49007.

165. *Women's Coven Newsletter*. Berkeley, CA. Issued irregu-
      larly.

166. *A Word to the Wise*. Mental Science Institute, Minneapo-
      lis, MN. Issued monthly.

167. *X*. Hampton, VA. Issued quarterly.

B. FOREIGN PERIODICALS

Of all the literature produced by British, Australian, and
Canadian Pagans and Witches, periodicals have the most influence in America as they circulate more freely than the books
and pamphlets. Those listed below have found their way into
the hands of American Pagans. As with the American periodicals,
the inclusion of a complete address indicates that the periodical was still being produced at the beginning of 1981.

1. BRITISH PERIODICALS

168. *Agape*. Bath, Avon. Issued irregularly.

169. *Aquarian Arrow*. Pallas-Aquariana, BCM-Opal, London
     WC1V 6XX. Issued quarterly.

170. *Azoth*. Sothis-Weirdglow, 30 Sandringham Road, London
     NW11. Issued irregularly.

171. *Balefire*. Coven of the Rhiannon and Merlin, 28 Claremont
     Road, Sale, Cheshire M33 1EF. Issued 8 times per year.

172. *The Coming Age*. Lux Madriana, 40 St. John Street, Ox-
     ford. Issued quarterly.

173. *The Daath Papers*. Order of the Serpents, 117 Scotia
     Road, Burslem, Stoke-on-Trent, Staffs. ST6 4HH.
     Issued quarterly.

174. *The Hermetic Journal*. 12 Antiqua Street, Edinburgh 1,
     Scotland. Issued quarterly.

175. *IG News*. BM Bulletin, London WC1V 6XX. Issued bi-
     monthly.

176. *Insight*. 118 Windham Road, Bournemouth, Hampshire.
     Issued quarterly.

177. *Isian News*. Fellowship of Isis, Cesara Publications, Huntington Castle, Clonegal, Enniscorth, Eire. Issued quarterly.

178. *The Kabbalist*. The International Order of Kabbalists, 25 Circle Gardens, Merton Park, London SW19 3JX. Issued quarterly.

179. *The Lamp of Thoth*. c/o The Sorcerer's Apprentice, 418 Burley Lodge Road, Leeds LS6 1QP.

180. *Matriarchy Newsletter*. Matriarchy Study Group, c/o Sisterwrite Bookshop, 190 Upper Street, London N1.

181. *Moonstone*. BM Moonstone, London W1N 3XX. Issued quarterly.

182. *New Celtic Review*. Golden Section Order Society, BM Oak Grove, London WC1V 6XX. Issued quarterly.

183. *The New Equinox*. Kaaba Publications, 12A Albert Road, Tamworth, Staffs. Issued quarterly.

184. *Pentagram*. London. Issued irregularly; only 4 issues appeared.

185. *Phoenix*. Concord of Cosmic People, c/o Sri Lokanath, 30 Sandringham Road, Golders Green, London.

186. *The Pipes of P.A.N.* Pagans Against Nukes, 69 Cranbury Road, Reading. Issued quarterly.

187. *Quadriga*. c/o Gareth Knight, "Wisteria," Runcton Lane, Runcton, N. Chichester, Sussex. Issued quarterly.

188. *Quest*. Spook Enterprises, BCM SCL, Quest, London WC1N 3XX. Issued quarterly.

189. *Raven Banner*. Odinist Committee, 10 Trinity Green, London E1. Issued quarterly.

190. *Round Merlin's Table*. Servants of Light, Box 215, St. Helier, Jersey, Channel Islands. Issued quarterly.

191. *Sangreal*. BM Sangreal, London WC1V 6XX. Issued quarterly.

192. *Spectrum*. Purley, Surrey. Issued quarterly.

193. *Waxing Moon*. 103 Mainly Road, Cardiff, Wales.

194. *The Wiccan*. Pagan Front, 90 'M,' 27 Moorlands Road, West Moores, Wimbourne, Dorset BH 220JN. Issued bi-monthly.

195. *Wood and Water*. 38 Exmouth Street, Swinden, Wiltshire SN1 3PU. Issued quarterly.

2. CANADIAN PERIODICALS

196. *Circle of Cerridwen*. 10196 152nd Street, Surrey, British Columbia V3R 6N7.

197. *The Gryphon*. c/o Acorn, Box 4144, Stn. D, Hamilton, Ontario L8V 4L5. Issued quarterly.

198. *Martinist Review*. Martinist Study and Research Group, Toronto, Ontario. Issued quarterly.

199. *Moon Rise*. Coven of the Risen Moon, Scarborough, Ontario.

200. *Sunwheel*. The Odinist Movement, Toronto, Ontario.

3. AUSTRALIAN PERIODICALS

201. *The Magus*. Magus Publications, GPO Box 321, Sydney 2001. Issued quarterly.

202. *The Wiccan*. Box 80, Land Court, N.S.W. 2066. Issued bi-monthly.

APPENDIXES

APPENDIX I (p. 195)

George F. Black, "List of Works in the New York Public
Library Relating to Witchcraft in the United States."
Bulletin of the New York Public Library, XII, no. 11
(November 1908), 658-75.

APPENDIX II (p. 213)

The Curriculum of the A.A.

The Curriculum of the A.A. printed below, as it appeared
in Aleister Crowley's *Magick in Theory and Practice* (item
459), remains in use by most O.T.O. magical lodges. As can
be seen by a quick perusal, it contains works of both Eastern
religion and Western occultism as well as an interesting
selection of popular literature including much occult
fiction.

Section III has been omitted here. It contained the works
of Crowley on magick which were official publications of the
A.A., and most of these items can be found in the volumes of
the *Equinox*, Crowley's book-length periodical.

APPENDIX I

LIST OF WORKS IN THE NEW YORK PUBLIC LIBRARY RELATING TO WITCHCRAFT IN THE UNITED STATES.

Compiled by George F. Black, of the Lenox staff.

This list is confined to printed material in the Library. Though without pretence to completeness as a bibliography, as an aid towards rounding out the record, titles of some 40 works not in the Library have been added at the end. For verification of some of the titles so noted the compiler is indebted to the kindness of Mr. Alfred C. Potter, assistant librarian of Harvard University.

Act (An) against conjuration, witchcraft, and dealing with evil and wicked spirits. [October, 1692.] (In: The Charters and General Laws of the Colony and Province of Massachusetts Bay... *Boston*, 1814. pp. 735–736. 8°.)

Adams (Brooks). The emancipation of Massachusetts. *Boston: Houghton, Mifflin & Co.*, 1887. vi, 382 p. 12°.
" The Witchcraft," pp. 216–236.

Adams (Sherman W.) *See under* **Stiles** (Henry R[eed]).

Alice: a story of Cotton Mather's time. (United States Magazine and Democratic Review. v. 25, pp. 249–256, 338–344. *New York*, 1849. 8°.)

Allen (Rowland H.) The New England tragedies in prose. I. The coming of the Quakers. II. The Witchcraft delusion. *Boston: Nichols & Noyes*, 1869. 156 p. 12°.
" The Witchcraft delusion " occupies pp. 69–156.

—— Salem Witchcraft. (Congregational Quarterly. v. 10, pp. 154–166. *Boston*, 1868. 8°.)
A review of Upham's *Salem Witchcraft*. 2 v. Boston, 1867.

American history told by contemporaries. v. 2. Building of the Republic. 1689–1783. Edited by A. B. Hart. *New York: Macmillan Co.*, 1901. xxi, 653 p. 12°.
Pp. 35–48, Salem Witches. Extracts from Deodat Lawson's *Christ's Fidelity*, London, 1704; " Witches' testimony," by clerk Ezekiel Cheever "; and " Guilt contracted by the Witch Judges (1697) by Chief Justice Samuel Sewall."

Andrews (E. Benjamin). History of the United States. *New York: Charles Scribner's Sons*, 1894. 2 v. 8°.
" The Salem Witchcraft " occupies pp. 92–102 of v. 1.

Ashton (John). The Devil in Britain and America. [*London:*] *Ward & Downey*, 1896. x, 363 p., ill. 8°.
Witchcraft in America, chaps. xxiii–xxiv, pp. 311–339.

Austin (George Lowell). The history of Massachusetts, from the landing of the Pilgrims to the present time... *Boston: B. B. Russell, Estes & Lauriat*, 1876. xviii, 1 l., 578 p., 8 pl. 8°.
" The Witchcraft delusion," chap. 8, pp. 154–174.

Bache (William). Historical sketches of Bristol borough, in the county of Bucks... *Pennsylvania. Bristol, Pa.*, 1853. 60 p. 12°.
Gives the trial, pp. 8–9, of Margaret Mattson, December, 1683, from the original record.

Bailey (Sarah Loring). Historical sketches of Andover... Massachusetts. *Boston: Houghton, Mifflin & Co.*, 1880. xxiv, 626 p., ill. 8°.
Account of Witchcraft trials at Andover, pp. 194–237. Among the authorities consulted are " Essex County Court Papers," Woodward's " Copies of Court Papers," " Suffolk County Court Papers," etc.

Bancroft (George). History of the United States of America, from the discovery of the continent. The author's last revision. *New York: D. Appleton & Co.*, 1890–'91. 6 v. 8°.
Vol 1, p. 568, case of Witchcraft in Pennsylvania; v. 2, pp. 51–66, Witchcraft in Salem.

—— The Salem Witchcraft. (In: Half-hours with American History. Selected and Arranged by Charles Morris. v. 1, pp. 233–243. *Philadelphia*, 1887. 12°.)

Barber (John Warner). The history and antiquities of New England, New Jersey and Pennsylvania... *Hartford: Allyn S. Stillman & Son*, 1856. 3. ed. 624 p., ill. 8°.
Witchcraft in Salem, mainly from Hutchinson, *History of Massachusetts*, on pp. 485–500.

Barry (John Stetson). The history of Massachusetts. The Provincial period. *Boston: Phillips, Sampson & Co.*, 1857. xii, 514 p. 8°.
" The Witchcraft delusion " forms ch. ii, pp. 25–44. A good summary.

Batchelder (H. M.) *See* **Osgood** (Charles S.)

Beard (George M.) The psychology of the Salem Witchcraft excitement of 1692, and its practical application to our own time. *New York: G. P. Putnam's Sons*, 1882. 112 p., 1 diagr. 12°.
An attempt to solve " the psychological problems that were the basis of that delusion."

Beaumont (John). An Historical, Physiological and Theological Treatise of Spirits, Apparitions, Witchcrafts, and other Magical Practices. Containing An Account of the Genii or Familiar Spirits... Likewise the Power of Witches, and the reality of other Magical Operations... *London: Printed for D. Browne, at the Black Swan*, 1705. 8 p.l., 400 p., 1 pl. 8°.
Pages 129–154 contain an account of Witchcraft in New England, based on the writings of Cotton Mather and Calef.

Benjamin (S. G. W.) Witchcraft in Salem and in Europe. (New England Magazine. new ser. v. 9, pp. 412–416. *Boston*, 1894. 4°.)

LIST OF WORKS RELATING TO WITCHCRAFT IN THE UNITED STATES

Bliss (William Root). The Old Colony town and other sketches. *Boston: Houghton, Mifflin & Co.,* 1893. 219 p. 12°.

Old Colony Witch stories, pp. 101-113. Superficial.

Bowditch (Nathaniel Ingersoll). Witchcraft papers, 1692. (Massachusetts Historical Society. Proceedings. 1860-62. v. 5, pp. 31-37. *Boston,* 1862. 8°.)

Gift of a file of original documents relating to witch trials. They probably once belonged to the files of the court of Salem.

Brattle (Thomas). Letter giving a full and candid account of the delusion called Witchcraft, which prevailed in New-England; and of the periodical trials and executions at Salem, in the county of Essex, for that pretended crime, in 1692. (Massachusetts Historical Society. Collections for the year 1798. pp. 61-80. *Boston,* 1798. 8°.)

The letter was communicated to the Society by his descendant, Thomas Brattle of Cambridge. Pages 79-80 contain the humble petition of Rebeccah Fox "to Hon Wm. Stoughton Chief Judge of their Majesties Special Court of Oyer and Terminer holden at Salem" in favor of her daughter Rebeccah Jacobs, accused of Witchcraft.

[Browne (William Hand).] Salem Witchcraft. (Southern Review. new ser. v. 3, pp. 306-332. *Baltimore,* 1868. 8°.)

Review of Upham's *Salem Witchcraft*. 2 v. Boston, 1867.

Bryant (William Cullen), *and* SYDNEY HOWARD GAY. A popular history of the United States, from the first discovery of the Western Hemisphere...to the end of the first century of the union of the States. *New York: Charles Scribner's Sons,* 1876-81. 4 v. 4°.

"The Witchcraft delusion" forms chap. xix, pp. 450-471 of v. 2. 1878.

Buckley (J. M.) Witchcraft. (Century Magazine. v. 43 (new ser. v. 21), pp. 408-422. *New York,* 1892.)

A general account of the belief, with particular reference to Witchcraft in New England.

Butler (Caleb). History of the town of Groton, including Pepperell and Shirley;...with appendices ... *Boston: T. R. Marvin,* 1848. xx, 9-499 p. 8°.

Witchcraft in Groton, pp. 254-257.

Byington (Ezra Hoyt). The Puritan as a colonist and reformer. *Boston: Little, Brown, & Co.,* 1899. xxvi, 1 l., 375 p., 3 ports. 12°.

Witchcraft in New England, pp. 176-178.

Calef (Robert). More | Wonders | of the | Invisible World: | Or, The Wonders of the Invisible World, Display'd in Five Parts. | Part I. An Account of the Sufferings of Margaret Rule, Written by | the Reverend Mr. C. M. | P. II. Several Letters to the Author, &c. and his Reply relating | to Witchcraft. | P. III. The Differences between the Inhabitants of Salem-Village, and | Mr. Parris their Minister, in New England. | P. IV. Letters of a Gentleman uninterested, Endeavouring to prove | the received Opinions about Witchcraft to be Orthodox. With short | Essays to their Answers. | P. V. A short Historical Accout [*sic*] of Matters of Fact in that Affair. | To which is added, A Postscript relating to a Book intitled, The | Life of Sir William Phips. | Collected by Robert Calef, Merchant of Boston in New-England. | *London:* | *Printed for Nath. Hillar, at the Princes-Arms, in*

Leaden-Hall-street, | *over against St. Mary-Ax, and Joseph Collyer, at the Golden-Bible,* | *on London-Bridge,* 1700. 6 l., 156 p., 1 p. errata. Small 4°.

Parts of this work, "A Warning to the Ministers" and "Touching the Supposed Witchcraft in New England," are reprinted in *A Library of American Literature from the earliest settlement to the present time*, v. 2, pp. 167-188 (New York, 1891. 4°).

The copy of the work in the New York Public Library appears to have been a gift from the author to Lord Bellomont. It bears the bookplate of Sir William Grace, Bart. There is also inserted in the volume a holograph letter from the author to Lord Bellomont. It reads as follows:

"Great Sr
I here lay at the foot of your Excellency the book intit. More Wonders of the Invisible World. had it not been too much presumt to afix so honourable a name to so mean a Work in stead of this had been a dedication to your Excelency. I expect it will meet with various reception in general yet under the influence of the best of Reigns and under your Excellncies Governmt. I cannot but promis to my selfe all Loyall ptection and security. your Exc. favourable construction of the whole will abundantly recompence, Great Sr one of the meanest tho. not least afectionat in yo. Goverment.
                                        Robert Calef."

This letter is also given in fac-simile in The *Memorial History of Boston*, edited by Justin Winsor, v. 2, p. 168, and in Fiske's *New France and New England*, Boston, 1904, p 147.

For a notice of this edition, see *North American Review*, v. 3, pp. 317-319, Boston, 1816.

—— More Wonders | of the | Invisible World: | or, | The Wonders of the | Invisible World, | Displayed | in Five Parts. | .... | *Printed in London in the Year 1700.* | *Re-printed in Salem, Massachusetts,* 1796, | *By William Carlton.* | *Sold at Cushing & Carlton's Book-Store, at the Bible* | *and Heart, Essex Street.* 318 p. 12°.

This is the first American edition of this work. The proofs were very carelessly read and the work has many typographical errors. The copy in the New York Public Library has been prepared for republication, as capitals and italics, etc., have been restored to make the volume correspond as nearly as possible to the original edition. The index which follows the preface in the first edition is omitted in this.

—— *Printed in London, A. D., 1700.* *Reprinted in Salem, by John D. and T. C. Cushing, Jr., for Cushing and Appleton,* 1823. xv, [17-] 312 p. 12°.

This edition appears to have been copied from that of 1796, with some slight departures. The publisher has added an article on Giles Corey, pp. 310-312.

—— The wonders of the invisible world displayed. In five parts... A new edition. *Boston: T. Bedlington,* 1828. xvi, [17-]333, 1 pl. 24°.

This edition has also an engraved title-page, which reads "Wonders of the invisible world or Salem Witchcraft. In five parts... Boston: Timothy Bedlington, Washington Street."

Carlier (Auguste). Histoire du peuple Américain... depuis la fondation des colonies anglaises jusqu'à la révolution de 1776. *Paris: Levy Frères,* 1864. 2 v. 8°.

'Sorcellerie, crime capital.—Executions,' v. 1, sect. xix, pp. 293-297.

Carpenter (William H.) The history of Massachusetts, from its earliest settlement to the present time. *Philadelphia: Lippincott, Grambo & Co.,* 1853. 330 p. 16°.

Witchcraft in Salem, pp. 145-149.

Chadwick (John W[hite]). Witches in Salem and elsewhere. (New England Society in the City of Brooklyn. First Annual Report. pp. 63-82. *Brooklyn,* 1885. 8°.)

C[hamberlain] (R[ichard]). Lithobolia: | or, the Stone-Throwing Devil. | Being | An Exact and True Account (by way of Journal) | of the various

LIST OF WORKS RELATING TO WITCHCRAFT IN THE UNITED STATES

Actions of Infernal Spirits, or (Devils Incarnate) | Witches, or both; and the great Disturbance and Amaze- | ment they gave to George Waltons Family, at a place call'd | Great Island in the Province of New-Hantshire in New- | England, chiefly in Throwing about (by an Invisible hand) | Stones, Bricks, and Brick-bats of all Sizes, with several other | things, as Hammers, Mauls, Iron-Crows, Spits, and other | Domestick Utensils, as came into their Hellish Minds, | and this for the space of a Quarter of a Year. | By R. C. Esq.; who was a Sojourner in the same | Family the whole Time, and an Ocular Witness | of these Diabolick Inventions. | The Contents hereof being manifestly known to the Inhabi- | tants of that Province, and Persons of the other Provinces, | and is upon Record in his Majesties Council-Court held | for that Province. | *London*, | *Printed, and are to be sold by E. Whitlook near | Stationers-Hall*, 1698. 4°.

Collation: Title (1) l., Epistle dedicatory "to the much Honoured Mart. Lumley, Esq." (1 l.), poetical address "to the much Honoured R. F., Esq." (1 p.), text 3-16 p.

——— ——— Reprint. (Historical Magazine. v. 5, pp. 321-327. *New York*, 1861. 8°.)

See *Historical Magazine*, v. 6, pp. 159-160, New York, 1862, for information about some of the persons and localities mentioned in the tract. An amusing version of the story related in the tract is to be found in Albee's *History of Newcastle, N. H.*, pp. 43-47. See also Drake, *A Book of New England Legends*, pp. 333-336.

Chancellor (William Estabrook) *and* FLETCHER WILLIS HEWES. The United States : a History of three centuries, 1607-1904... *New York: G. P. Putnam's Sons*, 1904. 2 v. 8°.

Witchcraft in Salem and New York. v. 1, pp. 457-462.

Chandler (Peleg W[hitman]). American criminal trials. *Boston: Charles C. Little and James Brown*, 1841. 2 v. 12°.

Trials for Witchcraft before the special court of Oyer and Terminer, Salem, Massachusetts, 1692, in v. 1, pp. 65-140, 426-434.

——— Communication in regard to the Witchcraft trials. (Massachusetts Historical Society. Collections. v. 20, pp. 395-400. *Boston*, 1884. 8°.)

A further defence of his position that the court for trying the Witches had been illegally instituted.

——— Letter about the Witch trials. (Massachusetts Historical Society. Collections. v. 20, pp. 327-330. *Boston*, 1884. 8°.)

A defense of his position, maintained in his *American Criminal Trials*, that the court for trying the Witches had been illegally instituted by Sir William Phips.

Channing (Edward). A history of the United States. *New York: Macmillan Co.*, 1905-'08. 2 v. 8°.

Witchcraft in United States, in v. 2, pp. 456-462.

Chever (George F.) The prosecution of Ann Pudeator for Witchcraft, A. D. 1692. (Essex Institute. Historical Collections. v. 4, pp. 37-42, 49-54. *Salem*, 1862. 8°.)

——— The prosecution of Philip English and his wife for Witchcraft. (Essex Institute. Historical Collections. v. 2, pp. 21-32, 73-85, 133-144, 185-204, 237-248, 261-272; v. 3, pp. 17-28, 67-79, 111-120. *Salem*, 1860-'61. 8°.)

Coffin (Joshua). A sketch of the history of Newbury, Newburyport, and West Newbury, from 1635 to 1845. *Boston: Samuel G. Drake*, 1845. 416 p. 8°.

Execution of Mary Johnston at Hartford in 1647, p. 48; trial of William Morse, 1679, pp. 122-125; trial of Elizabeth Morse, 1680, with original documents, pp. 126-134. See also pp. 61, 157.

Colden (Cadwallader). [Comments on the Witchcraft delusion in a letter on Smith's History of New York, dated July 5, 1759.] (New York Historical Society. Collections for 1869. pp. 209-210. *New York*, 1870. 8°.)

Complete (A) collection of state trials...from the earliest period to the year 1783... Compiled by T. B. Howell. *London: Longman [& Co.]*, 1816-28. 34 v. 8°.

Account of Witchcraft in New England, from Hutchinson's *History of Massachusetts*, is given in v. 6, pp. 647-682.

Cooke (John Esten). Grace Sherwood, the one Virginia Witch. (Harper's Magazine, v. 69, pp. 99-102. *New York*, 1884. 8°.)

For other titles relating to Grace Sherwood's trial see under J. P. Cushing, Elam, Howe, Ingle, James, and Witchcraft in Virginia.

Cotton Mather on Witchcraft. (Methodist Quarterly Review. 3. ser., v. 1, pp. 430-459. *New York*, 1841. 8°.)

Based on Mather's *Magnalia Christi Americana*.

Currier (Albert H.) Salem Witchcraft. (Congregational Review. v. 9, pp. 201-238. *Boston*, 1869. 8°.)

Review of *Salem Witchcraft* by C. W. Upham. 2 v. Boston, 1867.

Currier (John J.) . History of Newbury, Massachusetts, 1635-1902. *Boston: Damrell & Upham*, 1902. 755 p., ill. 8°.

Gives records of trial of Elizabeth Morse, 1680.

Cushing (Abel). Historical letters on the first charter of Massachusetts government. *Boston: J. N. Bang, Printer*, 1836. (3) 12-204 p. 16°.

Salem Witchcraft in letters 12-25, pp. 83-203.

Cushing ([Jonathan Peter]). Record of Grace Sherwood's trial for Witchcraft in 1705, in Princess Anne County, Virginia. Presented by President Cushing, to the Virginia Historical and Philosophical Society, on the 4th of February, 1833. (Virginia Historical and Philosophical Society. Collections. v. 1, pp. 67-78. *Richmond: T. W. White*, 1833. 8°.)

Davis (H. P.) Expose of Newburyport eccentricities, Witches and Witchcraft. The murdered boy, and the apparition of the Charles-St. Schoolhouse. [1873.] 24 p. 8°.

Chapter ii, Witches and Witchcraft in Newburyport; chapter iii, Modern Witchcraft.

Dean (John Ward). Lithobolia, or the Stone-Throwing Devil. (New England Historical and Genealogical Register. v. 43, pp. 183-185. *Boston*, 1889. 8°.)

On the authorship, etc., of the tract by Richard Chamberlain entitled *Lithobolia; or, the Stone-Throwing Devil* ... London, 1698 (q. v.).

[Deane (Charles).] Spurious reprints of early books. By Delta. *Boston: Privately Printed*, 1865. 12 p. Imp. 8°.

Surreptitious edition reprinted from the *Boston Advertiser*, March 24, 1865. A severe criticism of *Salem Witchcraft* as edited by S. P. Fowler. Seventy-five copies printed, of which 30 are on large paper.

Delta. *See* [**Deane** (Charles).]

Doyle (John A.) The English in America. The Puritan colonies. *London: Longmans, Green & Co.*, 1887. 2 v. 8°.

The Witchcraft delusion is dealt with in v. 2, pp. 130, 384-400.

LIST OF WORKS RELATING TO WITCHCRAFT IN THE UNITED STATES

Drake (Samuel G[ardner]). Annals of Witchcraft in New England, and elsewhere in the United States, from their first settlement. Drawn up from unpublished and other well-authenticated records of the alleged operations of Witches and their instigator, the Devil. *Boston: W. E. Woodward,* 1869. liii, 55–306 p. sm. 4°. (Woodward's Historical Series, No. 8.)

Only 275 copies printed, of which 25 are on large paper.

—— A book of New England legends and folklore in prose and poetry. *Boston: Roberts Brothers,* 1884. xviii, 461 p. sq. 8°.

Contains "Case of Mistress Ann Hibbins," pp. 28–35; "More Wonders of the Invisible World," pp. 60–65; "Calef in Boston," p. 65; "The escape of Philip English," pp. 176–180; "The Witchcraft tragedy," pp. 188–191; "Giles Corey, the Wizard," pp. 194–196; "Old Meg, the Witch," pp. 259–260; "The Stone-Throwing Devil," pp. 333–336.

—— The history and antiquities of Boston... ...from its settlement in 1630, to the year 1770... *Boston: Luther Stevens,* 1856. x, 840 p. 4°.

Witchcraft trials are referred to on pp. 308–310, 322–324, 493–502.

—— A memoir of the Rev. Cotton Mather, D.D., with a genealogy of the family of Mather. *Boston: Antiquarian Bookstore,* 1851. 16 p. 8°.

Reprinted in Mather's *Magnalia Christi Americana,* Hartford, 1855, v. 1, pp. xxix–xliii. Mather's connection with the witchcraft persecutions referred to on pp. 5, 6.

—— Nooks and corners of the New England coast. *New York: Harper & Brothers,* 1875. 459 p., ill. 8°.

Witchcraft, pp. 208–227. Superficial.

Elam (W. C.) Old times in Virginia and a few parallels. (Putnam's Magazine. New ser. v. 4, pp. 207–214. *New York,* 1869. 8°.)

Pages 207–209 deal with trial of Grace Sherwood.

Elliott (Charles W.) The New England history, from the discovery of the Continent...to the period when the Colonies declared their independence, A.D. 1776. *New York: Charles Scribner,* 1857. 2 v. 8°.

"The Salem Witchcraft. Spirits in the Year 1692," v. 2, chap. 3, pp. 41–56.

Ellis (George E[dward]). The Puritan age and rule in the Colony of the Massachusetts Bay, 1629–1685. *Boston: Houghton, Mifflin & Co.,* 1891. 3. ed. xix, 576 p. 8°.

"Note on the 'Salem Witchcraft,'" pp. 556–564.

Endicott (C. M.) Minutes for a genealogy of George Jacobs, Senior, of Salem Village, who suffered the utmost penalty of the law during the Witchcraft tragedy enacted in New England. (Essex Institute. Historical Collections. v. 1, pp. 52–55. *Salem,* 1859. 8°.)

Evans (Frederick W[illiam]). New England Witchcraft and Spiritualism. *Mt. Lebanon, N. Y.,* n. d. 8 p. 24°.

Shaker tract.

Everett (Edward). Orations and speeches on various occasions. *Boston: Little and Brown,* 1850–72. 4 v. 8°.

Witchcraft in New England dealt with in v. 2, pp. 129–133.

Felt (Joseph B.) Annals of Salem. *Salem: W. & S. B. Ives,* 1845–49. 2 v. 12°.

Witchcraft in v. 2, pp. 474–485.

—— The ecclesiastical history of New England ... *Boston: Congregational Library Association,* 1855–62. 2 v. 8°.

See particularly v. 2.

—— History of Ipswich, Essex, and Hamilton. *Cambridge: Charles Folsom,* 1834. xvi, 304 p. 8°.

Witchcraft cases, 1652–1693, on pp. 207–208.

Fiske (John). New France and New England. *Boston: Houghton, Mifflin & Co.,* 1902. xxiii, 1 l., 378 p. 12°.

"Witchcraft in Salem Village," pp. 133–196. An excellent summary of the subject.

—— —— Illustrated with portraits, maps, facsimiles [etc.]. *Boston & New York: Houghton, Mifflin and Co.,* 1904. xxx, 1 l., 338 p. 8°.

Witchcraft in Salem Village, pp. 121–180. Facsimile of verdict and death warrant of Ann Hibbins, May, 1656, on p. 133; portrait of Cotton Mather, p. 136; facsimile of title-page of Cotton Mather's "Memorable Providences," 1689; facsimile of Examination of Tituba, p. 143; Judge Corwin House, Salem (the so-called Witch house), p. 145; facsimile of order to arrest parties charged with Witchcraft, 1692, p. 146; facsimile of letter of Robert Calef, p. 147; facsimile of deposition of Mrs Ann Putnam and her daughter, May 31, 1692, p. 149; facsimile of title of Lawson's "A Brief and True Narrative," 1692, p. 151; the Jacobs house, Salem, p. 153; portrait of William Stoughton, p. 155; the Nourse house, Salem, p. 159; part of Gallow's Hill, Salem, p. 161; facsimile of end of examination of Martha Corey, p. 163; facsimile of title of Hale's "A Modest Enquiry," 1702, p. 167; facsimile of title of Increase Mather's "Cases of Conscience," 1693, p. 171; facsimile of title of Cotton Mather's "The Wonders of the Invisible World," 1693, p. 172; portrait of Samuel Sewall, p. 174.

Fogg (John S. H.) Witchcraft in New Hampshire in 1656. (New England Historical and Genealogical Register. v. 43, pp. 181–183. *Boston,* 1889.)

Account of the trial of Jane Walford at Portsmouth, New Hampshire. She was bound over to the next court, "but the complaint was probably dropped at the next term." Gives the charges against her from the original manuscript.

Foster (David Skaats). Rebecca the Witch and other tales in metre. *New York: G. P. Putnam's Sons,* 1888. iv, 198 p. 12°.

"Rebecca the Witch, in five parts," pp. 1–35. The scene is laid in Salem in 1692.

Fowler (Samuel P.) Account of the life, character, &c., of the Rev. Samuel Parris of Salem Village, and of his connection with the Witchcraft delusion of 1692. (Essex Institute. Proceedings for 1856–60. v. 2, pp. 49–68. *Salem,* 1862. 8°.)

—— —— *Salem: Wm. Ives and Geo. W. Pease,* 1857. 20 p. 8°.

Reprint of the foregoing with t.-p.

—— —— Reprinted in S. G. Drake's The Witchcraft delusion in New England... v. 3, Appendix, pp. 198–222. *Roxbury, Mass.,* 1866. sm. 4°.

—— —— Biographical sketch and diary of Rev. Joseph Green of Salem Village. (Essex Institute. Historical Collections. v. 8, pp. 91–96, 165–168. *Salem,* 1868. 8°.)

Has reference to his connection with the Witchcraft delusion.

—— —— Biographical sketches of Rev. Joseph Green, Rev. Peter Clark, and Rev. Benjamin Wadsworth, D.D., Ministers of Salem Village (now Danvers Centre). (Essex Institute. Historical Collections. v. 1, pp. 56–66. *Salem,* 1859. 8°.)

Gives several petitions to remove attainder and relieve those accused of Witchcraft, 1692.

—— —— Salem Witchcraft. (Historical Magazine. v. 2, pp. 11–12. *New York,* 1858. 8°.

Prints two original depositions of George Herrick as to finding witch marks on the body of George Jacobs.

See also under **Salem** Witchcraft.

LIST OF WORKS RELATING TO WITCHCRAFT IN THE UNITED STATES

Fullerton (Waldo L.) Anne: a tale of Old Salem. (The Outlook. v. 71, pp. 84–90. *New York*, 1902. 8°.)

Fiction. Cotton Mather, Sir William Stoughton, Sir William Phips, and Justice Sewall appear as characters in the story.

Furman (Gabriel). Antiquities of Long Island ...Edited by Frank Moore. *New York: J. W. Bouton*, 1875. 12°.

Pp. 121–124: Cases of Ralph Hall and his wife, 1665; and of the wife of Joshua Garlick, 1657.

Garcia Icazbalceta (Joaquin). Don Fray Juan de Zumárraga primer Obispo y Arzbispo de México. Estudio-biográfico y bibliográfico ... *México: Andrade y Morales*, 1881. 3 l., 371, 270, vii (1) p. 8°.

Pages 12–15 deal with Witchcraft in Massachusetts.

Gay (Sydney Howard). *See* **Bryant** (William Cullen).

Gill (Obadiah). *See* **Some** Few Remarks.

Goddard (Delano A.) The Mathers weighed in the Balances by Delano A. Goddard, M.A., and found not wanting. *Boston: Office of the Daily Advertiser*, 1870. 32 p. Square 16°.

In defense of the Mathers.

Goodell (Abner Cheney). Further notes on the history of Witchcraft in Massachusetts, containing additional evidence of the passage of the Act of 1711, for reversing the attainders of the Witches; also, affirming the legality of the special court of Oyer and Terminer of 1692: a heliotype plate of the Act of 1711, as printed in 1713, and an appendix of documents, etc. *Cambridge: John Wilson and Son*, 1884. 52 p., 1 pl. 8°.

200 copies printed. Reprinted with slight alterations from *Massachusetts Historical Society. Proceedings.* v. 20, pp. 280–326. Reviewed in *The Nation*, v. 38, p. 318 and v. 41, p. 470.

—— Letter from Sir William Phips and other papers relating to Witchcraft, including questions to ministers and their answers. (Massachusetts Historical Society. Proceedings for 1884–85. 2. ser. v. 1, pp. 339–358. *Boston*, 1885. 8°.)

—— Reasons for concluding that the Act of 1711, reversing the attainders of the persons convicted of Witchcraft in Massachusetts in the year 1692, became a law. Being a reply to Supplementary notes, etc., by George H. Moore, LL.D. *Cambridge: John Wilson and Son*, 1884. 21 p. 8°.

200 copies printed. This essay was previously published (without a title) in *Massachusetts Historical Society. Proceedings for 1884–1885.* 2. ser. v. 1, pp. 99–118. Reviewed in *The Nation*, v. 41, p. 470.

—— Witch trials in Massachusetts. (Massachusetts Historical Society. Proceedings. v. 20, pp. 280–326. 1 fac-sim. *Boston*, 1884. 8°.)

Republished as *Further notes on the history of Witchcraft in Massachusetts* ... Cambridge, 1884.

—— The Witch trials in Salem in 1692 further considered. (Massachusetts Historical Society. Proceedings for 1884–85. 2. ser. v. 1, pp. 65–70. *Boston*, 1885. 8°.)

—— Witchcraft considered in its legal and theological aspects. (Salem Press Historical and Genealogical Record, v. 2, pp. 151–167. *Salem*, 1892. 8°.)

[Goodrich (Samuel Griswold).]** Lights and shadows of American history. By the author of

Peter Parley's Tales. *Boston: Thompson, Brown & Co.* [1844] 320 p. ill. 12°.

Salem Witchcraft, pp. 218–236.

Goodwin (W. F.) Salem Witchcraft. From the Massachusetts Archives, cxxxiii, 169. (Historical Magazine. 2. ser. v. 6, pp. 298–299. *Morrisania*, 1869. 8°.)

Gordy (Wilbur F.) Colonial Days: a historical reader. *New York: Charles Scribner's Sons*, 1908. xii [i], 249 p., illus. 12°.

"The Salem Witchcraft." pp. 139–148, with illustration: "The Trial of a Witch," p. 145.

Gould (Elizabeth Porter). The home of Rebecca Nourse. (Essex Antiquarian. v. 4, pp. 135–137. *Salem*, 1900. 8°.)

—— The monument and homestead of Rebecca Nurse. (Bay State Monthly. v. 3, pp. 434–438. *Boston*, 1885. 8°.)

Grahame (James). The history of the United States of North America from the plantation of the British Colonies till their assumption of national independence. *Boston: Little & Brown*, 1845. 4 v. 8°.

Witchcraft in New England, v. 1, pp. 401–414.

—— —— 2. ed. *Philadelphia: Lea & Blanchard*, 1850. 2 v. 8°.

Witchcraft in v. 1, pp. 274–282.

Green (Samuel A.) Groton in Witchcraft times. *Groton*, 1883. 29 p. 8°.

Greene (Evarts Boutell). Provincial America, 1690–1740. *New York: Harper & Brothers*, 1905. xxi, 356 p., maps, port. (The American Nation: a History. v. 6.)

Witchcraft in Massachusetts, pp. 25–29, 332.

Greg (Percy). History of the United States from the foundation of Virginia to the reconstruction of the Union. *London: W. H. Allen & Co.*, 1887. 2 v. 8°.

Vol. 1, pp. 85–88, chap. vii, "The Witchcraft Mania."

Gunn (John A.) Witchcraft in Illinois. (Magazine of American History. v. 14, pp. 458–463. *New York*, 1885. 8°.)

Account of the execution of negro slaves for Witchcraft in 1779. Gives copy from original of sentence of negro slave to be burned alive and his ashes scattered, June, 1779.

H. (J. C.) Witchcraft on Long Island. (Historical Magazine. v. 6, p. 53. *New York*, 1862. 8°.)

Trial of Elizabeth Garlick, May, 1658. See also note in J. H. Trumbull's *The Public Records of the Colony of Connecticut prior to 1665*, Hartford, 1850, p. 573.

Hale (Edward Everett). The story of Massachusetts. *Boston: D. Lothrop Co.* [1871] 8°.

The Salem Witchcraft, pp. 176–180.

Hale (John). A | Modest Enquiry | Into the Nature of | Witchcraft, | and | How Persons Guilty of that Crime may be | Convicted: And the means used for their | Discovery Discussed, both Negatively and | Affirmatively, according to Scripture | and Experience. | By John Haie, | Pastor of the Church of Christ in Beverly, | Anno Domini, 1697. | ... | *Boston: Printed and Sold by Kneeland and Adams, next to | the Treasurer's Office, in Milk-Street.* | M,DCC,LXXI. 158 p. sm. 4°.

Reprint of the first edition, and said to be even more rare than it. The copy in the New York Public Library bears the inscription "Charles Deane Esqr. from his friend, George Livermore, Dana Hill, June, 1853."

LIST OF WORKS RELATING TO WITCHCRAFT IN THE UNITED STATES

Hanson (J. W.) History of the town of Danvers, from its early settlement to the year 1848. *Danvers*, 1848. 304 p. 12°.
" Salem Witchcraft," pp. 271-294.

Harris (William S.) Robert Calef, " Merchant, of Boston, in New England." (The Granite Monthly. v. 39, pp. 157-163. illus. *Concord, N. H.*, 1907. 8°.)

Hawks (Francis L[ister]). History of North Carolina. *Fayetteville, N. C.: E. J. Hale & Son*, 1857-58. 2 v. 8°.
Case of Susannah Evans in the county of Albemarle, in 1697.

Hewes (Fletcher Willis). *See* **Chancellor** (W. E.)

Hildreth (Richard). The history of the United States of America, from the discovery of the continent to the organization of government under the Federal Constitution. *New York: Harper & Brothers*, 1849. 3 v. 8°.
Salem Witchraft discussed in v. 2, pp. 145-167.

Hill (Hamilton Andrews). History of the Old South Church (Third Church), Boston, 1669-1884. *Boston: Houghton, Mifflin & Co.*, 1890. 2 v. 8°.
Witchcraft in New England, v. 1, pp. 284-293.

[Hinman (Royal Ralph).] The Blue Laws of New Haven Colony, usually called Blue Laws of Connecticut... Compiled by an Antiquarian. *Hartford: Case, Tiffany & Co.*, 1838. x, 1 l., (13-)336 p. 12°.
Witchcraft, pp. 296-336. "The only cases of trials for Witchcraft upon the Records of the Colony of Connecticut" are given on pp. 296-299. The remaining pages are devoted to Witchcraft in New England generally.

Hoadly (Charles J[eremiah]). A case of Witchcraft in Hartford. (The Connecticut Magazine. v. 5, pp. 557-561. *Hartford*, 1899. 8°.)
Case of Rebecca Greensmith and her husband in 1662.

—— Records of the Colony or Jurisdiction of New Haven, from May, 1653, to the Union... *Hartford: Printed by Case, Lockwood & Co.*, 1858. 8°.
Witchcraft in the Colony of New Haven, pp. 29-36, 77-89, 151-152, 224-226.

Holland (Josiah Gilbert). History of Western Massachusetts... *Springfield: Samuel Bowles & Co.*, 1855. 2 v. 8°.
Witchcraft in Hadley, v. 1, pp. 142-145.

Hopkins (   ). The Witchcraft in the American Colonies. (The Historical Magazine. v. 4, pp. 111-112. *New York*, 1860. 8°.)
Abstract only. Read before the New York Historical Society, March 6, 1860.

Howe (Henry). Historical collections of Virginia...relating to its history and antiquities... *Charleston, S. C.: Babcock & Co.*, 1845. 544 p. 8°.
Reprints Cushing's article on trial of Grace Sherwood, pp. 436-438.

Hubbard (William). A general history of New England from the discovery to MDCLXXX. *Cambridge: Hilliard & Metcalf*, 1815. 7 l., 676 p. 8°.
Account of trial and execution of Margaret Jones, of Charlestown, June, 1648. Hubbard's account is reproduced in the *North American Review*, v. 2, pp. 229-230, Boston, 1816.

Hurd (Hamilton). History of Essex county, Massachusetts... *Philadelphia: J. W. Lewis & Co.*, 1888. 2 v. 4°.
The pagination is continuous. Witchcraft at Salem,

pp. 165e-165h; trial of Mrs. Howe, at Ipswich, 1692, pp. 629-30; Witchcraft at Beverly, 1692, pp. 690-92; trial of John Willard of Middleton, 1692, pp. 931-32; trial of Rebecca Eames at Boxford, 1692, p. 958; Witchcraft in Peabody, pp. 995-98; trial of Wilmot Read, 1692, p. 1067; case of John Procter of Chebacco, 1692, pp. 1186-87; Andover in the Witchcraft delusion, 1692, pp. 1562-64; Witchcraft in North Andover, pp. 1685-87; Witchcraft at Haverhill, 1692, pp. 1965-96.

Hutchinson (Francis). An Historical Essay concerning Witchcraft. With Observations upon Matters of Fact; tending to clear the Texts of the Sacred Scriptures, and confute the vulgar Errors about that Point... *London: Printed for R. Knaplock, at the Bishop's Head, and D. Midwinter, at the Three Crowns in St. Paul's Church-yard*, 1718. xv, 2 l., 270 p. 8°.
Pages 72-94: "The Witchcrafts at Salem, Boston, and Andover in New-England."

—— —— 2. ed. *London: Printed for R. Knaplock, etc.*, 1720. (26), 336 p. 8°.
"The Witchcrafts at Salem," etc., pp. 95-122.

Hutchinson (Thomas), *Governor of Massachusetts*. The history of the Province of Massachusetts Bay, from the charter of King William and Queen Mary, in 1691, until the year 1750. *Boston: Thomas & John Fleet*, 1767. 2 v. 8°.
An account of New England Witchcrafts, with original documents, is printed in v. 2, pp. 15-62.

—— The Witchcraft delusion of 1692. From an unpublished manuscript (an early draft of his History of Massachusetts) in the Massachusetts archives. Communicated with notes by William Frederick Poole. (New England Historical and Genealogical Register. v. 24, pp. 380-414. *Boston*, 1870. 8°.)
This account is fuller than the one printed in his *History of Massachusetts Bay.*

—— (Separate Issue.) *Boston: Privately printed*, 1870. 43 p. sq. 8°.

Icazbalceta (Joaquin Garcia). *See* **Garcia Icazbalceta** (Joaquin).

Ingle (Edward). A Virginia Witch. (Magazine of American History. v. 10, pp. 425-427. *New York*, 1883. 8°.
An account of the trial of Grace Sherwood. She was tried by ducking and sent back to jail. Apparently there is no record of the end of this trial.

Ingram (M. V.) An authenticated history of the famous Bell Witch... The story of Betsy Bell, her lover and the haunting sphinx. *Clarksville, Tenn.: W. P. Titus* [cop. 1894]. 316 p., 12 pl., 3 port. 16°.

James (Edward W.) Grace Sherwood the Virginia Witch. (William and Mary College Quarterly. Historical Magazine. v. 3, pp. 96-101, 190-192, 242-245; v. 4, pp. 18-22. *Williamsburg, Richmond*, 1895-'96. 8°.)
The full records of the trial are given here. Reprinted in *The Lower Norfolk County Virginia Antiquary*, v. 2, pp. 88-94, 139-141; v. 3, pp. 34-38, 52-57. Baltimore, 1899, 1901.

[Johnson (Edward).] A History of New-England. From the English planting in the Yeere 1628 untill the Yeere 1652. Declaring the form of their Government, Civill, Military, and Ecclesiastique... *London: Printed for Nath: Brooke at the Angel in Corn-hill*, 1654. 236 p., 2 l. 4°.
In his account of the planting of the church at Springfield, under the year 1645, the author says: " There hath of late been more then one or two in this Town greatly suspected of witchcraft," and that they had "bewitched not a few persons." p. 199.

LIST OF WORKS RELATING TO WITCHCRAFT IN THE UNITED STATES

Judd (Sylvester). History of Hadley, including the early history of Hatfield, South Hadley, Amherst and Granby, Massachusetts... *Northampton: Printed by Metcalf & Co.*, 1863. 636 p. 8°.
Local Witchcraft cases are dealt with in chap. 21, pp. 232-241.

Kimball (Henrietta D.) Witchcraft illustrated. Witchcraft to be understood. Facts, theories and incidents. With a glance at Old and New Salem and its historical resources. *Boston: G. A. Kimball*, 1892. 135 p. 12°.
Popular and worthless. Has several illustrations among which are: (1) Tituba teaching the first act of Witchcraft; (2) Giles Corey's punishment and awful death; (3) Rebecca Nurse house, Danvers, Mass.; (4) the house where Witchcraft started, now Danvers, Mass.; (5) Court trial of Witches.

Kimball (James). Papers relating to the Witchcraft trials in Essex county. (Essex Institute. Historical Collections. v. 8, pp. 17-21. *Salem*, 1868. 8.)
The papers are: Petition of Philip English for remuneration, and petition of George Herrick for relief.

Kingsley (John S[terling]). Salem Witchcraft. (Nebraska State Historical Society. Transactions and Reports. v. 3, pp. 44-58. *Fremont, Nebraska*, 1892. 8°.)
A general survey of the subject.

Kittredge (George Lyman). Notes on Witchcraft. (American Antiquarian Society. Proceedings. v. 18, pp. 148-212. *Worcester, Mass.*, 1907. 8°.)
Has particular reference to the delusion in New England. See *The Evening Post*, New York, Sept. 20, 1907.

—— *Worcester: The Davis Press*, 1907. 67 p. 8°.
Separate issue of the above.

Lawson (Deodat). Christ's Fidelity | the only | Shield | Against | Satan's Malignity. | Asserted in a | Sermon | Deliver'd at Salem-Village the | 24th of March, 1692. Being Lecture- | day there, and a time of Publick | Examination, of some Suspected | for Witchcraft. | By Deodat Lawson, Minister | of the Gospel. | The Second Edition. | ... | Printed at Boston in New England, and Reprinted | in London, by R. Tookey, for the Author ...1704. (12) 120 p. 12°.
The appendix to this work, on Witchcraft in Salem, is reprinted in *A Library of American Literature from the earliest settlement to the present time*, v. 2, pp. 106-114 (New York, 1891. 4°).

—— A True Narrative of some | Remarkable Passages relating to sundry Persons | afflicted by Witchcraft at Salem Village in New- | England, which happened from the 19th. of | March to the 5th. of April, 1692. (In: INCREASE MATHER, A Further Account of the Tryals of the New-England Witches... London, 1693. pp. 1-9.)
A reprint of his *A Brief and True Narrative...* Boston, 1692.

Levermore (Charles H[erbert]). Witchcraft in Connecticut. 1647-1697. (New Englander and Yale Review. v. 44, pp. 788-816. *New Haven*, 1885. 8°.)
Excellent account of the delusion in Connecticut. Enumerates a total of 8, possibly 9, executions, of 3 more verdicts of "guilty" that were afterwards set aside, and of either 21 or 22 indictments altogether.

—— Witchcraft in Connecticut. (New England Magazine. new ser. v. 6, pp. 636-644. *Boston*, 1892. 8°.)
A condensation of the preceding essay.

Lewis (Alonzo), *and* JAMES R. NEWHALL. History of Lynn, Essex County, Massachusetts... *Boston: John L. Shorey*, 1865. 620 p. 8°.
Witchcraft in Lynn, pp. 293-296.

Longfellow (Henry Wadsworth). New England tragedies. Giles Corey of the Salem Farms. (Poetical Works. Riverside edition. *Boston*, 1889. v. 5, pp. 373-436. 8°.)
A dramatic rendering of Giles Corey's trial.

Lord (C. C.). Two Witches. (The Granite Monthly. v. 11 (v. 1, new series), pp. 32-34. *Concord, N. H.*, 1888. 8°.)
Witchcraft in the town of Hopkinton, New Hampshire. Of little importance.

Lowell (James Russell). Witchcraft. (North American Review. v. 106, pp. 176-232. *Boston*, 1868. 8°.)
Based on the works of Upham, Wier, Scot, de Thou, Glanvil, Webster, Mather, Sinclair, etc.

—— Among my books. *Boston: Fields, Osgood, & Co.*, 1870. 12°.
Witchcraft on pp. 81-150. Reprint of preceding article.

Martineau (Harriet). On Witchcraft. (Miscellanies. v. 2, pp. 389-402. *Boston: Hilliard, Gray, and Company*, 1836. 12°.)
Based on Upham's *Lectures*. Boston, 1831.

Marvin (Abijah P.). The life and times of Cotton Mather, D.D., F.R.S.; or, a Boston Minister of two centuries ago, 1663-1728. *Boston: Congregational Sunday School and Publishing Co.* [1892] v, 582 p., 2 ports., 1 pl. 8°.
Witchcraft on pp. 112-141, 256-266.

Mary, *Queen of William III.* Letter from Queen Mary to Sir William Phips respecting the trials for witchcraft. (Essex Institute. Historical Collections. 2 ser. v. 9, pt. 2, pp. 89-90. *Salem*, 1868. 8°.)

Mason (Edward G.) Illinois in the eighteenth century. Kaskaskia and its parish records; old Fort Chartres; and Col. John Todd's Record Book. *Chicago: Fergus Printing Co.*, 1881. 68 p. 12°.
Fergus Historical Series, no. 12. Todd's Record Book, which contains the account of witchcraft in Illinois, occupies pp. 49-68. See note under **Gunn** (John A.).

—— The Record book of Col. Todd. (Magazine of American History. v. 8, pp. 586-597. *New York*, 1882. 8°.)
Witchcraft on pp. 591-592.

Massachusetts--*General Court.* Records of the Governor and company of the Massachusetts Bay in New England. Edited by Nathaniel B. Shurtleff. *Boston: William White*, 1853-54. 5 v. in 6. f°.
Vol. 2, p. 242 (May 10, 1648), order by the court for discovery of witches.
Vol. 3, p. 126 (May 13, 1648), order by the court for discovery of witches and for watching of witch already in custody.
Vol. 3, p. 229 (May 22, 1651), bill of indictment found against "Mary Parsons of Springfield."
Vol. 3, p. 273, and vol. 4, pt. 1, p. 96 (May 27, 1652), Hugh Parsons found "not legally guilty of witchcraft, & so not to dy by or law."
Vol. 4, pt. 1, pp. 47-48 (May 23, 1651), case of Mary Parsons. The "evidences were not sufficient to proove hir a witch, and therfore she was cleered in that respect."
Vol. 4, pt. 1, p. 73 (Oct. 28, 1651), court to be convened at Boston for trial of those in prison accused of witchcraft.
Vol. 4, pt. 1, p. 269 (May 14, 1656), case of Mrs. Ann Hibbins. Found guilty and sentenced "to hang till she was dead."

LIST OF WORKS RELATING TO WITCHCRAFT IN THE UNITED STATES

Mather (Cotton). Autograph letter of Cotton Mather on Witchcraft. (Literary and Historical Society of Quebec. Transactions. v. 2, pp. 313–316. *Quebec,* 1831. 8°.)

The letter is addressed "For the Honourable John Foster, Esq." It was presented to the Literary and Historical Society by the Hon. Chief Justice Sewall.

—— Late | Memorable Providences | Relating to | Witchcrafts and Possessions, | Clearly Manifesting, | Not only that there are Witches, but | that Good Men (as well as others) | may possibly have their Lives shortned | by such evil Instruments of Satan. | Written by Cotton Mather Minister of the | Gospel at Boston in New-England. | The Second Impression. | Recommended by the Reverend Mr. Richard | Baxter in London, and by the Ministers of | Boston and Charlestown in New-England. | *London,* | *Printed for Tho. Parkhurst at the Bible and | Three Crowns in Cheapside near Mercers·| Chapel.* 1691. (22) 144 p. 12°.

This is the second issue of his *Memorable Providences*... Boston, 1689.

—— Magnalia Christi Americana: | Or, the | Ecclesiastical History | of | New England, | from | Its First Planting in the Year 1620, unto the Year | of our Lord, 1698. | In Seven Books | ... | By the Reverend and Learned Cotton Mather, M.A. | and Pastor· of the North Church in Boston, New England. | *London: Printed for Thomas Parkhurst, at the Bible and Three Crowns in Cheapside,* MDCCII. pp. (30), 38; (2), 75; (2), 238; (2), 125–222; 100; (2), 88; 118; errata (2). f°.

Case of Elizabeth Knap, Anne Cole, etc., Book 6, chap. 7.

—— First American edition, from the London edition of 1702. *Hartford: Silas Andrus,* 1820. 2 v. 8°.

Witchcraft in New England, v. 2, bk. 6, chap. 7, pp. 388–416.

—— With an introduction and occasional notes, by Thomas Robbins, and translations of the Hebrew, Greek, and Latin quotations by Lucius F. Robinson. *Hartford: Silas Andrus & Son,* 1853. 2 v. 8°.

—— With an introduction and occasional notes by Thomas Robbins, and translations of the Hebrew, Greek, and Latin quotations by Lucius F. Robinson. To which is added a memoir of Cotton Mather, by Samuel G. Drake... Also a comprehensive index, by another hand. *Hartford: Silas Andrus and Son,* 1855. 2 v. 8°.

Text is same in pagination, etc., as in 1853 ed. The errors in former editions are stated to have been carefully corrected according to an extensive errata prepared by Dr. Mather himself.

—— Pietas in Patriam: | The | Life | of His | Excellency | Sir William Phips, Knt., | Late Captain General, and Governour | in Chief of the Province of the Massachu·| set-Bay, | New England. | Containing the Memorable Changes Under·| gone, and Actions performed by Him | . | ... | *London: Printed by Sam. Bridge in Austin Friers, for Nath. Hiller at the Princes·Arms in Leaden-Hall Street, over·against St. Mary-Ax.* 1697. sm. 8°.

Collation: P. (1) Commendation; pp. (1–4) The Epistle Dedicatory, To his Excellency the Earl of Bellomont. April 27, 1697. Nath. Mather; pp. (1–4) The Contents of the Sections; pp. 1–100 The Life; pp. 1–6 Lines upon his Death; pp (1–2) Books printed for Nathaniel Hiller.

The work was published anonymously. Calef says: "Tho it bears not the Author's name, yet the Stile, manner and matter is such, that were there no other demonstration or token to know him by, it were no Witchcraft to determine that the said Mr. C[otton] M[ather] is the author of it"; and he sarcastically adds that the author assumed the guise of anonymity in order "that he might with the better grace extol the Actions of Mr. *Mather,* as Agent in *England,* or as President of *Harvard* College, not forgetting his own."—*More Wonders,* London, 1700. p. 145.

A second edition appears to have been printed in 1699. It was also reprinted in Mather's *Magnalia,* bk. ii.

—— The Wonders of the Invisible World. | Observations | as well Historical as Theological, upon the Nature, the | Number, and the Operations of the | Devils. | Accompany'd with, | I. Some Accounts of the Grievous Molestations, by Dæ·| mons and Witchcrafts, which have lately | annoy'd the Countrey; and the Trials of some eminent | Malefactors Executed upon occasion thereof: with several | Remarkable Curiosities therein occurring. | II. Some Councils, Directing a due Improvement of the ter·| rible things, lately done, by the Unusual & Amazing | Range of Evil Spirits, in Our Neighbourhood: & | the methods to prevent the Wrongs which those Evil | Angels may intend against all sorts of people among us; | especially in Accusations of the Innocent. | III. Some Conjectures upon the great Events, likely | to befall, the World in General, and New-En·| gland in Particular; as also upon the Advances of | the Time, when we shall see Better Dayes. | IV. A short Narrative of a late Outrage Committed by a | knot of Witches in Swedeland, very much Resem·| bling, and so far Explaining, That under which our parts | of America have laboured. | V. The Devil Discovered : in a Brief Discourse upon | those Temptations, which are the more Ordinary Devices | of the Wicked One. | By Cotton Mather. *Boston: Printed by Benj. Harris for Sam. Phillips,* 1693.

Collation: Title; "The Authors Defence," (3) pp.; Stoughton's Letter, (2) pp ; "Enchantments Encountred," (25) pp.; Text, 1–151 pp.; Errata, (1) p.; "The Devil Discovered," (24) pp.

This is the second separate publication relating to Salem Witchcraft, and though dated 1693 on the title-page, was, according to the late Justin Winsor, finished in the October preceding. It was no doubt printed and published before the end of the year. On the verso of the title is the order to print: "Published by the Special Command of His Excellency, the Governour of the Province of the Massachusetts-Bay in New-England."

A part of the book had been delivered in a Sermon on August 4, 1692. Following the "Discourse Proper" are transcripts of the Proceedings at the Trials of Witches executed at Salem.

1. "The Tryal of G[eorge] B[urroughs]." pp. 94–104.
2. "The Tryal of Bridget Bishop." June 2, 1692. pp. 104–114.
3. "The Tryal of Susanna Martin." June 29, 1692. pp. 114–126.
4. "The Trial of Elizabeth How." June 30, 1692. pp. 126–132.
5. "The Trial of Martha Carrier." August 2, 1692. pp. 132–138.

The pagination of "The Devil Discovered" runs 1–8, 17–32. Page 89 of the text is misnumbered 79. The copy in the New York Public Library has the last leaf in facsimile.

Portions of this work; "Of Beelzebub and his Plot," "The Trial of George Burroughs," "How Martha Carrier was tried," "The Invisibilizing of Witches," are reprinted in *A Library of American Literature,* ... v. 2, pp. 114–129 (New York, 1891. 4°).

—— The Wonders of the Invisible World: | Being an Account of the | Tryals of Several Witches, | Lately Executed in | New England: | And of several remarkable Curiosities therein Occurring. | Together with, | I. Observations upon the Nature, the Number, and the Operations of the Devils. | II. A short Narrative of a late out-

LIST OF WORKS RELATING TO WITCHCRAFT IN THE UNITED STATES

rage committed by a knot of Witches in | Swede-Land, very much resembling, and so far explaining, that under which | New-England has laboured. | III. Some Councels directing a due Improvement of the Terrible things lately | done by the unusual and amazing Range of Evil-Spirits in New-England. | IV. A brief Discourse upon those Temptations which are the more ordinary Devi- | ces of Satan. | By Cotton Mather. | Published by the Special Command of his Excellency the Governor of | The Province of the Massachusetts-Bay in New-England. | *Printed first, at Bostun in New England; and Reprinted at Lon- | don, for John Dunton, at the Raven in the Poultry.* 1693. 4°.

The first and only complete London edition, published in December, 1692, although dated 1693 on title. The last page is numbered 98, but the pagination is very irregular, the number of pages being in fact 110, including the preliminary leaves not numbered and the leaf preceding the title, with one leaf of book advertisements additional. The pagination runs as follows: (4 l.), pp. 5-16, [1]-16, 33-80, 41-56, 89-98. In one copy of this edition in the New York Public Library the pagination runs: (4 l.), pp. 5-16, [1]-11, 10-11, 14-16, 33-80, 41-56, 89-98. This English edition, instead of having been printed from an independent manuscript, was printed from a copy of the Boston Edition. The publisher, Dunton, wishing evidently to put the book upon the market as early as possible after he received the "copy," broke the book into several parts and distributed them among three printers. Taking the Boston edition as a basis, it seems evident from the page endings that one section included the preliminary pages and pages 1-32 of text. This when set in the English edition made the preliminary pages and pages 1-16 of text. The second section, taken in hand by another printer, included pages 33-68 of the Boston book. The printer began his numbering with 33 and carried it on to 48. The third section included pages 69-102, or in the English edition pages 49-64. The fourth section included pages 103-134, or in the English edition pages 65-80. The fifth section was the balance of the book. It is probable that the first, third and fifth sections were done by the same printer. The most notable differences in types are those of the head-lines. Of the seven errors pointed out in the list of Errata in the Boston book, five are repeated in the London edition. The other two were so obviously misprints that they seem to have been corrected by the printer himself. The leaf preceding the title has the half-title: "The | Tryals | of | Several Witches, | Lately Executed in | New-England: | Published by the Special Command of the Governor." | And on the verso, is the "Imprimatur. Decemb. 23. 1692. Edmund Bohun."

—— The Wonders of the Invisible World: | Being an Account of the | Tryals | of | Several Witches | Lately Executed in | New-England: | And of several Remarkable Curiosities | therein Occurring. | By Cotton Mather. | Published by the Special Command of his Excellency the | Governour of the Province of the Massachusetts Bay in New- | England. | The Second Edition. | *Printed first, at Boston in New-England, and reprinted at London, for | John Dunton, at the Raven in the Poultrey.* 1693. 4°.

The last page is numbered 62, but the pagination, like that of the first London edition, is very irregular, the number of pages being 64. The pagination runs: 9-24, 43-50, 41-46 [bis], 47-56, 47-62.

This edition omits much matter found in the first edition.

—— The Third Edition. *Printed first at Boston in New England, and reprinted at London, for John Duncon, at the Raven in the Poultrey,* 1693. 64 p. 4°.

"Duncon" is a misprint for "Dunton."

—— To which is added A Farther Account of the Tryals of the New-England Witches. By Increase Mather. *London: John Russell Smith,* 1862. xvi, 291 p., 1 port. 12°.

Mather (Increase). Cases of Conscience | Concerning evil | Spirits | Personating Men, | Witchcrafts, infallible Proofs of | Guilt in such as are accused | with that Crime. | All Considered according to the Scriptures, History, Experience, and the judgment | of Many Learned men. | By Increase Mather, President of Harvard Colledge at Cambridge, and Teacher of | a Church at Boston in New England. | ... *Boston: Printed and Sold by Benjamin | Harris at the London Coffee-House,* 1693. Title (4), 67, (7) p. 12°.

—— —— *Printed at Boston, and Re-printed at London, for John Dunton, at the Raven in the Poultrey.* 1693. (In: INCREASE MATHER, A Further Account of the Tryals of the New-England Witches... *London,* 1693.)

—— —— (In: COTTON MATHER. The Wonders of the Invisible World... *London,* 1862. pp. 219-291.)

Parts of this work, "Of the Workings of Satan" and "Of the Discovery of Witches" are reprinted in *A Library of American Literature* ..., v. 2, pp. 90-106 (New York, 1891. 4°).

—— An | Essay | for the | Recording | of | Illustrious Providences: | Wherein, | An Account is given of many Re- | markable and very Memorable Events, | which have happened in this last Age; | Especially in | New-England. | By Increase Mather, | Teacher of a Church at Boston in New- | England. | ... | *Printed at Boston in New-England, and are to | be sold by George Calvert at the Sign of the | Half-moon in Pauls Church-yard, London,* 1684.

Collation: Title; "The Preface," (19) pp.; "Remarkable Providences," 1-372 pp.; "The Contents," (8) pp., and 1 leaf of Advertisement.

A collection of remarkable sea deliverances, accidents, remarkable phenomena, Witchcrafts, apparitions, connected with the inhabitants of New England.

Sections of the above work, "Concerning Remarkable Judgments," "The Dæmon at William Morse his house," "That there be Dæmons and possessed Persons," are reprinted in *A Library of American Literature* ..., v. 2, pp. 76-90 (New York, 1891. 4°).

—— A Further | Account | of the | Tryals | of the | New-England Witches. | With the | Observations | Of a Person who was upon the Place several | Days when the suspected Witches were | first taken into Examination. | To which is added, | Cases of Conscience | Concerning Witchcrafts and Evil Spirits Per- | sonating Men. | Written at the Request of the Ministers of New-England. | By Increase Mather, President of Harvard Colledge. | Licensed and Entred according to Order. | *London: Printed for J. Dunton, at the Raven in the Poultrey,* 1693. 10, (4) 39, (5) p. and 2 l. book advt. 4°.

In a postscript Increase Mather says of the *Wonders of the Invisible World:* "Some I hear have taken up a Notion, that the Book newly published by my Son, is contradictory to this of mine. 'Tis strange that such Imaginations should enter into the Minds of Men: I perused and approved of that Book before it was printed; and nothing but my Relation to him hindered me from recommending it to the World."

—— —— (In: COTTON MATHER. The Wonders of the Invisible World... *London,* 1862. pp. 199-217.)

—— —— Remarkable Providences illustrative of the earlier days of American colonisation. With introductory preface by George Offor. *London: John Russell Smith,* 1856. xix, (18) 262 p., 1 port. 12°.

This is a modern issue of *An Essay for the Recording of Illustrious Providences* ... Boston, 1684.

Mather (The) Papers. (Massachusetts Historical Society. Collections. 4. ser., v. 8. xvi, 736 p. *Boston,* 1868 8°.)

Many references to Salem Witchcraft occur in these papers, for which see the index.

LIST OF WORKS RELATING TO WITCHCRAFT IN THE UNITED STATES

—— Cotton Mather and Salem Witchcraft. [By William Frederick Poole.] *Boston,* 1868. 23 p. 12°.

Reprinted from the *Boston Daily Advertiser* of October 28, 1868, One hundred copies printed.

Mathews (Cornelius). Witchcraft: a Tragedy, in five acts. *New York: S. French,* 1852. 99 p. 24°.

The scene is laid in Salem at the close of the seventeenth century. The *dramatis personæ* bear the names of individuals who figured prominently in the trials in 1692.

Mayberry (S. P.) A Witchcraft deposition. (Magazine of American History. v. 9, p. 67. *New York,* 1883. 8°.)

Deposition of Thomas Burnam in Boston, 1692.

Miller (John). New York considered and improved, 1695. Published from the original MS. in the British Museum, with introduction and notes by V. H. Paltsits. *Cleveland: The Burrows Brothers Company,* 1903. 8°.

'Miller and Witchcraft in New England,' App. D., pp. 123-125.

Moore (George Henry). Bibliographical notes on Witchcraft in Massachusetts. *Worcester: Printed for the Author,* 1888. 32 p. 8°.

Separate issue of the *Notes on the bibliography of Witchcraft in Massachusetts,* with title-page and repagination.

—— Final notes on Witchcraft in Massachusetts: a summary vindication of the laws and liberties concerning attainders with corruption of blood, escheats, forfeitures of crime, and pardon of offenders... *New York: Printed for the Author,* 1885. 120 p. 8°.

Read in part before the New York Historical Society, November 4, 1884. Reviewed in *Magazine of American History,* v. 13, p. 607, New York, 1885; *The Nation,* v. 41, pp. 470-471.

—— Notes on the bibliography of Witchcraft in Massachusetts. (American Antiquarian Society. Proceedings. new ser., v. 5, pp. 245-273. *Worcester,* 1889. 8°.)

—— Notes on the history of Witchcraft in Massachusetts; with illustrative documents. (American Antiquarian Society. Proceedings. new ser., v. 2, pp. 162-192. *Worcester,* 1883. 8°.)

The first of five papers published in a controversy between Dr. Moore and Mr. A. C. Goodell, relative to an alleged act of 1711 for reversing the attainders of the Witches.

—— (Separate issue.) *Worcester: Printed by Charles Hamilton,* 1883. 32 p. 8°.

Reviewed in *The Nation,* v. 38, p. 318, and in v. 41, pp. 470-471.

—— Supplementary notes on the history of Witchcraft in Massachusetts. (Massachusetts Historical Society. Proceedings. 2. ser., v. 1, pp. 77-118. *Boston,* 1885. 8°.)

—— Supplementary notes on Witchcraft in Massachusetts: a critical examination of the alleged law of 1711 for reversing the attainders of the Witches of 1692. *Cambridge: John Wilson and Son,* 1884. 25 p., 1 l. 8°.

Reprint of the preceding article. Reviewed in *The Nation,* v. 41, pp. 470-471.

Morgan (Forrest). Witchcraft in Connecticut. (American Historical Magazine. v. 1, pp. 216-238. *New York,* 1906. 8°.)

Morgan (Forrest) [*and others*]. Connecticut as a colony and as a state, or one of the original thirteen. *Hartford: The Publishing Society of Connecticut,* 1904. 4 v. 8°.

"Witchcraft in Connecticut," v. 1, chap. xi, pp. 205-229. The chapter is signed "F. M."

Morse (Jedidiah), *and* ELIJAH PARISH. A compendious history of New England, designed for schools and private families. *Charlestown: Samuel Etheridge,* 1804. 388 p. 12°.

Witchcraft, chap. 23, pp. 307-317.

—— —— 2. ed. *Newburyport: Thomas & Whipple,* 1809. 336 p. 12°.

Witchcraft, pp. 287-296.

—— —— 3. ed. *Charlestown: Printed by S. Etheridge,* 1820. 324 p. 12°.

Witchcraft, pp. 254-261.

Morse (Willard H.) The first New England Witch. (Bay State Monthly. v. 3, pp. 270-277. *Boston,* 1885. 8°.)

Trials of Caleb Powell, schoolmaster, and Elizabeth Morse, 1679.

—— —— An unpublished page of New England history. (The Granite Monthly. v. 10, pp. 347-354. *Concord, N. H.,* 1887. 8°.)

Reprint of the foregoing article.

Moulton (Joseph). Giles Corey's will. (New England Historical and Genealogical Register. v. 10, p. 32. *Boston,* 1856. 8°.)

Giles Corey is generally said to have been pressed to death because he would not plead guilty to the indictment. The original record shows that he *did* plead "Not Guilty," but his refusal to answer the further query "How will you be tried?" involved the infliction of the penalty *peine forte et dure* of the Common Law. Had he replied "By God and my Country" the case would have been sent to the Jury, but if he had desired to be tried by the Judges alone, the case would have proceeded in that manner to final judgment.

Neal (Daniel). The history of New England, containing an impartial account of the civil and ecclesiastical affairs of the country to the year of our Lord 1700... *London: Printed for J. Clark at the Bible & Crown in the Poultry,...*1720. 2 v. 8°.

The pagination is continuous. Chapter xii, pp. 495-541, treats "Of the suspected witchcrafts of New England."

—— —— 2. ed. *London: Printed for A. Ward,* ...1747. 2 v. 8°.

Witchcraft, v. 2, chap. xii, pp. 124-170.

Neal (John). Rachel Dyer: a North American story. *Portland: Shirley and Hyde,* 1828. 276 p. 1828. 12°.

Based on Witch trials in Salem. On pp. 265-276 the author "has thought it adviseable to give a few of the many facts upon which the tale is founded, in the very language of history," in order that the reader may not be led to suppose the work a "sheer fabrication."

Nevins (John L.) Demon possession and allied themes; being an inductive study of phenomena of our own times... *New York: Fleming H. Revel Co.* [1894] x, 482 p. 12°.

Salem Witchcraft, on pp. 303-310, 355.

Nevins (Winfield S.) Stories of Salem Witchcraft. (New England Magazine. new ser., v. 5, pp. 517-533, 664-680, 717-729; v. 6, pp. 36-48, 217-230. *Boston,* 1891-'92. 8°.)

With numerous illustrations.

—— Witchcraft in Salem village in 1692 together with some account of other witchcraft prosecutions in New England and elsewhere. *Salem, Mass.: North Shore Publishing Co.,* 1892. 273 p. 12°.

Newhall (James R.) *See under* **Lewis** (Alonzo).

Noble (Frederick A.) The Pilgrims. *Boston: The Pilgrim Press,* 1907. xvi, 483 p. 8°.

Chap. 18, "Witches and Quakers."

LIST OF WORKS RELATING TO WITCHCRAFT IN THE UNITED STATES

Noble (John). Some documentary fragments touching the Witchcraft episode of 1692. (Colonial Society of Massachusetts. Publications. v. 10, pp. 12–26. *Boston*, 1907. 8°.)

The first set of documents referred to deal with the case of Elizabeth Colson; the second series concerns the case of Philip English and his wife, Mary. Some notes "showing the history of witchcraft, as it appears in the records of the highest Court of Massachusetts" are added.

Northend (William Dummer). Address before the Essex Bar Association. (Essex Institute. Historical Collections. v. 22, pp. 257–278. *Salem*, 1885. 8°.)

The legal procedure at the Witchcraft trials in Salem and before the provincial courts is discussed on pp. 264–270.

—— The Bay Colony: a civil, religious and social history of the Massachusetts Colony... *Boston: Estes and Lauriat* [1896]. viii, 349 p., ports. 12°.

Chap. xviii, pp. 297-302, deals with "Beginnings of Witchcraft in the Colony."

O'Callaghan (E. B.) The documentary history of the State of New York. *Albany: The Public Printers*, 1850–51. 4 v. 4°.

v. 4, pp. 85-88, trial of Ralph Hall and Mary his wife, 1665; trial of Katherine Harrison, July, 1670.

Old-time (The) Spirits. The strangest chapter in the history of New England. (The Galaxy. v. 19, pp. 358–367. *New York*, 1875. 8°.)

Based on Upham's *Salem Witchcraft*. 2 v.

Ollier (Edmund). Cassell's history of the United States. *London: Cassell, Petter & Galpin*, n. d. 4°.

Witchcraft in New England. v. 1, chap. xlv, pp. 389–401.

Orcutt (Samuel). A history of the old town of Stratford, and the city of Bridgeport, Connecticut. [*New Haven, Conn.: Tuttle, Morehouse & Taylor, printers*,] 1886. 2 v. 4°.

"Witches and Witchcraft," v. 1, pp. 145-157.

Order in Council respecting the trials for Witchcraft in New England, Jan. 26, 1692–'93. (Essex Institute. Historical Collections. v. 9, part 2, pp. 88–89. *Salem*, 1868. 8°.)

Osgood (Charles S.), *and* H. M. BATCHELDER. Historical sketch of Salem, 1626–1879. *Salem: Essex Institute*, 1879. viii, 280 p., ports., ill. 8°.

Chap. ii, pp. 21-37, "Sketch of the Witchcraft delusion, with an account of the trials and executions."

Page (A) from a sad book. (Household Words. v. 5, pp. 474–476. *London*, 1852. 8°.)

Gives "the examination of Susannah Martin, May 2, 1692."

Palfrey (John Gorham). History of New England. *Boston: Little, Brown and Co.*, 1865–1892. 5 v. 4°.

v. 2, p. 376. Witchcraft in Connecticut; v. 4, pp. 96-133, Witchcraft in Salem.

—— A compendious history of New England from the discovery by Europeans to the first general Congress of the Anglo-American Colonies. *Boston: H. C. Shepard*, 1873. 4 v. 12°.

Witchcraft in Salem, v. 3, pp. 90-124.

Parish (Elijah). *See* **Morse** (Jedidiah).

[**Parkman** (Francis).] The Salem Witchcraft. (Christian Examiner. v. 11, pp. 240–259. *Boston*, 1831. 8°.)

A review of C. W. Upham's *Lectures on Witchcraft*. Boston, 1831.

Peabody (Oliver William Bourn). Popular Superstitions. (North American Review. v. 34, pp. 198–220. *Boston*, 1832. 8°.)

Review of Upham's *Lectures on Witchcraft*, Boston, 1831, and Thacher's *Essay on Demonology*, Boston, 1831.

Peabody (William Bourn Oliver). Life of Cotton Mather. (In: The Library of American Biography. Conducted by Jared Sparks. *Boston*, 1836. v. 6, pp. 163–350. 16°.)

The author of this article was the twin brother of the preceding author.

Peareson (P. Edward). [Letter on two cases of Witchcraft in South Carolina.] (In: COOPER, The Statutes at Large of South Carolina. v. 2, pp. 742–743. *Columbia, S. C.*, 1837. 8°.)

In the first case Barbara Powers was accused of transforming a young woman into a horse, and using her as a beast of burden. This case was tried at Lancaster in 1813 or 1814, but was thrown out of court by the presiding judge. The second case was tried at Fairfield in 1792. Four persons were tried, found guilty, and punished by stripes and burning their feet at a bare fire so that the soles came off.

There is preserved in the Charleston Library a manuscript volume containing eight charges delivered by Chief Justice Nicholas Trott to the General Sessions; one of these, delivered about the year 1700, is upon the subject of Witchcraft, "and is a most learned and elaborate defence of the theory of the existence of Witchcraft as a crime" (McCrady, *History of South Carolina under the Proprietary Government*, 1670–1719, p. 449. New York, 1897. 12°).

Perley (Sidney). The history of Boxford, Essex County, Massachusetts, from the earliest settlement known to the present time. *Boxford, Mass.: The Author*, 1880. 418 p. 8°.

Trial of Rebecca Eames, 1692, pp. 120–124. She was sentenced to death but finally reprieved.

Persons arrested by warrant in 1692 [for Witchcraft]. (Essex Institute. Historical Collections. v. 3, pp. 119–120. *Salem*, 1861. 8°.)

Phips (*Sir* William). Extract from a letter of Sir William Phips to Mr. Blathwayt. Oct. 12, 1692. (Essex Institute. Historical Collections. 2 series, v. 9, part 2, pp. 86–88. *Salem*, 1868. 8°.)

Relates his finding the province "miserably harassed with a most Horrible Witchcraft or Possession of Devills."

Pike (James S.) The new Puritan: New England 200 years ago; some account of the life of Robert Pike, the Puritan who defended the Quakers, resisted clerical domination, and opposed the Witchcraft prosecution. *New York: Harper & Brothers*, 1879. 237 p. 12°.

Salem Witchcraft dealt with in ch. xxiii-xxiv, pp. 147-165.

Pond (Enoch). The lives of Increase Mather and Sir William Phips... *Boston: Massachusetts Sabbath School Society*, 1847. 12°.

For Mather and Witchcraft, see chapters 8 and 10.

Poole (Fitch). Giles Corey & Goodwyfe Corey. A ballad of 1692. (Essex Institute. Bulletin. v. 2, pp. 113–115. *Salem*, 1871. 8°.)

This ballad is also printed in *The Witchcraft Delusion in New England*. v. 3, appendix no. 2.

Poole (William Frederick). Cotton Mather and Salem Witchcraft. (North American Review. v. 108, pp. 337–397. *Boston*, 1869.)

A review of the *Mather papers*, Upham's *Salem Witchcraft*, etc.

—— —— *Boston*, 1869. 63 p. 8°.

Reprinted from the *North American Review*, v. 108. One hundred copies printed. Reviewed in *Historical Magazine*, v. 16, p. 129 (by C. W. Upham); *Boston Daily Advertiser*, April 9, 1870 (by Delano A. Goddard); *Boston Journal*, Jan. 28, 1870.

LIST OF WORKS RELATING TO WITCHCRAFT IN THE UNITED STATES

—— Witchcraft in Boston. (The Memorial History of Boston, including Suffolk County, Massachusetts, 1630–1880. Edited by Justin Winsor. In four volumes. *Boston: James R. Osgood & Co.*, 1880–'81. 4°. vol. 2, pp. 131–172.)

—— *See also under* **Hutchinson** and the **Mather** Papers.

Prime (Nathaniel S.) History of Long Island, from its first settlement by Europeans to the year 1845... *New York: Robert Carter*, 1845. xii, 420 p. 12°.

The trials of John Garlicke, Mary Wright, and Ralph Hall and his wife are dealt with on pp. 88–89. The substance of Prime's account is given in Silas Wood's *Sketch of the first settlement of the several towns on Long Island*, Brooklyn, 1865, p. 24. 4°.

Proposed (The) memorial "Lookout" on Gallows Hill. (Putnam's Monthly Historical Magazine. v. 1, pp. 295–296. *Salem*, 1893. 8°.)

Quincy (Josiah). The history of Harvard University. *Boston: Crosby, Nichols, Lee & Co.*, 1860. 2 v. 8°.

For the connection of the Mathers with the Witchcraft delusion, see v. 1, pp. 61–65, 88, 147–8, 177–9, 407–8, 413–14.

Quincy (Josiah P.) Cotton Mather and the supernormal in New England history. (Massachusetts Historical Society. Proceedings. 2 ser., v. 20, pp. 439–453. *Boston*, 1907. 8°.)

Rantoul (Robert S.) Remarks at the meeting in Salem commemorative of the Witchcraft delusion of 1692. (Salem Press Historical and Genealogical Record. v. 2, pp. 168–170. *Salem*, 1892. 8°.)

Recantation of confessors of Witchcraft. (Massachusetts Historical Society. Collections. 2 ser., v. 3, pp. 221–225. *Boston*, 1815. 8°.)

Prepared for publication by Dr. Belknap and apparently intended to follow Brattle's article (q. v.). This document agrees in substance with the recantation printed in Hutchinson, v. 2, p. 40.

Records of Salem Witchcraft, copied from the original documents. *Roxbury, Mass.: Privately printed for W. Elliott Woodward*, 1864. 2 v. (v. 1, x, [9–]279 p.; v. 2, 287 p.) sm. 4°. (Woodward's Historical Series, Nos. 1 and 2.)

Only 215 copies printed, of which 15 are on large paper.

Reynolds (John). Pioneer history of Illinois. ... *Belleville, Ill.: N. A. Randall*, 1852. 347 p. 16°.

Witchcraft on p. 143. See the note under **Gunn** (John A.)

Rice (Charles B.) Proceedings at the celebration of the two hundredth anniversary of the first parish at Salem Village, now Danvers, October 8, 1872. *Boston: Congregational Publishing Co.*, 1874. 272 p. 8°.

The Witch trials are referred to on pp. 39–43, 186, 209–215 247–256.

Richardson (Abbey Sage). The history of our country from its discovery by Columbus... *Boston: H. O. Houghton & Co.*, 1875. 8°.

"Salem Witchcraft," chap. 26, pp. 141–146.

Ridpath (John Clark). The new complete history of the United States of America. *Washington: Ridpath History Co.*, n. d. 4°.

Publication still in progress. v. 3, pp. 1326–1344, deals with the Witchcraft delusion. Gives facsimile of the order and certificate of execution of Bridget Bishop for Witchcraft in Salem in 1692. There is also a facsimile of a page of MS. of Increase Mather's Cases of Conscience and facsimile of signatures of New England ministers to a commendation of the same work.

Roads (Samuel). The history and traditions of Marblehead. *Marblehead: N. Allen Lindsay*, 1897. xxiv, 595 p. 8°.

Trial of Wilmot Redd [Read], wife of Samuel Redd, 1692, on pp. 34–36. She was executed.

Robbins (Chandler). History of the Second Church, or Old North, in Boston... *Boston: Printed by John Wilson & Son*, 1852. viii, 320 p. 8°.

Defends action of the Mathers in the Witchcraft persecutions.

Robbins (R. D. C.) Cotton Mather and the Witchcraft delusion. (Bibliotheca Sacra. v. 34, pp. 473–513. *Andover*, 1877. 8°.)

Robinson (Therese Albertina Louise von Jakob). Geschichte der Colonisation von Neu-England. Von den ersten Niederlassungen daselbst im Jahre 1607 bis zur Einführung der Provinzialverfassung von Massachusetts im Jahre 1692. *Leipzig: F. A. Brockhaus*, 1847. xviii, 709 p., 1 map. 8°.

Witchcraft in New England, pp. 680–707.

Salem Witchcraft. (American Review. v. 3, pp. 60–67. *New York*, 1846. 8°.)

General account of the persecutions.

—— (Harpers' Popular Cyclopædia of United States History. v. 2, pp. 1537–38. *New York*, 1892. 4°.)

—— (Massachusetts Historical Society. Collections. 3d ser., v. 3, pp. 169–180. *Cambridge*, 1833. 8°.)

Extracts from the records of the church in Danvers.

Salem Witchcraft: Comprising More Wonders of the invisible world, collected by Robert Calef; and Wonders together with the invisible world, by Cotton Mather; together with notes and explanations, by Samuel P. Fowler. *Salem, Mass.: H. P. Ives and A. A. Smith*, 1861. xxi, [23–]450 p. 12°.

—— (Another issue). *Boston: William Veazie*, 1865. sq. 8°.

Printed from the stereotype plates of the edition of 1861. 100 copies on large paper and 250 on small paper.

Salem (The) Witchcraft madness (LARNED, History for ready reference. v. 3, pp. 2113–15. *Springfield, Mass.*, 1895. 4°.)

Savage (Gertrude). Witchcraft in New England. (Bostonian. v. 1, pp. 197–205. *Boston*, 1894. 8°.)

Based on the writings of Upham, Drake, Coffin, Wendell, and Lossing.

Schenck (Elizabeth Hubbell). The history of Fairfield, Fairfield County, Connecticut, from the settlement of the town in 1639 to 1818. *New York: The Author*, 1889. 2 v.

Witchcraft in Fairfield, v. 1, pp. 274–275.

Scott (*Sir* Walter). Letters on Demonology and Witchcraft, addressed to J. G. Lockhart, Esq. *London: John Murray*, 1830. (4) ix, 402 p. 12°.

New England Witchcraft is discussed in the 8th letter. There are other and later editions of this work.

Seip (Elisabeth Cloud). Witchfinding in Western Maryland. (Journal of American Folklore. v. 14, pp. 39–44. *Boston*, 1901.)

Magic rather than Witchcraft.

Sener (S. M.) Local Superstitions. (Lancaster County Historical Society. Papers. v. 9, pp. 233–246. *Lancaster, Pa.*, 1905. 8°.)

Trial of Margaret Mattson, 1683. pp. 238–239.

LIST OF WORKS RELATING TO WITCHCRAFT IN THE UNITED STATES

Sewall (Samuel). The Judge's confession. (Library of American Literature. *New York*, 1891. v. 2, pp. 188.)

From the *Sewall Papers*. The confession or recantation is also printed in Currier's *Ould Newbury*, p. 246. Boston, 1896.

Sibley (John Langdon). Biographical sketches of graduates of Harvard University, in Cambridge, Massachusetts. *Cambridge: Charles William Sever*, 1873-1885. 3 v. 8°.

See the references under "Witchcraft" in the index to each volume.

Smith (E. Vale). History of Newburyport; from the earliest settlement of the country to the present time.. *Newburyport*, 1854. v, 414 p. 8°.

Witchcraft, pp. 28-37.

Smith (William). History of New York, from its discovery to the year MDCCXXXII... With a continuation...to the commencement of the year 1814. *Albany: Printed by Ryer Schermerhorn*, 1814. 512 p. 8°.

Gives the trial of Ralph Hall and Mary, his wife, from the original record, pp. 509-511. They were acquitted.

Soldan (Wilhelm Gottlieb). Geschichte der Hexenprozesse. Neu bearbeitet von Heinrich Heppe. *Stuttgart: Verlag der J. G. Cotta'schen Buchhandlung*, 1880. 2 v. 8°.

Witchcraft in Massachusetts, v. 2, pp. 152-160.

Some Few | Remarks, | upon | A Scandalous Book, against the | Government and Ministry of | New England. | Written, | by one Robert Calef. | Detecting the Unparrallel'd Malice & Falsehood | of the said Book; | And | Defending the Names of several particular | Gentlemen by him therein aspersed & abused. | Composed and Published by several Persons | belonging to the Flock of some of the | Injured Pastors, and concerned for their Just Vindication. | *Boston, N. E.: Printed by T. Green, Sold by Nicholas Boone*, 1701. Title, 1 l., pp. 5-71. 8°.

The postscript (pp. 67-71) is signed by Increase and Cotton Mather, who disavow their authorship of the work, which purports to have been drawn up by Obadiah Gill and six other members of the Old North Church.
Sabin says, quoting from "a Boston catalogue," that this work was answered by "Remarks on Some Few Remarks upon a Scandalous Book against the Government and Ministry of New England. Boston, 1701. 16°."

Sorciers (Les) de Salem dans les possessions Anglaises, en Amérique. (Causes célèbres étrangères publiées...par une société de Jurisconsultes et de gens de lettres. v. 1, pp. 368-370. *Paris*, 1827. 8°.)

Spirits (The) in 1692, and what they did at Salem. (Putnam's Monthly Magazine. v. 7, pp. 505-511. *New York*, 1856. 8°.)

Spofford (Harriet Prescott). New England legends. *Boston: James R. Osgood & Co.*, 1871. 40 p., double cols. 8°.

Witchcraft in Salem, pp. 15-23.

Stiles (Henry R[eed]). The history of ancient Wethersfield, Connecticut... Based upon the manuscript collections of the late Judge Sherman W. Adams... *New York: The Grafton Press*, 1903-04. 2 v. 4°.

Witchcraft in Wethersfield, v. 1, pp. 679-686. Cases of Margaret Johnson, 1648; John Carrington and Joane his wife, 1650-51; Catharine Harrison, 1668-69; Philip Smith, 1684.

—— The history and genealogies of ancient Windsor, Connecticut...1635-1891. *Hartford,*

**Conn.: *Case, Lockwood & Brainard Co.*, 1891-92. 2 v. 8°.

"Witchcraft in Windsor," v. 1, pp. 444-450.

Stone (Lincoln R.). An account of the trial of George Jacobs, for Witchcraft. (Essex Institute. Historical Collections. v. 2, pp. 49-57. *Salem*, 1860. 8°.)

Talvj, *pseud. See* **Robinson.**

Taylor (John M[etcalf]). The Witchcraft delusion in colonial Connecticut, 1647-1697. *New York: The Grafton Press* [1908]. xv, 1 l., 172 p., 1 facsim. 12°.

Reviewed in *The Nation*, v. 87, pp. 188-189.

Thacher (James). An essay on demonology, ghosts and apparitions, and popular superstitions. Also, an account of the Witchcraft delusion at Salem, in 1692. *Boston: Carter and Hendee*, 1831. v, 234 p. 16°.

Reviewed in *North American Review*, v. 34, pp. 198-220. Boston, 1832.

Thompson (Benjamin F.) The history of Long Island from its discovery and settlement to the present time. *New York*, 1843. 2 v. 8°.

Vol. 1, p. 302: Trial of the wife of Joshua Garlick, 1657.

[Thornton (J. Wingate).] Witchcraft in Maine. (New England Historical and Genealogical Register. v. 13, pp. 193-196. *Boston*, 1859. 8°.)

Todd (Mabel Lewis). The Witch of Winnacunnett. (New England Magazine. new ser., v. 3, pp. 587-592. *Boston*, 1891. 8°.)

Towne (Mrs. Abbie W.) William Towne, his daughters, and the Witchcraft delusions. (Topsfield Historical Society. Historical Collections. v. 1, pp. 12-14. *Topsfield, Mass.*, 1895. 8°.)

Of little importance.

[Trial of Margaret Mattson and Yeshro Hendrickson. December, 1683.] (Minutes of the Provincial Council of Pennsylvania. v. 1, pp. 93, 95-96. *Philadelphia*, 1852. 8°.)

Turell (Ebenezer). Detection of Witchcraft. (Massachusetts Historical Society. Collections. 2 ser., v. 10, pp. 6-22. *Boston*, 1823. 8°.)

The author was minister of Bedford, Mass. An abstract of his essay is given in Hutchinson, *History of Massachusetts Bay*, v. 2, pp. 20-22. Boston, 1767.

[Underwood (F. H.).] Curiosities of Puritan history. Witchcraft. (Putnam's Monthly Magazine. v. 2, pp. 249-259. *New York*, 1853. 8°.)

From her *Salem Witchcraft in outline*.

Upham (Caroline E.) The bewitched children of Salem, 1692. Beginnings of the Witchcraft tragedy. (Magazine of American History. v. 26, pp. 143-144. *New York*, 1891.)

From her *Salem Witchcraft in outline*.

—— Salem Witchcraft in outline. *Salem: The Salem Press Publishing and Printing Co.*, 1891. 3. ed. 11, 161 p. ill. 8°.

A summary of the narrative in C. W. Upham's *Salem Witchcraft*. 2 v. 1867.

Upham (Charles W[entworth]). Lectures on Witchcraft, comprising a history of the delusion in Salem in 1692. *Boston: Carter, Hendee and Babcock*, 1831. vii, 280. 16°.

Reviews: *Christian Examiner*, v. 11, pp. 240-259. Boston, Nov., 1831 (by Francis Parkman); *North American Review*, v. 34, pp. 198-220. Boston 1832; by Harriet Martineau, *Miscellanies*, v. 2, pp. 389-402. Boston, 1836.

—— *Boston: Carter and Hendee*, 1832. 2. ed. 300 p. 16°.

LIST OF WORKS RELATING TO WITCHCRAFT IN THE UNITED STATES

—— Salem Witchcraft; with an account of Salem village, and a history of opinions on Witchcraft and kindred subjects. *Boston: Wiggin and Lunt*, 1867. 2 v. 8°.

Fifty copies printed on large paper, and one hundred in small quarto as four volumes with separate title-page for each half volume.
Reviews: *The Nation*, v. 5, pp. 391, 392, New York, 1867 (by G. E. Ellis); *Edinburgh Review*, v. 128, pp. 1–47, London, 1868 (reprinted in *Littell's Living Age*, 4 ser., v. 10 (consecutive v. 98), pp. 387–411, Boston, 1868); *Congregational Quarterly*, v. 10, pp. 154–166, Boston, 1868; *Congregational Review*, v. 9, pp. 201–238 (by A. H. Currier); *Southern Review*, new ser. v. 3, pp. 306–332, Baltimore, 1868.

—— Salem Witchcraft and Cotton Mather. (The Historical Magazine. new ser., v. 6, pp. 129–219. *Morrisania*, 1869. 8°.

Reply to Poole. Shows clearly that Cotton Mather was largely responsible for instigating the persecutions "by fostering a morbid condition in the public mind."—*Winsor*.

—— *Morrisania*, 1869. 3 l., 91 p., double columns. 8°.

A separate issue of the preceding.

Upham (William Phineas). Account of the Rebecca Nourse Monument. (Essex Institute. Historical Collections. v. 23, pp. 151–160, 201–229. *Salem*, 1886. 8°.)

Also issued in separate form.

—— House of John Procter, Witchcraft martyr, 1692. *Peabody: C. H. Shepard*, 1904. 17 p., 1 l., 1 diagr. 8°.

—— The "Rebecca Nurse House," Danvers. (Essex County Historical and Genealogical Register. v. 1, pp. 63. *Ipswich*, 1894. 8°.)

With plate illustration of the house.

—— Suffolk Early Files. No. 48343. (Essex Institute. Historical Collections. v. 28, pp. 181–182. *Salem*, 1891. 8°.)

Depositions, made in 1738, relating to Philip English and the trials of 1692.

Walsh (Robert), jr. An appeal from the judgments of Great Britain respecting the United States of America. Part first, containing an historical outline of their merits and wrongs as colonies; and strictures upon the calumnies of the British writers. *London: John Miller*, 1819. lvi, 505 p. 8°.

Pp. 52–55 defend the colonists from the charge of intolerance, and show that the belief in Witchcraft was epidemic in the seventeenth century and could not fail to extend to New England.

—— American ed. *Philadelphia: Ames and White*, 1819. lvi, 512 p. 8°.

Ward (May Alden). Old Colony days. *Boston: Roberts Bros.*, 1896. 280 p. 12°.

The fourth chapter, pp. 187–231, "Some delusions of our forefathers," deals with Witchcraft in New England.

Washburn (Emory). Sketches of the Judicial history of Massachusetts, from 1630 to the Revolution in 1775. *Boston: C. C. Little & James Brown*, 1840. 8°.

Deals with courts for trial of Witchcraft in Massachusetts.

Waters (Stanley). Witchcraft in Springfield, Mass. (New England Historical and Genealogical Register. v. 35, pp. 152–153. *Boston*, 1881. 8°.)

Testimonies of witnesses in the trial of Hugh Parsons and his wife, 1651.

Waters (Thomas Franklin). Ipswich in the Massachusetts Bay Colony... *Ipswich, Mass.: Ipswich Historical Society*, 1905. vii, 586 p. 8°.

Particulars relating to several local Witchcraft trials, from the original records, are given in chap. xvi, pp. 287–300.

Watkins (Walter K.) Mary Watkins; a discolored history of Witchcraft, cleansed by modern research. (New England Historical and Genealogical Society. Register. v. 44, pp. 168–170. *Boston*, 1890. 8°.)

On charges against Mary Watkins in Suffolk County, Mass., 1693.

Waylen (Edward). Ecclesiastical reminiscences of the United States. *New York: Wiley and Putnam*, 1846. 8°.

The Salem Witch trials are dealt with on pp. 68–112.

Wendell (Barrett). Cotton Mather, the Puritan priest. *New York: Dodd, Mead & Co.* [copyright, 1891.] vi, 321 p., 1 port. 12°. ("Makers of America" Series.)

Chapter 6, pp. 88–123, discusses Cotton Mather's connection with the New England Witch trials.

—— Were the Salem Witches guiltless? (Essex Institute. Historical Collections. v. 29, pp. 129–147. *Salem, Mass.*, 1892. 8°.)

His conclusions are that the accused persons used an apparently supernatural power over their victims, akin to what is now known as hypnotism.

—— *Salem*, 1892. 19 p. 8°.

Separate issue of the foregoing.

—— Stelligeri, and other essays concerning America. *New York: Charles Scribner's Sons*, 1893. 217 p. 16°.

His *Were the Salem Witches guiltless?* is reprinted in this volume.

White (Andrew Dickson). A history of the warfare of Science with Theology in Christendom. *New York: D. Appleton*, 1896. 2 v. 8°.

The Witchcraft delusion in Salem discussed in v. 2, pp. 146–154.

White (Henry). The early history of New England, illustrated by numerous interesting incidents. *Boston: Sanborn, Carter, Bazin & Co.* [1841.] 9. ed. 412 p. 12°.

"Witchcraft," pp. 381–392.

Whiting (John). An account of a remarkable passage of divine providence that happened in Hartford, in the yeare of our Lord 1662. (Massachusetts Historical Society. Collections. 4. ser., v. 8, pp. 466–469. *Boston*, 1868. 8°.)

This account of the case of Anne Cole was communicated to Increase Mather by Whiting in 1682. Mather relates the case in a condensed form and different words in his "Essay for the Recording of Illustrious Providences," chap. 5.

Whittemore (James O.) The Witch's curse: a legend of an old Maine town. (New England Magazine. New ser. v. 27, pp. 111–113. *Boston*, 1902. 8°.)

With two illustrations.

Whittier (John Greenleaf). Literary recreations and miscellanies. *Boston: Ticknor & Fields*, 1854. 12°.

"Magicians and Witchfolk," pp. 273–287. Of no importance.

—— The supernaturalism of New England. By the author of "The Stranger in Lowell." *New York: Wiley & Putnam*, 1847. ix, 71 p. 12°.

—— The Witch of Wenham. (Atlantic Monthly. v. 39, pp. 129–134. *Boston*, 1877. 8°.)

Poetry.

Wilkins (Mary E.) Giles Corey, Yeoman. (Harpers' Magazine. v. 86, pp. 20–40. *New York*, 1893. 8°.)

Drama founded on the trial of Giles Corey in 1692. 4 illustrations.

LIST OF WORKS RELATING TO WITCHCRAFT IN THE UNITED STATES

Willard (Samuel). Account of the strange case of Elizabeth Knapp of Groton. (Massachusetts Historical Society. Collections. 4 ser., v. 8, pp. 555–570. *Boston*, 1868. 8°.)

His account forms a part of the *Mather papers* published in the above volume.

—— Some Miscellany | Observations | On our present Debates respecting | Witchcrafts, in a Dialogue | Between S. & B. | By P. E. and J. A. | *Philadelphia, Printed by William Bradford, for Hezekiah Usher,* | 1692. 16 p. 4°.

As this tract bears internal evidence of having been written sometime after the 19th of July, 1692, to be a production of Bradford's press it must have been issued in the latter end of that month or in the month following; for in the latter part of August or beginning of September, Bradford's printing-press and type had been seized by the authorities. They were not restored to him until after the 27th April, 1693. Dr. G. H. Moore appeared to have had doubts about this tract being a production of Bradford's press and suggested "Was it not printed in Boston—and the imprint a fictitious one? Was not Hezekiah Usher *at that time* a fugitive, as well as P. E. and J. A.? A careful examination of the typography confirms my doubt that it was printed from Bradford's types."—*Biographical Notes on Witchcraft in Massachusetts,* p. 6 n.

S. and B., who carry on the dialogue, probably stand for Salem and Boston, or, as has been suggested, for Stoughton and Brattle. S. takes the part of the Magistrates, B. that of the Clergy.

—— (Reprinted in: The Congregational Quarterly. v. 11 (v. 1, new ser.), pp. 400–415. *Boston,* 1869. 8°.

Williams (Howard). The superstitions of Witchcraft. *London: Longman, Green,* 1865. xi, 278 p. 12°.

Witchcraft in the English Colonies in North America, pp. 259–269.

Winsor (Justin). The literature of Witchcraft in New England. (American Antiquarian Society. Proceedings. new ser., v. 10. pp. 351–373. *Worcester, Mass.,* 1896. 8°.)

—— *Worcester, Mass.: Printed by Charles Hamilton,* 1896. 25 p. 8°.

Reprint of the foregoing with title-page. One hundred copies printed.

Winthrop (John). The history of New England from 1630 to 1649. From his original manuscripts. With notes. [Edited] by James Savage. *Boston: Printed by Phelps and Farnham,* 1825–26. 2 v. 8°.

v. 2, p. 307, reference to an unnamed, executed at Hartford, 1647; v. 2, p. 326, account of Margaret Jones of Charlestown, executed in 1648.

—— New edition. *Boston: Little, Brown and Company,* 1853. 2 v. 8°.

—— Another edition. *New York: Charles Scribner's Sons,* 1908. 2 v. 8°. (Original Narratives of Early American History.)

Witch (The). (The Parterre; or, Universal Story-teller. v. 1. pp. 135–138. *London* [1834]. 8°.

Legend of Ann Jones, in New Haven, 1669. Reprinted from *The Legendary.*

Witch (The) of New Haven. A tale of the early Colonists. By the author of "Kit Carson." (Holden's Dollar Magazine. v. 2. pp. 516–519. *New York,* 1848. 8°.

Witchcraft. (Boston Monthly Magazine. v. 1, pp. 251–264. *Boston,* 1825. 8°.)

General. Of little value.

Witchcraft (The) delusion in New England: its rise, progress and determination, as exhibited by Dr. Cotton Mather in The Wonders of the In-

visible World; and by Mr. Robert Calef, in his More Wonders of the Invisible World. With preface, introduction, and notes by Samuel G. Drake. *Roxbury, Mass.,* 1866. 3 v. sm. 4°. (Woodward's Historical Series. Nos. 5, 6, 7.)

In three sizes: 280 copies on small paper, 70 copies large paper, and 50 copies largest paper (roy. 4°). V. 1, The Wonders of the Invisible World. Introductory, Memoir of the author, text. V. 2, More Wonders of the Invisible World. Prefatory by the editor, memoir of Robert Calef, text of first half of the work. V. 3, Calef's More Wonders continued; Appendices.

[**Witchcraft** at Fairfield, Connecticut, September, 1692.] (Connecticut Historical Society. Collections. v. 3, pp. 233–235. *Hartford,* 1895. 8°.)

Cases of Mercy Disborough and Elizabeth Clawson. Documents referring to these trials were published in the *New York Commercial Advertiser,* July 14, 15, 1820; *New York Spectator,* July 18, 1820; and in the *Times and Weekly Advertiser,* Hartford, August 8, 1820.

Witchcraft in Hingham, 1708–9. (New England Historical and Genealogical Society. Register. v. 5, p. 263. *Boston,* 1851. 8°.)

Testimonials in favor of Mahitabel Warren, accused of being a witch.

Witchcraft [in New Hampshire]. (Documents and Records relating to the Province of New Hampshire. 1623–1686. Compiled and edited by Nathaniel Bouton. v. 1, pp. 415–419. *Concord,* 1867. 8°.

Trial of Rachel Fuller in 1680. Also published in *New Hampshire Historical Society. Collections.* v. 8, pp. 45–49, 133–134. Concord, 1866.

Witchcraft in New Hampshire, 1656. Complaint of Susannah Trimmings, of Little-Harbour, Pescataqua. (New Hampshire Historical Society. Collections. v. 1, pp. 255–257. *Concord,* 1824. 8°.)

Reprinted in *Documents and Records relating to the Province of New Hampshire... 1623–1686.* v. 1, pp. 217–219. Concord, 1867. 8°.

Witchcraft in New Mexico. (Journal of American Folklore. v. 1, pp. 167, 168. *Boston,* 1888. 8°.)

From the *St. Louis Globe-Democrat.*

Witchcraft in New York. (New York Historical Society Collections for 1869. Publication Fund Series. pp. 273–276. *New York,* 1870. 8°.)

Witchcraft Papers, 1692. (New England Historical and Genealogical Register. v. 27, p. 55. *Boston,* 1873. 8°.

The first paper contains Mary Herrick's account of the manner in which she was afflicted by Mrs. Hayle; the second is a writing sent out for signatures by persons opposed to the further prosecution of the "suspected witches."

Witchcraft in Pennsylvania. (Minutes of the Provincial Council of Pennsylvania. v. 2, p. 20. *Philadelphia,* 1852. 8°.)

The charge against Robert Guard and his wife "being found trifling, was dismissed." Reprinted in *Notes and Queries,* 5 Ser., v. 9, p. 226, London, 1877.

Witchcraft in 1665. (Niles' Weekly Register. v. 20 (v. 8, new ser.), pp. 379–380. *Baltimore,* 1821. 4°.)

Case of Ralph Hall and Mary his wife in New York, October, 1665. Reprinted from the *National Advocate,* New York, 2 August, 1821.

Witchcraft in Virginia. (William and Mary College Quarterly. Historical Papers. v. 1, pp. 127–129. *Williamsburg, Va.,* 1893. 8°.)

1. 20 November, 1656, William Harding sentenced to receive ten stripes on the bare back and to be forever banished

LIST OF WORKS RELATING TO WITCHCRAFT IN THE UNITED STATES

the county. 2. January 1678-9, Alice Cartwrite searched by a jury of women for the witch's mark. She was acquitted on her husband's bond. 3. Note on the charges against Grace Sherwood.

The records of the case against Alice Cartwrite were reprinted in *The Lower Norfolk County Virginia Antiquary*, v. 1, pp. 56-57.

—— (William and Mary College Quarterly. Historical Papers. v. 2, pp. 58-60. *Williamsburg, Va.*, 1894. 8°.)

Original records of cases in Lower Norfolk County, May 1655 and 1659, and in Princess Anne County, 1698. Reprinted in *The Lower Norfolk County Virginia Antiquary*, v. 1, pp. 20-21; v. 3, p. 152; v. 4, p. 36, Richmond, [1895], and Baltimore, 1902, 1904.

—— (William and Mary College Quarterly. Historical Magazine. v. 3, pp. 164-165. *Williamsburg*, 1895. 8°.)

A jury of women were appointed 16 June, 1675, to make a search on the body of Jone Jenking "according to the 118 chapter of doulton" for the witch's mark. The allusion here is to Michael Dalton's *Country Justice containing the practice, duty, and power of justices of the peace*, which was the authority for the English practice in such trials. It contains a chapter dealing with Witchcraft. The first edition appeared in 1619 and the twelfth in 1746.

Witches (The) of Salem. (Harpers' Popular Cyclopædia of United States history. v. 2, pp. 1538-39. *New York*, 1892. 4°.)

With illustrations of Rebecca Nourse's house and Witches' Hill.

Wood (Silas). *See under* **Prime.**

Wright (Thomas). Narratives of sorcery and magic from the most authentic sources. *London*, 1851. 2 v. 12°.

"The doings of Satan in New England," v. 2, pp. 284-314.

Supplement.

The works named in the following list are not in the New York Public Library, but have been added in order to make the bibliography as nearly complete as possible.

[Boulton (Richard).] A compleat history of magick, sorcery, and Witchcraft. *London: E. Curll*, 1715-16. 2 v. 12°.

V. 2, contains "The Tryals of several Witches at Salem in New England."

Byington (Ezra Hoyt). The Puritan in England and New England. With a chapter on Witchcraft in New England. *Boston: Little, Brown & Co.*, 1900. 4. ed. 457 p., ports. 8°.

Castleton (D. R.), *pseud.* Salem: a tale of the seventeenth century. *New York: Harper*, 1874. 336 p. 12°.

Child (Frank Samuel). A colonial Witch: being a study of the black art in the Colony of Connecticut, 1640-63. *New York: The Baker & Taylor Co.* [1897.] 307 p. 12°.

Portrays, with the aid of a slight thread of a story, a remarkable phase of life that had its rise and final climax between the years 1640 and 1660 in the American colonies.

Deane (Charles). Bibliographical tracts, number one. Spurious reprints of early books. *Boston*, 1865. 19 p. Imp. 8°.

Reprinted from the *Boston Advertiser*, March 24, 1865. A severe criticism of *Salem Witchcraft* as edited by S. P. Fowler. Four copies were issued on India paper, eight copies on vellum paper, and 131 copies on ordinary paper.

Delusion; or the Witch of New England. *Boston: Hilliard, Gray, & Co.*, 1840. iv, 160 p. 16°.

Disosway (E. T.) South Meadows: a tale of long ago. *Philadelphia: Porter and Coates* [1874]. 2 p.l., 280 p. 12°.

Fiction. Deals with Salem Witchcraft.

Ferguson (Henry). Essays in American history. *New York: James Pott & Co.*, 1894. 211 p. 12°.

"The Witches," pp. 61-110. "Presents a severe indictment of the Puritans for their treatment of the Witches, yet treats the subject with calmness and impartiality."

Hale (John). A Modest Enquiry | Into the Nature of | Witchcraft, | and | How Persons Guilty of that Crime | may be Convicted: and the means | used for their Discovery Discussed, | both Negatively and Affirmatively, | according to Scripture and | Experience. | By John Hale, | Pastor of the Church of Christ in Beverley, | Anno Domini 1697 | ... | *Boston in N. E.:* | *Printed by B. Green, and J. Allen, for | Benjamin Eliot, under the Town House,* 1702. 176 p. sm. 8°.

Collation: pp. 3-7, An Epistle to the Reader, March 23d, 1697-8, signed by John Higginson, Pastor of the Church of Salem; pp. 8-12, The Preface to the Christian Reader, Beverly, Decemb. 15th, 1697, John Hale; Text pp. 13-176. This is one of the rarest of all the works relating to the Witchcraft delusion in New England. A fac-simile of the title-page is given by Fiske, p. 167.

Herbert (Henry William). Ruth Whalley; or the fair Puritan. A romance of the Bay Province. *Boston: H. L. Williams*, 1845. 72 p. 8°.

Fiction. Relates to the Salem Witch trials.

Lawson (Deodat). A Brief and True | Narrative | of some Remarkable Passages Relating to sundry Persons | Afflicted by | Witchcraft, | at | Salem Village: | Which happened from the Nineteenth of March, to the | Fifth of April, 1692. | Collected by Deodat Lawson. | *Boston: Printed for Benjamin Harris and are to be sold at his | Shop, over against the Old Meeting-House.* 1692. 10 pp. 4°.

This is the earliest publication on the Witchcraft delusion in Salem.

—— Christ's Fidelity The only Shield against Satan's Malignity. Asserted in a Sermon Deliver'd at Salem-Village, the 24th of March, 1692. Being Lecture-day there, and a time of Publick Examination, of some Suspected for Witchcraft. By Deodat Lawson, Minister of the Gospel. *Boston Printed by B. Harris, & Sold by Nicholas Buttolph, next to Guttridges Coffee-House.* 1693. (16) 79 p. 16°.

Mather (Cotton). Memorable Providences, | Relating to | Witchcrafts | And Possessions. | A Faithful Account of many Wonderful and Surprising Things, | that have befallen several Bewitched and Possessed Persons in New-England. | Particularly, a Narrative of the marvellous | Trouble and ¦Releef Experienced by a pious Family in Boston, very lately and sadly molested | with Evil Spirits. | Whereunto is added, | A Discourse delivered unto a Congregation in | Boston, on the Occasion of that Illustrious Pro- | vidence. As also | A Discourse delivered unto the same Congrega- | tion; on the occasion of an horrible Self-Mur- | der Committed in the Town. | With an Appendix, in vindication of a Chapter | in a late Book of Remarkable Providences, from | the Calumnies of a Quaker at Pen-silvania. | Written by Cotton Mather, Minister of the Gospel. | And Recommended by the Ministers | of Boston and Charlestown. | *Printed at Boston in N. England by*

LIST OF WORKS RELATING TO WITCHCRAFT IN THE UNITED STATES

R. P.[*ierce*], *1689.* | Sold by Joseph Brunning, at his Shop at the Cor- | ner of the Prison-Lane next the Exchange. Small 8°.

Collation: Title, 1 l., verso blank; the epistle dedicatory "To the Honorable Wait-Wintchrop [sic] Esq.," signed " C. Mather," 2 pp ; " To the Reader," 4 pp.; " The Introduction," 2 pp ; " Witchcraft and Possessions," 75 pp.; " A Discourse on the Power and Malice of the Devils," 21 pp.; " A Discourse on Witchcraft," 40 pp.; "Notandum," 1 p., verso blank; " Appendix," 14 pp.

—— *Printed at Boston in New England, and Reprinted at | Edinburgh by the Heirs and Successors of Andrew Anderson, Printer to His Most Excellent Majesty, Anno Dom.* 1697, [6] 102 p. Sm. 12°.

—— Speedy Repentence Urged. | A | Sermon | preached at Boston, Decemb. 29, 1689. | In the Hearing and at the Request of | One Hugh Stone; | A Miserable Man | Under a just Sentence of Death, for a | Tragical and Horrible Murder. | To- gether with some Account concern- | ing the Char- acter, Carriage, and | Execution of that Unhappy Ma· | lefactor | To which are added certain Memor- able | Providences Relating to some other Mur- | ders; & some great Instances of Repen- | tance which have been seen among us. | By Cotton Mather, Pastor of a | Church in Boston. | *Boston: Printed by Samuel Green, and Sold by Joseph Browning at the corner of the Prison Lane, and Benj. Hcrris at the London Coffee-House,* 1690. (6), 87, (8), 15, 75, 21, 40, (2), 14 p. 12°.

This volume contains " A little history of several very astonishing Witchcrafts and Possessions, which partly from my ocular observation, and partly my undoubted information, hath enabled me to offer unto the publick notice of my neigh* bours," which occupies 75 pp. Then follows " A Discourse on the Power and Malice of Devils," and " A Discourse on Witchcraft "; the volume concluding with an Appendix in defence of Increase Mather's " Remarkable Providences." This is probably the first appearance of Cotton Mather's essay on Witchcraft. The latter part of this volume is in fact an- other issue of Mather's *Memorable Providences*.

Mather (Increase). An Essay | for the | Re- cording | of Illustrious | Providences: | Wherein an Account is given of many Re- | markable and very Memorable Events, | which have hapned this last Age; | Especially in | New-England. | By In- crease Mather.... | *Boston in New-England. Printed by Samuel Green for Joseph Browning, and are to be sold at his shop at the Corner of the Prison-Lane next the Town-House.* 1684. (21), 372, (9) p. 8°.

The London edition is the same as this, with another title- page.

—— An | Essay | For the Recording of | Illus- trious | Providences, | Wherein an Account is given of | many Remarkable and very Me- | morable Events, which have hap- | pened in this last Age: | Especially in | New-England. | By Increase Ma- ther, | Teacher of a Church at Boston in | New- England. | ... | *Boston in New-England* | *Printed by Samuel Green for Joseph Browning,* | *And are to be sold at his Shop at the corner of* | *the Prison Lane.* 1684. (21), 372, (9) p. Sm. 8°.

Maule (Thomas). Truth Held forth | and Maintained | According to the testimony of the holy | Prophets, Christ and his Apostles | recorded in the Holy Scriptures. | With some Account | of the | Judgements of the Lord lately inflicted upon | New England by Witchcraft. | To which is added | Something concerning the Fall of Adam |

... | [*New York:*] Printed [*by William Brad- ford*] *in the Year,* 1695. xvi, 260 p. sm. 4°.

Chapter xxix: " Concerning the Great Judgements of God upon the inhabitants of New England by Witchcraft." For the knowledge of the above volume I am indebted to Mr. George Parker Winship, Librarian, John Carter Brown Library, Providence. The only other known copy of the work in the United States is in the Library of the Essex Institute.

Mudge (Zachariah Atwell). Witch Hill: a History of Salem Witchcraft, including illustrative sketches of persons and places. *New York: Carlton & Lanahan* [1870]. 322 p., 3 pl. 16°.

Old (The) Witchcrafts. [*Edinburgh: W. & R. Chambers,* n. d.] 32 p. 8°.

The Salem Witchcraft trials are discussed on pp. 14-31.

P. (W.) The history of witches and wizards, giving a true account of all their tryals in England, Scotland, Sweedland, France, and New England, with their confession and condemnation. Collected from Bishop Hall, Bishop Morton [and others] by W. P. *London: Printed for C. Hitch and L. Haws, at the Red Lion in Paternoster Row...*[1700 ?] (10) 144 p., ill. sm. 12°.

Peterson (Henry). Dulcibel: a tale of old Salem. *Philadelphia: John C. Winston Co.,* 1907. 4. 402 p. 12°.

The Witchcraft delusion in Salem is the theme of the story. The trials of the accused persons are given in detail.

Philip English's two cups. " 1692." *New York: A. D. F. Randolph & Co.,* 1869. 109 p. 12°.

Fiction. Relates to the Witchcraft delusion in Salem.

[Poole (William Frederick).] Cotton Mather and Witchcraft. Two notes of Mr. Upham; his reply. *Boston,* 1870. 30 p. sq. 16°.

Reprinted from *Watchman and Reflector,* Boston, May 5, 1870, and *Christian Era,* Boston, April 28, 1870.

Putnam (Allen). Mesmerism, spiritualism, Witchcraft and miracle. A brief treatise, showing that mesmerism is a key which will unlock many chambers of mystery. *Boston,* 1858. 74 p. 8°.

—— Witchcraft of New England explained by modern spiritualism. *Boston: Colby & Rich,* 1880. 482 p. 8°.

Riley (E. S.), *Jr.* Witchcraft in early Mary- land. (Southern Magazine. v. 12, pp. 450. *Baltimore.*)

Salem (The) Belle; a tale of 1692. *Boston: Tappan & Dennet,* 1842. 238 p. 16°.

—— A tale of love and witchcraft, in the year 1692. *Boston,* 1847. 238 p. 16°.

Another issue of the above, with altered title.

Salem Witchcraft; or the adventures of Parson Handy, from Punkapog Pond. *New York: Elam Bliss,* 1827. 2. ed. 70, (1) pp. 12°.

Scott (Jonathan M.) The Sorceress, or Salem delivered. A poem in four cantos. *New York: Charles N. Baldwin,* 1817. 120 p. 18°.

Taylor (M. Imlay). New England Witch- craft. (The Four Track News. v. 7, pp. 271-274. *New York,* 1904. 8°.)

A | **True** Account | of the | Tryals, Examina- tions, Confessions, Condemnations, | and Execu- tions of divers | Witches, | at Salem, in New England, | for Their Bewitching of Sundry Peo- ple and Cattel | to Death, and doing other great Mischiefs, | to the Ruine of many People about

LIST OF WORKS RELATING TO WITCHCRAFT IN THE UNITED STATES

them. | With the Strange Circumstances that attended | their Enchantments: | And | Their Conversation with Devils, and other | Infernal Spirits. | In a Letter to a Friend in London. | Licensed according to Order. | *London: Printed for J. Conyers, in Holborn.* 8 pp., including title. 4°.

The letter is signed "C. M.," with the place and date "Salem, 8th Month, 1692." It has been credited to Cotton Mather, but Dr. G. H. Moore says "it requires little examination to prove that this tract was not written" by him. Dr. Moore considers it "a bookseller's catchpenny, stolen mainly from the *Wonders of the Invisible World* and issued early in 1693, shortly after the publication of that book in London."—*Bibliographical Notes on Witchcraft in Massachusetts,* pp. 14–15.

The New York Public Library possesses a modern MS. copy of this work.

Upham's Lectures on Witchcraft. (American Monthly Review. v. 1, pp. 140–142. *Cambridge,* 1832. 8°.)

Willard (Samuel). Some Miscellany Observations on our present Debates respecting Witchcrafts, in a Dialogue between S. & B. By P. E. and J. A. Philadelphia, Printed by William Bradford, for Hezekiah Usher, 1692. "Congregational Quarterly" Reprint.—No. 1. *Boston,* 1869. 24 p. sm. 4°.

One hundred copies only reprinted from the *Congrega-*

tional Quarterly, v. 11. **Pages 3–4 contain Introduction by "Editors, 1869."**

—— Useful Instructions | for a professing People in Times of great | Security and Degeneracy: | Delivered in several | Sermons | on Solemn Occasions. | By Mr. Samuel Willard Pastor of the Church of Christ | at Groton. | *Cambridge: Printed by Samuel Green,* 1673. (4) 80 p. 4°.

The second sermon is upon the Witchcraft delusion at Groton, and particularly the case of Elizabeth Knap.

Witch (The) of New England; a Romance. *Philadelphia: H. C. Carey & I. Lea,* 1824. 217 p. 24°.

Reviewed in *United States Literary Gazette,* Boston, 1825, v. 1, pp. 168–170; *The Atlantic Magazine,* New York, 1824, v. 1, p. 392; *North American Review,* v. 10, pp. 96–98. "The scene of course is laid in New England, but in what part, we are at a loss to imagine; possibly somewhere in Connecticut. The principal character in the story is an old woman, who pretends to witchcraft, commits certain horrid crimes, and is executed accordingly."—*No. Amer. Rev.*

Witches (The): a Tale of New England. *Bath* [*Me.*]: *R. L. Underhill,* 1837. 72 p. 18°.

Wright (Thomas). Narratives of sorcery and magic. *New York: Redfield,* 1852. 12°.

Chap. 31, pp. 385–403, "The doings of Satan in New England."

CURRICULUM OF A∴ A∴

COURSE I.

GENERAL READING.

SECTION 1. — Books for Serious Study:

The Equinox. The standard Work of Reference in all occult matters. The Encyclopædia of Initiation.

Collected Works of A. Crowley. These works contain many mystical and magical secrets, both stated clearly in prose, and woven into the Robe of sublimest poesy.

The Yi King. (S.B.E. Series, Oxford University Press.) The "Classic of Changes"; gives the initiated Chinese system of Magick.

The Tao Teh King. (S.B.E. Series.) Gives the initiated Chinese system of Mysticism.

Tannhäuser, by A. Crowley. An allegorical drama concerning the Progress of the Soul; the Tannhäuser story slightly remodelled.

The Upanishads. (S.B.E. Series.) The Classical Basis of Vedantism, the best-known form of Hindu Mysticism.

The Bhagavad-Gita. A dialogue in which Krishna, the Hindu "Christ", expounds a system of Attainment.

The Voice of the Silence, by H. P. Blavatsky, with an elaborate commentary by Frater O. M.

The Goetia. The most intelligible of the mediaeval rituals of Evocation. Contains also the favorite Invocation of the Master Therion.

The Shiva Sanhita. A famous Hindu treatise on certain physical practices.

The Hathayoga Pradipika. Similar to The Shiva Sanhita.

Erdmann's "History of Philosophy". A compendious account of philosophy from the earliest times. Most valuable as a general education of the mind.

The Spiritual Guide of Molinos. A simple manual of Christian mysticism.

The Star of the West. (Captain Fuller.) An introduction to the study of the Works of Aleister Crowley.

The Dhammapada. (S.B.E. Series, Oxford University Press.) The best of the Buddhist classics.

The Questions of King Milinda. (S.B.E. Series.) Technical points of Buddhist dogma, illustrated by dialogues.

Varieties of Religious Experience. (James.) Valuable as showing the uniformity of mystical attainment.

Kabbala Denudata, von Rosenroth: also the Kabbalah Unveiled, by S. L. Mathers.

The text of the **Kabalah,** with commentary. A good elementary introduction to the subject.

Konx om Pax. Four invaluable treatises and a preface on Mysticism and Magick.

The Pistis Sophia. An admirable introduction to the study of Gnosticism.

The Oracles of Zoroaster. An invaluable collection of precepts mystical and magical.

The Dream of Scipio, by Cicero. Excellent for its Vision and its Philosophy.

The Golden Verses of Pythagoras, by Fabre d'Olivet. An interesting study of the exoteric doctrines of this Master.

The Divine Pymander, by Hermes Trismegistus. Invaluable as bearing on the Gnostic Philosophy.

The Secret Symbols of the Rosicrucians, reprint of Franz Hartmann. An invaluable compendium.

Scrutinium Chymicum, by Michael Maier. One of the best treatises on alchemy.

Science and the Infinite, by Sidney Klein. One of the best essays written in recent years.

Two Essays on the Worship of Priapus, by Richard Payne Knight. Invaluable to all students.

The Golden Bough, by J. G. Frazer. The Text-Book of Folk Lore. Invaluable to all students.

The Age of Reason, by Thomas Paine. Excellent, though elementary, as a corrective to superstition.

Rivers of Life, by General Forlong. An invaluable text-book of old systems of initiation.

Three Dialogues, by Bishop Berkeley. The Classic of subjective idealism.

Essays of David Hume. The Classic of Academic Scepticism.

First Principles, by Herbert Spencer. The Classic of Agnosticism.

Prolegomena, by Emanuel Kant. The best introduction to Metaphysics.

The Canon. The best text-book of Applied Qabalah.

The Fourth Dimension, by H. Hinton. The text-book on this subject.

The Essays of Thomas Henry Huxley. Masterpieces of philosophy, as of prose.

The object of this course of reading is to familiarize the student with all that has been said by the Great Masters in every time and country. He should make a critical examination of them; not so much with the idea of discovering where truth lies, for he cannot do this except by virtue of his own spiritual experience, but rather to discover the essential harmony in those varied works. He should be on his guard against partisanship with a favourite author. He should familiarize himself thoroughly with the method of mental equilibrium, endeavouring to contradict. any statement soever, although it may be apparently axiomatic.

The general object of this course, besides that already stated, is to assure sound education in occult matters, so that when spiritual illumination comes it may find a well-built temple. Where the mind is strongly biased towards any special theory, the result of an illumination is often to inflame that portion of the mind which is thus overdeveloped, with the result that the aspirant, instead of becoming an Adept, becomes a bigot and fanatic.

The A∴ A∴ does not offer examination in this course, but recommends these books as the foundation of a library.

SECTION 2. — Other books, principally fiction, of a generally suggestive and helpful kind:

Zanoni, by Sir Edward Bulwer Lytton. Valuable for its facts and suggestions about Mysticism.

A Strange Story, by Sir Edward Bulwer Lytton. Valuable for its facts and suggestions about Magick.

The Blossom and the Fruit, by Mabel Collins. Valuable for its account of the Path.

Petronius Arbiter. Valuable for those who have wit to understand it.

The Golden Ass, by Apuleius. Valuable for those who have wit to understand it.

Le Comte de Gabalis. Valuable for its hints of those things which it mocks.

The Rape of the Lock, by Alexander Pope. Valuable for its account of elementals.

Undine, by de la Motte Fouqué. Valuable as an account of elementals.

Black Magic, by Marjorie Bowen. An intensely interesting story of sorcery.

La Peau de Chagrin, by Honoré de Balzac. A magnificent magical allegory.

Number Nineteen, by Edgar Jepson. An excellent tale of modern magic.

Dracula, by Bram Stoker. Valuable for its account of legends concerning vampires.

Scientific Romances, by H. Hinton. Valuable as an introduction to the study of the Fourth Dimension.

Alice in Wonderland, by Lewis Carroll. Valuable to those who understand the Qabalah.

Alice Through the Looking Glass, by Lewis Carroll. Valuable to those who understand the Qabalah.

The Hunting of the Snark, by Lewis Carroll. Valuable to those who understand the Qabalah.

The Arabian Nights, translated by either Sir Richard Burton or John Payne. Valuable as a storehouse of oriental magick-lore.

Morte d'Arthur, by Sir Thomas Mallory. Valuable as a storehouse of occidental magick-lore.

The Works of François Rabelais. Invaluable for Wisdom.

The Kasidah, by Sir Richard Burton. Valuable as a summary of philosophy.

The Song Celestial, by Sir Edwin Arnold. "The Bhagavad-Gita" in verse.

The Light of Asia, by Sir Edwin Arnold. An account of the attainment of Gotama Buddha.

The Rosicrucians, by Hargrave Jennings. Valuable to those who can read between the lines.

The Real History of the Rosicrucians, by A. E. Waite. A good vulgar piece of journalism on the subject.

The Works of Arthur Machen. Most of these stories are of great magical interest.

The Writings of William O'Neill (Blake). Invaluable to all students.

The Shaving of Shagpat, by George Meredith. An excellent allegory.

Lilith, by George MacDonald. A good introduction to the Astral.

Là-Bas, By J. K. Huysmans. An account of the extravagances caused by the Sin-complex.

The Lore of Proserpine, by Maurice Hewlett. A suggestive enquiry into the Hermetic Arcanum.

En Route, by J. K. Huysmans. An account of the follies of Christian mysticism.

Sidonia the Sorceress, by Wilhelm Meinhold.

The Amber Witch, by Wilhelm Meinhold.
These two tales are highly informative.

Macbeth; Midsummer Night's Dream; The Tempest, by
W. Shakespeare. Interesting for traditions treated.

Redgauntlet, by Sir Walter Scott. Also one or two other
novels. Interesting for traditions treated.

Rob Roy, by James Grant. Interesting for traditions treated.

The Magician, by W. Somerset Maugham. An amusing hotch-
pot of stolen goods.

The Bible, by various authors unknown. The Hebrew and
Greek Originals are of Qabalistic value. It contains also many
magical apologues, and recounts many tales of folk-lore and magical
rites.

Kim, by Rudyard Kipling. An admirable study of Eastern
thought and life. Many other stories by this author are highly
suggestive and informative.

For Mythology, as teaching Correspondences:

    Books of Fairy Tales generally.
    Oriental Classics generally.
    Sufi Poetry generally.
    Scandinavian and Teutonic Sagas generally.
    Celtic Folk-Lore generally.

This course is of general value to the beginner. While it is not
to be taken, in all cases, too seriously, it will give him a general
familiarity with the mystical and magical tradition, create a deep
interest in the subject, and suggest many helpful lines of thought.

It has been impossible to do more, in this list, than to suggest a
fairly comprehensive course of reading.

AUTHOR INDEX

Abercrombie, Sharon 816
Abernathy, Harold 614
Abragail 817
Achad, Frater 482-493
Adams, Frederick C. 1152-1154
Adcock, Joe 1256
Adefumni, Baba Oseijeman 1408
Adler, Margot 818, 1060
Agassi, Joseph 22
Ahl, Henry Curtis 146
Aima 317, 819
Alan, Jim 1129
Albertus, Frater 318-321
Alderman, Clifford Lindsey
  147, 820
Allsopp, Fred W. 1366
Altar 510
Amber 1061-1062
Anandakipila, Swami 426
Anderson, Alan 148
Anderson, Robert D. 1, 149
Anderson, Victor 1130
Andrius 1155-1156
Arboo, Madam 1277
Arduine 1106
Asbury, Herbert 1278
Asherah 1157
Ashlag, Yehuda 294
Aurand, A. Monroe, Jr. 664
Aylesworth, Thomas G. 150
Ayres, D. Drummond 1409

Bach, Charlotte M. 407
Bach, Marcus 1279-1281
Baily, Henry D.B. 706
Baker, Aleta Blanche 494-500
Banis, Victor 2

Baphomet X° 501
Bardon, Franz 195-197
Baritz, Loren 615
Barker, Dennis 1344
Baroja, Julio Caro 151
Barreiro, Jose 822
Barrère, Dorothy B. 1416
Barrett, Francis 198
Bascom, William 1345-1356
Baskin, Wade 158
Bastasz, Bob 1257
Bayard, S.P. 665
Beam, Maurice 1282
Beard, George M. 616
Beardwoman, Helen 1063
Beckley, Timothy 1283
Beculhimer, Marvin 824
Beguin, Rebecca 1143a
Bella, Rick 1158
Bender, Deborah 1064-1065
Benninghoff, Mary 825
Berg, Philip S. 295
Best, Michael R. 277
Beth-Shin-Tau 502
Beyerl, Paul 1159
Bidart, Gay-Darlene 826
Black, George Fraser 3-4
Blavatsky, Helen Petrovna
  199, 323
Bokser, Ben Zion 296
Bond, Bligh 297
Bonewits, P.E. Isaac 5, 827
Bonfant, Leo 618
Booth, Sally Smith 619
Boreas 1106
Borino, Bob 1440
Botkin, B.A. 1367

Bourke, John G. 1441
Bowles, John E. 707
Bowman, James 829, 1162
Boyer, Paul 620-621
Bracelin, Jack 758
Bramly, Serge 1402
Brandon, Fran 157
Brennan, J.H. 6
Brennan, T. Casey 504
Breslin, Jack 1163-1164
Brier, Bob 112
Briggs, Katherine Mary 279
Brightman, Frank H. 277
Brissenden, Constance 830
Brittan, Emma Hardinge 708
Broad, Sally 1258
Brooks, Amanda 1410
Brown, C.F. 676
Brown, Dennise C. 1066
Brown, Robert T. 324
Brown, Steve 1229
Bruce, Philip Alexander 592
Brunswick, N. 831
Bryant, James 832
Bryn, Katherine 622
Buckland, Raymond 759-770
Buckley, Edmund 408
Buczynski, Edmund M. 833
Budapest, Zsuzsanna Emese
  1067-1076, 1143b
Burgoyne, Thomas H. 325-327
Burland, C.A. 505
Burnett-Rae, Alan 466
Burr, George H. 623
Burr, George Lincoln 593
Burridge, Gaston 328
Burt, Al 1295
Butler, E.M. 200
Butler, Patrick 1165, 1230
Butler, William E. 201-202

Canavan, Kathy 834
Canet, Carlos 1411
Canon, W. 1368
Caporael, Linnda R. 624
Cappannari, Stephen C. 1369
Carlson, John 835

Carol, Chris 1077-1078, 1131
Carr, Gary 1259
Carrington, Hereward 467
Carson, Michael 1048
Carter, Carl 836, 1166
Case, Paul Foster 329-335
Cassidy, Hugh J.B. 1285
Castleberry, Brett 1167
Caulfield, Ernest 625
Cavendish, Richard 7, 60
Chappell, Helen 837
Chavez, Tibo J. 1442
Chevalier, Georges 203
Chew, Willa C. 1168
Choyke, Bill 838
Christ, Carol P. 1079-1080
Christensen, Cheryl JoAnne
  336
Christianson, Penny 839
Clark, Carolyn 1172
Clement, Carol 1143b
Clymer, R. Swinburne 337,
  468, 506
Cocke, Ed 1286
Cohen, Daniel 8-9, 842
Cohn, Norman 152
Colburn, Marcia Froelke 1232
Cole, Donna 1173
Cole, Henry 1370
Colin, Paul 27
Colquhoun, Ithell 204
Combs, Josiah Henry 709
Connor, John W. 153
Conway, David 10
Cordova, Gabriel 1443
Crabb, Judy 339
Crabb, Riley 339
Crammell, C.R. 469
Crosby, John R. 666
Cross, Tom Peete 710-711
Crow, W.B. 61
Crowley, Aleister 439-465
Crowther, Arnold 790, 792
Crowther, Patricia 790-792
Culin, Stewart 1287
Culling, Louis T. 507-509
Cunningham, Sara 843-844
Cutner, H. 409

Dale-Green, Patricia 113
Dalton, David 470
Damon 510
Danforth, Florence G. 626
Daniels, Mary 1174, 1414
d'Argent, Jacques 1288
Dart, John 845
Davis, Ann 340
Davis, Frank 1289
Davis, Hubert J. 712
Davis, Richard Beale 594
Dawson, Johnny 1175
Dayhoof, Eleanor 1290
Debus, Allen G. 62
de Camp, L. Sprague 298
de Claremont, Lewis 341-343
de Lama, George 1348
de Laurence, L.W. 280-283
Demos, John 595
Denning, Melita 511-514,
  1291
de Placy, Collin 154
Dequer, John H. 344
Desmangles, Leslie G. 1292-
  1293
Devine, John W. 1924
Dew, Joan 846
Dexter, T.F.G. 114
Dey, Charmaine 847
Dickinson, Alice 628
Dickson, Larry 848
Diederich, Bernard 1295
DiPalo, James 849
Dixon, James 850
Dixon, Jo 850
Dodson, Ruth 1445
Donovan, Frank 155
Dorson, Richard M. 1372-
  1374
Douglas, Albert 596
Douglas, Mary 98
Douglas, Nik 410
Downey, Tab 851
Drake, Frederick C. 597
Drake, Samuel Gardner 598,
  629
Drury, Neville 205-207

Drylie, A. 477
Dugan, Donald S. 852
Dulaure, Jacques Antoine 411
Dumézil, Georges 115
Durdin-Robertson, Lawrence
  793-794
Dyer, B.R. 156
Dykstra, Dirk 853

Early, Eleanor 630
Ebon, Martin 854-855
Eddison, Robert 856
Edwards, C. Taliesin 1144
Edwards, David 208, 268
Eklund, Christopher 857
Eliade, Mircea 11, 63
Ellwood, Robert S. 12, 345,
  1178
Elvidge, Marcia 858
Emmerettae 516
Encausse, Gerard 259
Enderle, Herman 1173
Epstein, Perle 299
Erwin, Milo 713
Evans, Arthur 859
Evans, Wick 1446
Evans-Pritchard, E.E. 99
Evans-Wentz, W.Y. 116

Fabricio, Roberto 1349-1350
Fair, London 714
Fairgrove, Rowan 1180
Farrar, Stewart 771
Farren, David 860-862
Federmann, Reinhard 64
Feldman, Mark 517
Feley, Bob 1296
Firth, Violet Mary. See
  Fortune, Dion
Fitzgerald, Arlene J. 863
Fleeson, Lucinda 864
Fleming, John 518
Fludd, Robert 403
Folsom, Joseph Fulford 599
Forbes, Esther 715
Forfreedom, Ann 1082-1083
Fortier, Alcee 1375

Fortune, Dion 209-218
Fossier, Albert A. 1297
Fowler, Samuel P. 631
Fox, Jack D. 519
Fox, Selena 810, 1084-1085, 1129
Franck, Adolphe 300
Frankfort, Henri 117
Frazier, James G. 118
Frazier, Paul 667
Frisbie, Tom 1251
Fritscher, John 866
Frost, Gavin 867-872
Frost, Yvonne 868-872
Frye, Rod 873
Fuller, J.F.C. 471
Fuller, Jean Overton 472

Galbreath, Robert 13, 219
Galvin, James A.V. 1447
Gamache, Henri 346-348
Gamble, Eliza Burt 412
Gandee, Lee R. 668-670
Gannon, Frederick Augustus 632
Garcia, Raquel 1351
Gardner, Gerald B. 772-775
Gardner, Helena 65
Garrison, Omar 520
Gastman, Gloria 1352
Gauthier, Xaviere 1086
Gawr, Rhuddlwn 811, 874
Gearhart, Sally 1087
Geist, Bill 875
Gentile, Don 876
Gewurz, Elias 301
Ghishba, Ohoyo Osh 1107
Gibson, Richard 1262
Gidlow, Elsa 1088
Gilbert, Andrea 1182
Gilbert, Robert A. 220-221, 473
Giles, Carl H. 877
Gilfond, Henry 1298
Ginsburg, Christian D. 302
Glass, Justine 878
Gleadow, Rupert 520

Gleason, Judith 1353-1354
Godwin, John 14
Godwin, Joscelyn 66
Goldberg, Ben Zion 413
Golden, M.D. 1376
Goldenberg, Naomi R. 1089-1090
Gonzalez-Wippler, Migene 15, 303, 1355
Good, Sandy 1183
Goramson, Mark 880
Gordon, Raymond 148
Gorham, Melvin 1184
Goshko, John 633
Gottlieb, Jack 556
Graham, Arthur 881
Grammary, Ann 882
Grant, Kenneth 222-224, 521-524
Graves, Robert 119-120, 776, 883
Graves, Samuel 884
Gray, David C. 1185
Gray, William G. 225-236
Gray-Cobb, Geoff 525
Greeley, Andrew 16, 885
Green, Marian 795-796
Greene, Daniel St. Albin 1412
Gregor, Arthur S. 17
Gregor, Paul 1403
Griffin, Jean Latz 886
Gross, R. 1186
Grossinger, Richard 526
Gruberger, Philip S. 304
Gruen, John 1187
Grunder, Hartnett 777
Gundella 887
Gunn, John H. 716
Gunther, Max 888
Gupta, Marie 157
Guthrie, Kenneth Sylvan 121
Gutmanis, June 1417
Guy, Don 634
G'Zell, Otter 1108

H.I., Soror 237
Haining, Peter 158, 889-891

Haldane, Claudia 892, 1188
Halevi, Z'ev ben Shimon 305-307
Hall, J.A. 1378
Hall, Manly P. 18, 349-353
Hammond, Ruth 893
Hanna, Pat 894
Hannay, J.B. 414
Hansen, Chadwick 635-636
Haraszti, Zolton 637
Hark, Ann 671
Harper, Clive 159
Harper, George Mills 238
Harris, Anthony 160
Harris, Jesse W. 717
Harrison, Jane Ellen 122
Harrison, Michael 161
Hartman, Franz 67, 239-240
Hartman, Patricia 19
Harvey, Gerald 718
Harvey, Steve 1092
Haskins, James 1299-1300
Hatch, David Patterson 354-355
Hefferman, Bill 1356
Heflin, Lee 527
Heidrick, Bill 528
Heinzmann, Louis J. 672
Henry, Stuart C. 638
Herdegen, Lance J. 1249
Herrmann, Pat 896
Herron, Patricia 1093
Hershberger, Barbara 897
Hershberger, Hersh 897
Hershman, Florence 898
Hicks, Darryl E. 899
Hildebrand, Norb 1302
Hilken, Glen A. 900
Hill, Dave 901
Hill, Douglas 20
Hill, Greg 1271
Hillinger, Charles 1418
Hinterberger, John 529
Hiroa, Te Rangi 1419
Hitchcock, Ethan Allen 357-359
Hoch, Edward D. 639
Hoeller, Stephen A. 360, 902

Hoffbower, Henry F. 673-674
Hoffman, Enid 1420
Hoffman, Lisa 778
Hohman, Johann Georg 675-676
Holden, William Curry 1448
Holdredge, Helen 1303-1304
Hole, Christina 162
Holman, Nancy 903
Holmes, Richard 163
Holzer, Hans 904-908, 1189
Howard, Clifford 415
Howard, Michael 1250
Howe, Ellic 241
Hudson, Alisha S. 429
Huebner, Louise 909-911
Hueffer, Oliver Madox 164
Humphrey, Christopher C. 1190
Hundingsbani, Helgi 1251
Hurley, Phillip 361
Hurston, Zora Neale 1378
Hurt, Wesley R., Jr. 1449
Huson, Paul 912-913
Hutin, Serge 68
Huxley, Elspeth 21
Hyatt, Harry Middleton 719
Hyman, Tom 914

Interollo, Lisa 1404

Jackson, Joy J. 1306
Jackson, Shirley 640
Jacobs, Dorothy 916-917
Jaffé, Aniela 69
James, E.W. 600
James, Edward R. 601
James, Edwin Oliver 123-124
Janz, M.L. 1094
Jarvie, I.C. 22
Jeanne 918
Jennings, Hargrave 70, 416
Johns, June 779
Joiner, Robert L. 919
Jones, Charles S. See Achad, Frater
Jones, Marc Edmund 362
Jordan, Wilvert C. 1380
Joseph, Greg 920

Kabouter, Jomo 1192
Kamakau, Samuel Manaiakalani
  1421-1422
Kasdin, Simon 363
Kearton, Michael 242
Kelley, George M. 1307
Kelly, Aidan 780
Kelly, Tom 1193
Kennedy, L. 1308
Kenyon, Richard L. 23, 921,
  1095
Kenyon, Theda 720
Khedemel, Frater 364
Kieckhefer, Richard 165
Kiev, Ari 1450
Kimball, C. 1381
King, Frances 243-246, 417-
  418, 474
King, Grace 1309-1310
Kittredge, G.L. 602
Klauder, J.I. 24
Klemesrud, Judy 922
Knight, Gareth 247-249
Knight, Richard Payne 419
Kohn, Bernice 166
Kok, T.R. 530
Kors, Alan C. 167
Kotula, Denise 923
Kraemer, Ross S. 125
Krakovsky, Levi Isaac 308
Krishnar, Maravedi el 420
Kriss, Marika 924
Krochmal, Pat 925
Kulp, Radelle 531, 1195
Kulp, Thomas 531, 1195
Kuna, Ralph R. 1382
Kushner, Lawrence 309

Lacy, Edward F. 926
Lafarque, André, 1311
Laidlaw, William K. 721
LaJoie, Raymond A. 927
Langden, Carolyn S. 603
Langguth, A.J. 1405
Larner, Christina 25
Laurel, Alicia Bay 1210
Laurent, Emile 421

Lavender, Curtis 928
Lawrence, Lynda 929-930
Layne, Meade 532
Lea, H.C. 168
Lea, Thomas Simcox 297
LeBlanc, Rena Dictor 1313
Le Breton, John 722
Leek, Sybil 915, 931-942
Le Gros, George Cardinal 723
Leininger, Madeline 26, 943
Leland, Charles G. 126-129
Lesh, Cheri 1096-1098
Lethbridge, T.C. 169
Levi, Eliphas 250-254
Levin, David 641-642
Lewis, Arthur H. 677
Lewis, David A. 899
Lewis, Sharon 944
Leyburn, James G. 1314
Lightman, Herb A. 945
Lippman, Deborah 27
Lloyd, J. William 422
Lloyd, Susannah Liller 946
Long, Max Freedom 1423-1429
Long, Richard B. 423
Longworth, R.C. 1359
Ludwig, Arnold M. 1447
Luptak, Gene 535
Lyon, John 604
Lyons, Delphine 947

McBride, L.R. 1430
McCormick, Jane 170
McFarland, Morgan 1099-1100
MacFarlane, A.D.J. 171
McFerran, Douglas 28, 948
McGraw, Walter J. 781
McGregor, Pedro 1406
McIntosh, Christopher 71,
  255
McKenna, Peter 949
McKern, Sharon 644
McLean, Adam 402, 405-406
McLean, Patricia 1383
McNallen, Stephen A. 1253
McNeil, Brownie 1452
MacPhail, Ian 72, 365

McQuillin, Cynthia A. 1139
McTeer, J.E. 1384
Madsen, Claudia 29
Madsen, William 29
Magus Incognito 73
Maior, Ursa 1101
Malaclypse the Younger 1271
Malchus, Marius 284
Malinowski, Bronislaw 100
Mallowe, Mike 950
Manduro, Reynaldo J. 1385
Manning, Al G. 951-953
Mannix, Daniel P. 475-476
Maple, Eric 172
Mari, Seagull 1102
Mariechild, Diane 1103
Mars, Dina Acosta 1104
Marshburn, Joseph H. 173
Martello, Leo L. 954-963,
  1133
Martin, Frances Louise 724
Martin, Kevin 174
Martinez, Raymond J. 1315
Marty, Martin 30
Marwick, Max 101
Masters, Robert E.L. 31
Mather, Cotton 643
Mathers, S.L. MacGregor 256,
  285-286
Mathis, J. 1385
Maughan, T. 1263
Mauss, Marcel 32
Maxwell, C.N.W. 797, 678
Maynard, Jim 1147
Mead, George R.S. 74, 366
Meara 964
Melton, J. Gordon 33-36, 679
Meltzer, David 310
Melville, Leinani 1431
Mestel, Sherry 965-966
Métraux, Alfred 1316
Michaelson, Mike 1387
Michelot, Jules 175
Middleton, John 102, 1453
Midelfort, H.C. Erik 176
Miller, David L. 1198
Miller, Elliot 967
Miller, George Noyes 424-425

Miller, Richard Alan 537
Miller, William Marion 605,
  725
Minerva 1199-1200
Minor, Mary Y. 1388
Minor, Marz 726
Mitchell, Faith 1389
Mohan, Rusheed 367
Monter, E. William 177
Moore, Martin 968
Moraud, Paul 1317
Moreau, John Adam 1360
Morgan, Fred T. 727
Morgan, Robin 1105
Morgana 1106
Morning Glory 1107-1108
Morrish, Furze 257
Morrison, Sarah Lyddon 969
Morrow, Darrell 970
Motta, Marcelo Ramos 538-540
Moutray, Eva Martin 1318
Mumford, John 426
Murphy, Joseph M. 1361
Murray, Jack 645
Murray, Margaret A. 783-784
Muses, Charles Arthur 427

Nahigan, Ken 287
Nalesnyk, E. Linder 680
Nash, June 103
Neifert, William W. 681
Neill, Edward D. 606
Nelson, Norman E. 1264
Nemo 510
Neruda, James 1246
Nesnick, Mary 782
Neumann, Eric 130
Nevins, Winfield S. 646
Newell, Venetia 104
Newell, W.W. 1319
Newley, Joanne 728
Newsom, Ted 471
Nichols, Dudley 682
Nichols, Woodrow 972
Nicolaus 75
Nilsson, Martin P. 131
Nissenbaum, Stephen 620-621
Norling, Rita 973

Noyes, John Humphrey   428
Nugent, Donald   37, 178

Oak   1109
Oakes, Philip   256
O'Connell, Margaret F.   179
O'Donnell, Franklin   1265
Oliver, Betty   607
Ophiel   541-544
Osirus   974
O'Sullivan, Gerry   875
O'Toole, Thomas J.   545
Overton, Marion F.   729
Owens, Ethel   730
Owens, Mary Alice   1390-1391

Pagel, Walter   369
Paine, Lauran   180
Palmer, John Phillips   546
Papus   259
Parfitt, Will   477
Parke, Francis Neal   608
Parrinder, Geoffrey   105-106
Parsley, Ron   517
Parsons, Jack   547-548
Parzival, Frater   538-540
Passmore, Nancy   1148
Patai, Raphael   132
Paulsen, Kathryn   978
Paxton, Henry D.   683
Peach, Edmund   541-544
Pearson, Ann   980
Pearson, Karl   133
Peck, Mrs. M.S.   1392
Pelton, Robert W.   1320-1325
Pendderwen, Gwydion   1136
Pendleton, Louis   1393
Penneck, Rupert   647
Pennell, Elizabeth R.   134
Pepper, Elizabeth   979
Perley, M.V.B.   648
Peters, Edwards   167
Petry, Ann   649
Phillips, Osborne   511-512,
    1291
Phylotus   370-371
Picard, Barbara Leonie   135

Pick, Bernhard   311
Picone, Patricia   981
Pitney, Emmanuel Marpin   550
Plaskow, Judith   1080
Plowman, Edward E.   982
Poole, William E.   650
Poppy, John   1204
Potts, Billie   1110
Prose, Francine   1326
Puckett, Niles   1394
Pullin-Burry, Henry   312
Pumara, Hazel J. Diaz   1432
Putnam, Allen   651

Raine, Kathleen   260-261
Raleigh, Albert Sidney   372-
    385
Randolph, Paschal Beverly
    551-553
Randolph, Vance   731-733
Raskin, Edith   734
Raskin, Joseph   734
Redgrove, H. Stanley   76
Redmond, Jeffery R.   1254
Reed, Ishmael   1327
Regardie, Israel   479, 554-
    572
Renslow, Charles   1244
Reynard   573
Richmond, Arline L.   386
Richmond, Olney H.   387-388
Richler, Mordecai   985
Riddell, William Renwick
    609-610
Rigaud, Milo   1320
Ringel, Faye   652
Riva, Anna   735, 987-990,
    1329
Roback, C.W.   389
Robbins, Peggy   653
Robbins, Rossell Hope   181-
    182
Roberts, Houston   1208
Roberts, Mark   1112-1113
Roberts, Susan   478, 991
Robertson, Olivia   798-802
Robotti, Francis Diane   654

Rocco, Sha 429
Rodman, Julius Scammon 1433
Rohmer, Sax 77
Ronan, Margaret 78
Rony, Jerome-Antoine 40
Rose, Donna 736-741, 1362
Rose, Elliott 183
Rose, Ronald 107
Rosnek, Carl E. 1455
Ross, Lilla 1209
Rowley, Peter 41
Rubinton, Noel 992
Ruether, Rosemary 1114
Rush, Anne Kent 1115
Russell, C.F. 514
Russell, Jeffery Burton 184-185

S.M.R.D., Frater 262
Sachse, Julius Friedrich 684
Sadhu, Mouni 263-264
Sadoul, Jacques 79
St. Clair, David 1116, 1407
Samuel, Jack 994
Sandbach, John 575
Sargeant, Philip W. 186
Saunders, Maxine 786
Saxon, Harry O. 576
Saxon, Lyle 1330-1331
Schafer, Ed 995
Schieneman, Thomas J. 186a
Scholem, Gershom 313-314
Schul, Bill D. 742
Schultz, C.P. 685
Schurmacher, Emile C. 996
Scott, George Ryley 430
Scott, Gini Graham 42
Seabrook, William 43, 743, 1332
Seagull 1117
Seip, Elizabeth Cloud 744
Selene 997
Seleneicthon 998-999
Selig, Godfrey 390
Seligmann, Kurt 80
Sellon, Edward 430
Sena 1118
Sender, Ramon 1210

Sepharial 44, 315
Seth, Ronald 187-189
Sevarg, Luba 1000
Seymour, St. John D. 190
Shah, Sayed Idries 288
Shaner, Richard H. 686-687
Sharon, Douglas 108
Sharp, Daisy 1001
Shea, Robert 1272
Sheba, Lady 1002-1005
Shen, Yao 1434
Sheridan, Jack 1267
Sherwood, Debbie 1006
Shirota, Jon 1007
Shoemaker, Alfred L. 688
Shoemaker, Henry Wharton 689
Shumaker, Wayne 81
Siegal, Benjamin 655
Sigl, Susan T. 1211
Silberer, Herbert 82
Simbro, William 1008
Simmons, Marc 1456
Simon 289
Simor, George 1009
Simpson, Damien 1010
Singer, Dale 45, 1334
Sisters of the Owl 1119
Skinner, Charles M. 754
Skinner, Stephen 207, 246, 265
Slagle, Alton 1011
Slinger, Penny 410
Smith, Mary 782
Smith, Robert T. 1012-1014
Smith, Suzy 1015
Smyth, Frank 1016
Sneed, Michael 1414
Snell, John E. 1395
Snow, Loudell F. 1335
Soiret, Eve 1198-1199
Sommers, Robert 578
Spanos, Nicolas P. 656
Spare, Austin Osman 266
Speare, Eva A. 746
Spence, Lewis 136-138
Squire, Charles 139
Stahl, Annie Lee West 1336
Stanton, Herb 1337

Starhawk   1120-1121
Starkes, M. Thomas   1017
Starkey, Marion Lena   657-
    659
Starr, Bill   1457-1459
Steagall, Archie   1460
Steedman, Marguerite   611
Steiger, Brad   1435
Steiner, Roland   1396
Steiner, Rudolf   140
Stephensen, P.R.   479
Stewardson, Jack   1246
Stockham, Alice B.   432
Stone, Lee Alexander   433
Stone, Margaret   1436
Stone, Merlin   1122-1123
Stowe, Caryl   1212
Stowers, Carlton   1018
Strabo, Mikhail   580
Strathloch, Lord   802
Strauch, Art   1019
Straughn, R.A.   392
Sullivan, Ronald   1363
Summers, Montague   191-192
Suro, Roberto   1364
Symon, Jon   582-584
Symonds, John   480-481
Sympson, Ron   1415

Tahil, Patricia   404
Tallant, Robert   1338
Tanith, Soror   585
Tapley, Charles Sutherland
    660
Taylor, Barney C. (Eli)
    1020-1021
Taylor, John M.   660a
Tegarden, J.B. Hollis   1339
Thanet, O.   1397
Thibodeau, Robert   393-394
Thomas, Ed   1022
Thomas, Keith   83
Thomas, M. Wynn   661
Thomas, Veronica   1023
Thompson, C.J.S.   84, 141
Thompson, R. Campbell   85
Thorndike, Lynn   86
Three Initiates   395

Tiling, David   1398
Tiryakian, Edward A.   46
Tonn, Martin   1024
Torrens, Robert George   267
Tortora, Vincent R.   700
Touchstone, Blake   1340
Toups, Oneida   587
Town, Sandra   1025
Trachtenberg, Joshua   87
Trent, Bill   1026
Trevor-Roper, H.R.   193
Truzzi, Marcello   47-49, 1028
Turner, Robert   268
Tyler, Sarah   747

Upham, Charles W.   662
Uranus   1215

Vachon, Brian   1029
Valarie   817
Valiente, Doreen   803-807
Vega, Antonio   1461
Vetter, George B.   51

Wagner, Belle   396, 397
Wagner, Henry   396a-397
Wagstaff, Beverly   1217
Waite, Arthur Edward   88-90,
    269-270, 290-291, 316
Wake, C. Stanisland   437
Wakin, Edward   1285
Walker, D.P.   91
Walker, Deward E., Jr.   109
Wall, Don   788
Wall, Otto Augustus   434
Wallace, C.H.   1030
Wallace, Kevin   1269
Wallis-Budge, E.A.   142
Wang, Robert   271-272
Ward, Ken   815
Warner, Charles Dudley   1342
Warner, Marina   143
Wax, Murray   52
Wax, Rosalie   52
Wayne, Philip   1139
Webb, James   92-93
Webb, Julie Yvonne   1343
Webb, Wheaton P.   748

Webster, Hutton 53
Wedeck, Harry E. 54, 144
Weinstein, Marion 1031, 1124
Wellesley, Gordon 435
Welsh, Roger 749
Wentler, William 589
Weschcke, Carl L. 1033
West, Robert H. 1034
Westervelt, William D. 1437
Westkoff, Marcia 701
Westropp, Hodder M. 436-437
White, Anne 292-293, 590
White, Nelson 292-293, 590
White Witchdoctor 750-751
Whittemore, James O. 752
Whitten, Norman E. 1399
Wilcox, John 979
Wilgus, Neal 1273
Wilkerson, Clark 1438-1439
Wilkinson, Ronald Sterne 398-399
Wille, Lois 1219
Williams, Barbara Ann 877
Williams, Charles 194
Williams, David 273
Williams, Pat 20
Williams, Thomas A. 274
Williams, Wentworth 1036
Wilson, Arnold W. 55
Wilson, Robert Anton 1037, 1272, 1274-1276
Winsor, Justin 612
Wiltse, H.M. 1400
Winter, E.H. 102
Winter, Murray 1212
Wintrob, Ronald M. 1401
Wisby, Gary 1038
A Witch 808
Witt, Robin 1042
Wittemans, Frans 94
Wolfe 964, 1043
Woods, Richard 57
Woodside, Jeani 1044
Woodward, W.E. 663
Worley, Elizabeth 1045
Worth, Valerie 1046
Worthen, Samuel Capp 613
Wright, Dudley 145

Wright, Elbee 755
Wright, Harry B. 111
Wright, Thomas 438
Wright, Walter 58
Wyoming, Anona D. 1128

Yates, Frances A. 95-97
Yeats, William Butler 275-276
Yoder, Don 703-704

Zain, C.C. 400-401
Zakatarious 1222
Zalasin, Paul 1047
Zarathustra, Frater 591
Zell, Tim 1108, 1172, 1223-1227
Zell, Otter 1108
Zientara, Bob 1048
Ziomek, Jon 1228
Zolar 59
Zook, Jacob 705
Zook, Jane 705
Zubryn, Emil 1463

PERIODICAL INDEX

Item numbers refer to periodicals listed
on pages 178-191 of this bibliography.

Discordians   15, 40, 116 128

Druid   117

Egyptian   25

Feminist   31, 61, 105, 141, 158, 165, 180

Huna   19, 62

Norse   5, 10-11, 18, 43, 91, 100, 126-127, 150-151, 189,
200

Paganism   9, 12, 14, 21, 24, 34, 41, 44, 50-52, 56, 65, 67,
71, 73, 75, 86-88, 93, 95-96, 108, 110, 114, 117, 119,
124, 130, 145-147, 149, 182, 186

Ritual Magic   2, 26, 48, 54, 64-64a, 68, 70, 72, 83, 92,
103-104, 107, 131, 138, 140, 143, 155, 173-174, 178-179,
183, 187, 190-191, 197-198, 201

Witchcraft   3-4, 17, 20, 22, 27-28, 32, 38, 45-47, 49, 53,
60, 74, 77-78, 81, 84, 89, 94, 106, 109, 112-113, 122,
129, 133, 135-137, 139, 142, 144, 154, 156-157, 159-163,
166, 171-172, 177, 184, 188, 193-196, 199, 202